KOBA THE DREAD

Martin Amis is the author of eighteen books, fiction and non-fiction, including *London Fields*, *Money*, *The Information*, *Experience*, *The War Against Cliché* and, most recently, *Yellow Dog*. He lives in London.

ALSO BY MARTIN AMIS

Fiction

The Rachel Papers
Dead Babies
Success
Other People
Money
Einstein's Monsters
London Fields
Time's Arrow
The Information
Night Train
Heavy Water
Yellow Dog

Non-Fiction

Invasion of the Space Invaders
The Moronic Inferno
Visiting Mrs Nabokov
Experience
The War Against Cliché

Martin Amis

KOBA THE DREAD

Laughter and the Twenty Million

V

VINTAGE

Published by Vintage 2003

2 4 6 8 10 9 7 5 3 1

First published in Great Britain in 2002 by
Jonathan Cape

Vintage
Random House, 20 Vauxhall Bridge Road,
London SW1V 2SA

Random House Australia (Pty) Limited
20 Alfred Street, Milsons Point, Sydney
New South Wales 2061, Australia

Random House New Zealand Limited
18 Poland Road, Glenfield,
Auckland 10, New Zealand

Random House (Pty) Limited
Endulini, 5A Jubilee Road, Parktown 2193,
South Africa

The Random House Group Limited Reg. No. 954009
www.randomhouse.co.uk

A CIP catalogue record for this book
is available from the British Library

ISBN 0 099 43802 X

Papers used by Random House are natural, recyclable
products made from wood grown in sustainable forests.
The manufacturing processes conform to the environ-
mental regulations of the country of origin

Printed and bound in Great Britain by
Bookmarque Ltd, Croydon, Surrey

To Bob and Liddie
—and to Clio

Contents

PART III

When We Dead Awaken   **243**

Index   **283**

PART I

THE COLLAPSE OF
THE VALUE
OF HUMAN LIFE

Preparatory

Here is the second sentence of Robert Conquest's *The Harvest of Sorrow: Soviet Collectivization and the Terror-Famine*:

> We may perhaps put this in perspective in the present case by saying that in the actions here recorded about twenty human lives were lost for, not every word, but every letter, in this book.

That sentence represents 3,040 lives. The book is 411 pages long.

'Horse manure was eaten, partly because it often contained whole grains of wheat' (1,340 lives). 'Oleska Voytrykhovsky saved his and his family's . . . lives by consuming the meat of horses which had died in the collective of glanders and other diseases' (2,480 lives). Conquest quotes Vasily Grossman's essayistic-documentary novel *Forever Flowing*: 'And the children's faces were aged, tormented, just as if they were seventy years old. And by spring they no longer had faces. Instead, they had birdlike heads with beaks, or frog heads – thin, wide lips – and some of them resembled fish, mouths open' (3,880 lives). Grossman goes on:

> In one hut there would be something like a war. Everyone would keep close watch over everyone else . . . The wife turned against her husband and the husband against his wife. The

mother hated the children. And in some other hut love would
be inviolable to the very last. I knew one woman with four
children. She would tell them fairy stories and legends so that
they would forget their hunger. Her own tongue could hardly
move, but she would take them into her arms even though she
had hardly the strength to lift her arms when they were empty.
Love lived on within her. And people noticed that where there
was hate people died off more swiftly. Yet love, for that matter,
saved no one. The whole village perished, one and all. No life
remained in it.

Thus: 11,860 lives. Cannibalism was widely practised – and widely
punished. Not all these pitiable anthropophagi received the
supreme penalty. In the late 1930s, 325 cannibals from the Ukraine
were still serving life sentences in Baltic slave camps.

The famine was an enforced famine: the peasants were
stripped of their food. On 11 June 1933, the Ukrainian paper *Visti*
praised an 'alert' secret policeman for unmasking and arresting a
'fascist saboteur' who had hidden some bread in a hole under a
pile of clover. That word *fascist*. One hundred and forty lives.

In these pages, guileless prepositions like *at* and *to* each represent the murder of six or seven large families. There is only one
major book on this subject – Conquest's. Again: it is 411 pages long.

Credentials

I am a fifty-two-year-old novelist and critic who has recently read
several yards of books about the Soviet experiment. On 31
December 1999, along with Tony Blair and the Queen, I attended
the celebrations at the Millennium Dome in London. Touted as
a festival of high technology in an aesthetic dreamscape, the evening resembled a five-hour stopover in a second-rate German

airport. For others, the evening resembled a five-hour attempt to *reach* a second-rate German airport – so I won't complain. I knew that the millennium was a non-event, reflecting little more than our interest in zeros; and I knew that 31 December 1999 wasn't the millennium anyway.* But that night did seem to mark the end of the twentieth century; and the twentieth century is unanimously considered to be our worst century yet (an impression confirmed by the new book I was reading: *Reflections on a Ravaged Century*, by Robert Conquest). I had hoped that at midnight I would get some sort of chiliastic frisson. And I didn't get it at the Dome. Nonetheless, a day or two later I started to write about the twentieth century and what I took to be its chief lacuna. The piece, or the pamphlet, grew into the slim volume you hold in your hands. I have written about the Holocaust, in a novel (*Time's Arrow*). Its afterword begins:

> This book is dedicated to my sister Sally, who, when she was
> very young, rendered me two profound services. She awakened
> my protective instincts; and she provided, if not my earliest
> childhood memory, then certainly my most charged and radiant.
> She was perhaps half an hour old at the time. I was four.

It feels necessary to record that, between Millennium Night and the true millennium a year later, my sister died at the age of forty-six.

Background

In 1968 I spent the summer helping to rewire a high-bourgeois mansion in a northern suburb of London. It was my only taste

*The millennial moment was midnight, 31 December 2000. This is because we went from B.C. to A.D. without a year nought. Vladimir Putin described the (pseudo) millennium as 'the 2000th anniversary of Christianity'.

of proletarian life. The experience was additionally fleeting and qualified: when the job was done, I promptly moved into the high-bourgeois mansion with my father and stepmother (both of them novelists, though my father was also a poet and critic). My sister would soon move in too. That summer we were of course monitoring the events in Czechoslovakia. In June, Brezhnev deployed 16,000 men on the border. The military option on 'the Czech problem' was called Operation Tumour . . . My father had been to Prague in 1966 and made many contacts there. After that it became a family joke – the stream of Czechs who came to visit us in London. There were bouncing Czechs, certified Czechs, and at least one honoured Czech, the novelist Josef Skvorecky. And then on the morning of 21 August my father appeared in the doorway to the courtyard, where the rewiring detail was taking a break, and called out in a defeated and wretched voice: 'Russian tanks in Prague.'

I turned nineteen four days later. In September I went up to Oxford.

The first two items in *The Letters of Kingsley Amis* form the only occasion, in a book of 1,200 pages, where I find my father impossible to recognize. Here he is humourlessly chivvying a faint-hearted comrade to rally to the cause. The tone (earnest, elderly, 'soppy-stern') is altogether alien: 'Now, really, you know, this won't do at all, leaving the Party like that. Tut, tut, John. I am seriously displeased with you.' The second letter ends with a hand-drawn hammer and sickle. My father was a card-carrying member of the CP, taking his orders, such as they were, from Stalin's Moscow. It was November 1941: *he* was nineteen, and up at Oxford.

1941. Kingsley, let us assume, was sturdily ignorant of the

USSR's domestic cataclysms. But its foreign policies hardly cried out for one's allegiance. A summary. August 1939: the Nazi-Soviet Pact. September 1939: the Nazi-Soviet invasion-partition of Poland (and a second pact: the Soviet-German Treaty on Borders and Friendship). November 1939: the annexation of Western Ukraine and Western Belorussia, and the attempted invasion of Finland (causing the USSR's expulsion, the following month, from the League of Nations). June 1940: the annexation of Moldavia and Northern Bukovina. August 1940: the annexation of Lithuania, Lativa and Estonia; and the murder of Trotsky. These acquisitions and decapitations would have seemed modest compared to Hitler's helter-skelter successes over the same period. And then in June 1941, of course, Germany attacked the Soviet Union. My father rightly expected to participate in the war; the Russians were now his allies. It was then that he joined the Party, and he remained a believer for fifteen years.

How much did the Oxford comrades know, in 1941? There were public protests in the West about the Soviet forced-labour camps as early as 1931. There were also many solid accounts of the violent chaos of Collectivization (1929–34) and of the 1933 famine (though no suggestion, as yet, that the famine was terror-istic). And there were the Moscow Show Trials of 1936–38, which were open to foreign journalists and observers, and were moni-tored worldwide. In these pompous and hysterical charades, renowned Old Bolsheviks 'confessed' to being career-long enemies of the regime (and to other self-evidently ridiculous charges). The pubescent Solzhenitsyn was 'stunned by the fraud-ulence of the trials'. And yet the world, on the whole, took the other view, and further accepted indignant Soviet denials of fam-ine, enserfment of the peasantry, and slave labour. 'There was no reasonable excuse for believing the Stalinist story. The excuses which can be advanced are irrational,' writes Conquest in *The Great Terror*. The world was offered a choice between two realities; and the young Kingsley, in common with the overwhelming majority of intellectuals everywhere, chose the wrong reality.

The Oxford Communists would certainly have known about the Soviet decree of 7 April 1935, which rendered children of twelve and over subject to 'all measures of criminal punishment', including death. This law, which was published on the front page of *Pravda* and caused universal consternation (reducing the French CP to the argument that children, under socialism, became grownups very quickly), was intended, it seems, to serve two main purposes. One was social: it would expedite the disposal of the multitudes of feral and homeless orphans created by the regime. The second purpose, though, was political. It applied barbaric pressure on the old oppositionists, Kamenev and Zinoviev, who had children of eligible age; these men were soon to fall, and their clans with them. The law of 7 April 1935 was the crystallization of 'mature' Stalinism. Imagine the mass of the glove that Stalin swiped across your face; imagine the mass of it.*

---

*It will be as well, here, to get a foretaste of his rigour. The fate of Mikhail Tukhachevsky, a famous Red commander in the Civil War, was ordinary enough, and that of his family was too. Tukhachevsky was arrested in 1937, tortured (his interrogation protocols were stained with drops of 'flying' blood, suggesting that his head was in rapid motion at the time), farcically arraigned, and duly executed. Moreover (this is Robert C. Tucker's précis in *Stalin in Power: The Revolution from Above, 1928–41*): 'His wife and daughter returned to Moscow where she was arrested a day or two later along with Tukhachevsky's mother, sisters, and brothers Nikolai and Aleksandr. Later his wife and both brothers were killed on Stalin's orders, three sisters were sent to camps, his young daughter Svetlana was placed in a home for children of "enemies of the people" and arrested and sent to a camp on reaching the age of seventeen, and his mother and one sister died in exile.'

On 7 April 1935, my father was nine days away from his thirteenth birthday. Did he ever wonder, as he continued to grow up, why a state should need 'the last line of defence' (as a secret reinforcing instruction put it) against twelve-year-olds?

Perhaps there *is* a reasonable excuse for believing the Stalinist story. The real story – the truth – was entirely unbelievable.

More Background

It was in the following summer of 1969, I think, that I sat for an hour in the multi-acre garden of the fascist mansion in southern Hertfordshire with Kingsley Amis and Robert Conquest. A scrap of the conversation sticks in my mind, because I pulled off a mildly successful witticism at a time when I was still (rightly) anxious about my general seaworthiness in adult company. Kingsley and Bob (a.k.a. 'Kingers' and 'Conquers', just as Bob's future translatee, Aleksandr Solzhenitsyn, would be referred to as 'Solzhers' – pronounced *soldiers*), were deploring a recent production of *Hamlet* in which the Prince was homosexual and Ophelia was played by a man. In retrospect that sounds almost staid, for 1969. Anyhow, I said, 'Get thee to a monastery.' No great thing; but it seemed to scan.

In 1967 Kingsley had published the article called 'Why Lucky Jim Turned Right'. The ex-Communist was developing into a reasonably active Labourite – before becoming (and remaining) a markedly noisy Tory. In 1968 Bob had published *The Great Terror*, his classic study of Stalin's purges of the 1930s, and was on the way to assembling a body of work that would earn him the title, bestowed at a plenum of the Central Committee in

Moscow in 1990, of 'anti-Sovietchik number one'. Both Kingsley and Bob, in the 1960s, were frequently referred to as 'fascists' in the general political debate. The accusation was only semi-serious (as indeed was the general political debate, it now seems. In my milieu, policemen and even traffic wardens were called fascists). Kingers and Conquers referred to their own weekly meetings, at Bertorelli's in Charlotte Street, as 'the fascist lunch'; here they would chat and carouse with other fascists, among them the journalist Bernard Levin, the novelists Anthony Powell and John Braine (an infrequent and much-feared participant), and the defector historian Tibor Szamuely. What united the fascist lunchers was well-informed anti-Communism. Tibor Szamuely knew what Communism was. He had known them: purge, arrest, gulag.

I didn't read *The Great Terror* in 1968 (I would have been more likely, at that time, to have read Conquest's poetry). But I spent an hour with it, and never forgot the cold elegance of the following remark about 'sources': '1. *Contemporary official accounts* require little comment. They are, of course, false as to essentials, but they are still most informative. (It is untrue that Mdivani was a British spy, but it is true that he was executed.)' I have recently read the book twice, in the first edition (which I must have successfully stolen from my father), and in its revised, post-*glasnost* form, *The Great Terror: A Reassessment.* When asked to suggest a new title for the revised work, Conquest told his publisher, 'How about *I Told You So, You Fucking Fools*?' Because the book, itself revolutionary at the time of its appearance, has since been massively vindicated. In the mid-1960s I joined in hundreds of conversations like the following (the interlocutors here are my father and A. J. Ayer):

'In the USSR, at least they're trying to forge something positive.'

'But it doesn't *matter* what they're trying to forge, because they've already killed five million people.'

'You keep going back to the five million.'

'If you're tired of that five million, then I'm sure I can find you another five million.'

And one can, now. One can find another 5 million, and another, and another.

Alongside all this there was, in England then, a far hotter debate: the one about Vietnam. A certain urbanity was maintained in arguments about the USSR. It was in arguments about Vietnam that people yelled, wept, fought, stalked out. I watched my father forfeit two valuable friendships over Vietnam (those of A. Alvarez and Karl Miller). For he, and most but not all of the frequenters of the fascist lunch, broadly backed American policy. And this was, of course, the position of a minuscule and much-disliked minority. In my first term at Oxford (autumn, 1968) I attended a demonstration against the resuppression of Czechoslovakia. About a hundred people were there. We heard speeches. The mood was sorrowful, decent. Compare this to the wildly peergroup-competitive but definitely unfakeable emotings and self-lacerations of the crowds outside the American Embassy in Grosvenor Square, where they gathered in their tens of thousands.

In 1968 the world seemed to go further left than it had ever gone before and would ever go again. But this left was the New Left: it represented, or turned out to represent, revolution as play. The 'redeemer' class was no longer to be found in the mines and factories; it was to be found in the university libraries and lecture halls. There were demonstrations, riots, torchings, street battles in England, Germany, Italy, Japan and the USA. And remember the Paris of 1968: barricades, street theatre, youth-worship ('The young make love; the old make obscene gestures'), the resurgence of Marcuse (the wintry dialectician), and Sartre standing on street corners handing out Maoist pamphlets . . . The death throes of the New Left took the form of vanguard terrorism (the Red Brigades, the Baader-Meinhof gang, the Weathermen). And its afterlife is anarchistic, opposing itself to the latest mutation of capital: after imperialism, after fascism, it now faces globalization. We may note here that militant Islam cannot be made to fit into this 'model' – or into any other.

But red wasn't dead, in 1968. During my time at Oxford they used to come to your room: the believers, the steely ones – the proselytizing Communists. One might adapt the old joke. Q: What's the difference between a Communist car and a Commu-nist proselytizer? A: You can close the door on a Communist pros-elytizer. To glance quickly at a crucial dissonance: it has always been possible to joke about the Soviet Union, just as it has never been possible to joke about Nazi Germany. (Hitler attracts mockery, but his actions repel it).This is not merely a question of decorum. In the German case, laughter automatically absents itself. *Pace* Adorno, it was not poetry that became impossible after Auschwitz. What became impossible was laughter. In the Soviet case, on the other hand, laughter intransigently refuses to absent itself. Immersion in the facts of the Bolshevik catastrophe may make this increasingly hard to accept, but such an immersion will never cleanse that catastrophe of laughter . . .

I have to say that for a while I rather creepily, but very loyally, toed my father's line on Vietnam. Soon I changed my mind and we argued about it, often bitterly, for thirty years.* As I now see it, America had no business involving itself in a series of distant convulsions where the ideas, variously interpreted, of a long-dead German economist were bringing biblical calamity to China, North Korea, Vietnam, Laos and Cambodia. The prosecution of the war by America, I came to think, was clearly intolerable, impossible, not only because of what it was doing to Vietnam, but also because of what it was doing to America. There was a ghostly epiphany, a ghostly confirmation, when, in the late 1980s, the number of home casualties in the war was officially exceeded by the number of suicides among its veterans. That is strong evidence of an ideological brutalization of the motherland. The veterans returned, as we know, not to flowers and embraces, but to isolation.

The Szamuelys. All four Szamuelys – Tibor, Nina, Helen and George – were staying at the fascist mansion on the day I drove from there to Oxford, in 1972, to be orally judged for my degree. When it was over I crowed the news home by telephone, and returned to a scene of celebration. At about one o'clock that night I made a cordially unrequited pass at Helen Szamuely and then blacked out on the chaise longue in the drawing room. I awoke at about five, and stood up wonderingly, and headed for the door. When I opened it, all the fascist burglar alarms went off and I

---

*Conquest was strongly anti-Vietcong, but his support for the American conduct of the war was never emphatic, and has evolved in the direction of further deemphasis. (Here we may recall that, despite his donnish accent and manner, Conquest is an American. Well, American father, English mother; born in the UK; dual nationality; now a resident of California.) Kingsley was never less than 100 per cent earnest on Vietnam, right up until his death in 1995.

roused everyone in the house, my father, stepmother, step-uncle, and all four Szamuelys.

The Politicization of Sleep

Having analysed a particularly violent tackle by a particularly violent player, the ex-footballer Jimmy Greaves remarked: 'Put it this way. He's a lovely boy when he's asleep.' With the Bolsheviks, there was no such respite. In 1910 a political opponent said of Lenin that you couldn't deal with a man who 'for twenty-four hours of the day is taken up with the revolution, who has no other thoughts but thoughts of the revolution, and who, even in his sleep, dreams of nothing but revolution'. The actual Revolution, of course, had no effect on this habit. As the young secretary Khrushchev said to a cheering audience of Party members, 'A Bolshevik is someone who feels himself to be a Bolshevik even when he's sleeping!' That's how a Bolshevik felt about sleep,

> The death of each day's life, sore labour's bath,
> Balm of hurt minds, great nature's second course,
> Chief nourisher in life's feast.

Sleep was just another opportunity to feel like a Bolshevik.

But that is what they want, the believers, the steely ones, that is what they live for: the politicization of sleep. They want politics to be going on everywhere all the time, politics permanent and circumambient. They want the ubiquitization of politics; they want the politicization of sleep.

Soon we will look at what Stalin did to the Meyerholds: the extreme example of the politicization of sleep.

*   *   *

This is from a letter addressed to Maxim Gorky concerning the status of intellectuals under the new regime:

> The intellectual strength of workers and peasants grows in the struggle to overturn the bourgeoisie and their acolytes, those second-rate intellectuals and lackeys of capitalism, who think they are the brains of the nation. They are not the brains of the nation. They're its shit.

That isn't Stalin. (That is Lenin.) Stalin hated intellectuals too, but he cared about what we call creative writing and had an uneasy feel for it. His famous and much-mocked remark, 'writers are the engineers of human souls', is not just a grandiose fatuity: it is a description of what he wanted writers to be under his rule. He didn't understand that talented writers cannot go against their talent and survive, that they cannot be engineers. Talentless writers can, or they can try; it was a very good thing to be a talentless writer in the USSR, and a very bad thing to be a talented one.

Stalin personally monitored a succession of novelists, poets and dramatists. In this sphere he wavered as in no other. He gave Zamyatin his freedom: emigration. He menaced but partly tolerated Bulgakov (and went to his play *Days of the Turbins* fifteen times, as the theatre records show). He tortured and killed Babel. He destroyed Mandelstam. He presided over the grief and misery of Anna Akhmatova (and of Nadezhda Mandelstam). He subjected Gorky to a much stranger destiny, slowly deforming his talent and integrity; next to execution, deformity was the likeliest outcome for the post-October Russian writer, expressed most eloquently in suicide. He endured Pasternak; he silenced him, and took a lover and a child from him; still, he spared him ('Do

not touch this cloud-dweller'). But this is what he did to the
Meyerholds.

The world-famous Vsevolod Meyerhold had displeased
Stalin, at the height of the Great Terror, with his production of
a play about the Civil War. Meyerhold was savaged by *Pravda*
(that was a ritual, something like a promissory note of disaster)
and his theatre was shut down. After a while he was given some
employment and protection by Stanislavsky. Stanislavsky died in
August 1938. Just under a year later Meyerhold was given an official opportunity to recant at a conference organized by the
Committee on Art Affairs. He did not recant. He said, among
other things:

> I, for one, find the work of our theatres pitiful and terrifying
> . . . Go to the Moscow theatres and look at the colourless,
> boring productions which are all alike and differ only in their
> degree of worthlessness . . . In your effort to eradicate
> formalism, you have destroyed art!

A few days later he was arrested. The file on Meyerhold
contains his letter from prison to Molotov:

> The investigators began to use force on me, a sick, sixty-five-
> year-old man. I was made to lie face down and then beaten
> on the soles of my feet and my spine with a rubber strap . . .
> For the next few days, when those parts of my legs were covered
> with extensive internal haemorrhaging, they again beat the
> red-blue-and-yellow bruises with the strap and the pain was
> so intense that it felt as if boiling water was being poured on
> these sensitive areas. I howled and wept from the pain . . .
> [which] caused my eyes to weep unending streams of tears.
> Lying face down on the floor, I discovered that I could wriggle,
> twist and squeal like a dog when its master whips it . . . When
> I lay down on the cot and fell asleep, after eighteen hours of

interrogation, in order to go back in an hour's time for more,
I was woken up by my own groaning and because I was jerking
about like a patient in the last stages of typhoid fever.

You know that your sleep has been politicized – when that is
what wakes you. The interrogator, he added, urinated in his
mouth. Meyerhold wrote this letter on 13 January 1940, having
confessed to whatever it was they wanted him to confess to
(spying for the British and the Japanese, among other charges).
Stalin needed confessions; he followed the progress of certain
interrogations (lasting months or even years), and couldn't sleep
until confessions were secured. So *his* sleep, of course, was also
politicized.

A few days after Meyerhold's arrest his young wife, the actress
Zinaida Raikh, was found dead in their apartment. She had seventeen knife wounds. The neighbours had heard her screams; they
thought she was *rehearsing*. It is reported that her eyes, presumably closed in sleep when the doorbell rang, had been cut out.

Meyerhold was shot on 2 February 1940.

I had just begun this book when I came across the following, in
an account of the Soviet-exported Hungarian 'revolution' of 1919:

With some twenty of 'Lenin's Boys' [the terror wing of the
Revolutionary Council], Tibor Szamuely . . . executed several
locals accused of collaborating with the Romanians . . . One
Jewish schoolboy who tried to plead for his father's life was
killed for calling Szamuely a 'wild beast' . . . Szamuely had
requisitioned a train and was travelling around the country
hanging any peasant opposed to collectivization . . .

My first thought was to fax Bob Conquest with the question:
'Was Tibor Szamuely related to Tibor Szamuely?' Then I recalled

the piece about Tibor, our Tibor, written by my father in his *Memoirs*. I settled down to it, thinking that I knew Tibor's story pretty well, and thinking, moreover, that it was a happy story, a story of struggle, heroic cunning, luck, escape, subversive triumph. And I finished the piece with a pain in my throat. This is not a Meyerhold story; but it is another story about the politicization of sleep.

Tibor Szamuely was Tibor Szamuely's *uncle*, and a famous associate of Lenin's. Tibor, our Tibor, 'had a framed photograph, prominently displayed, of the two monsters side by side facing a crowd from a platform', my father writes. It was, then, as a scion of an émigré Hungarian political family that Tibor was born in Moscow in 1925. When he was eleven his father disappeared into the mouth of 1936. Tibor fought in the Red Army while still in his teens. In the early 1950s Tibor happened to say, in the hearing of somebody he thought he could trust, that he was sick of the sight of that 'fat pig' Georgi Malenkov (Prime Minister of the USSR, 1953–55). Representatives of 'the Organs' came for him in the middle of the night. He got eight years, to be served in the northern camp of Vorkuta – a name that means as much to a Russian, perhaps, as the name Dachau means to a Jew. Or means more. I choose Dachau advisedly and maybe pusillanimously. Many people died in it but Dachau did not have time to become a death camp (its gas chambers were built too late). Vorkuta was not a death camp. The gulag had no death camps of the Nazi type, no Belzec, no Sobibor (though it had execution camps). But all the camps were death camps, by the nature of things. Those not immediately killed at Auschwitz, which was a slave camp and a death camp, tended to last three months. Two years seems to have been the average for the slave camps of the gulag archipelago.

'Write to your mother' were Tibor's last words to his wife as he was led away at three o'clock in the morning. It used to be his boast that he was the only prisoner ever freed by Stalin – by Stalin personally. Nina Szamuely's mother had apparently had close relations with Hungary's Stalinist dictator Matyas Rakosi. Stalin was duly called or cabled by the Stalinist; orders were dispatched to Vorkuta. The KGB man sent to liberate Tibor apologized to him, on the railway platform by *kissing his shoes*. The convicted slanderer of the state was now in favour. And Tibor, by a series of wonderful feints and flukes, escaped to the England he had visited as a boy. He escaped with his wife, his two children, and also (a great coup) his vast and irreplaceable library. So this was a happy story, I thought: a happy story.

It didn't take Tibor long to establish himself: historian, academic, journalist, USSR-watcher. When his naturalization papers came through, the fascists held a celebratory lunch. Of his new citizenship he later said to my father, 'You know, this means I have no more worries. Nothing matters to me now. Not even dying. I'll be able to say to myself, well, at least it's in England.' And it *was* in England: two years later, at the age of forty-seven. And Nina died two years after that: the same day, the same cancer. I remember her with greater clarity and feeling than I remember him. I used to smile at it: her air of worry, her constant *activity* of worry. And I remember her funeral, too, and 'one of the most harrowing sights imaginable,' as my father writes, 'that of the two young orphaned children, Helen and George, there at the top of the church steps to greet the mourners, standing completely alone . . .'

Tibor was an unusually late riser, and Kingsley once complained to Nina about it. She said that her husband sometimes needed to see the first signs of dawn before he could begin to contemplate sleep. Even in England. He needs, said Nina, 'to be absolutely certain that they won't be coming for him that night'.

We cannot understand it, and there is no reason why we should. It takes a significant effort of imagination to guess at the 'fear that millions of people find insurmountable', in the words of Vasily Grossman, 'this fear written up in crimson letters over the leaden sky of Moscow – this terrible fear of the state'.

More Background

'Hugh MacDiarmid: what a bastard,' said my father in about 1972, referring to the man widely believed to be the greatest Scottish poet of the twentieth century. 'He became a Communist in 1956 – *after* Hungary.'

'And what's his stuff like?' I asked.

'Oh, you know. Nothing but Marxist clichés interspersed with archaic "Scotch" expletives.'

'For instance?'

He thought for a moment. My memory exactly vouches for lines two and four, though it can't do the same for lines one and three, where, for that matter, any old rubbish would have done. He said something like:

Every political system is a superstructure over a determining
        socioeconomic base.
Whah-hey!
The principle of distribution according to need precludes the
    conversion of products into goods and their conversion
        into value.
Och aye!

> The objective conditions for the transfer to socialism can
>   only—

'Enough,' I said – though now I wish I had let him go on a bit. It was easy to joke about Communism. That was one of the things the Russians, too, had always done about Communism. On the other hand you could serve years for joking about Communism, under Communism (as Tibor knew). Joke. Q: Why are the USSR and America the same? A: Because in the USSR you can joke about America and in America you can joke about America.

During the mid-1970s I worked for the famous and historic and now perhaps obsolescent Labour weekly, the *New Statesman* (or the NEW STATESMAN, in its own house style).* My contemporaries there were Julian Barnes (novelist and critic), Christopher Hitchens (journalist, essayist, political man of letters), and James

---

*The *New Statesman* was founded in 1913 by, among others (and the others included Maynard Keynes), the century's four most extravagant dupes of the USSR: H. G. Wells, George Bernard Shaw, and Sidney and Beatrice Webb. Wells, after an audience with Stalin in 1934, said that he had 'never met a man more candid, fair and honest'; these attributes accounted for 'his remarkable ascendancy over the country since no one is afraid of him and everyone trusts him'. Shaw, after some banquet diplomacy, declared the Russian people uncommonly well-fed at a time when perhaps 11 million citizens (Martin Malia, *The Soviet Tragedy: A History of Socialism in Russia*, 1917–1991) were in the process of dying of starvation. The Webbs, after extensive study, wrote a book which, 'seen as the last word in serious Western scholarship, ran to over 1,200 pages, representing a vast amount of toil and research, all totally wasted. It was originally entitled *Soviet Communism: A New Civilisation?*, but the question mark was triumphantly removed in the second edition – which appeared in 1937 at precisely the time the regime was in its worst phase' (Conquest). Sidney and Beatrice Webb swallowed the great Show Trials of 1936–38, and the *New Statesman* was not much less sceptical: 'We do not deny . . . that the confessions may have contained a substratum of truth'; 'there had undoubtedly been much plotting in the USSR'; and so on.

Fenton (journalist, critic, essayist and, above all, poet). Politically we broke down as follows. Julian was broadly Labour – though Christopher Hitchens would tirelessly ridicule him for having once voted Liberal. I was quietist and unaligned. Fenton and Hitchens, on the other hand, were proselytizing Trotskyists who (for instance) spent their Saturdays selling copies of the *Socialist Worker* on impoverished London high streets.

'What do I call you if I write this piece?' I said to Christopher, on the phone to him in Washington, D.C. 'Trotskyites or Trotskyists?'

'Oh, Trotskyists. Only a Stalinist would have called us Trotskyites.'

I laughed. I laughed indulgently. We talked on.

At the *New Statesman* in the mid-1970s we used to argue about Communism. I was unaligned, but I was, in a sense, a congenital anti-Communist, inoculated not at birth but at the age of six or seven, in 1956, when the Amises settled into honest atheism with the Labour Party. And, anyway, the argument was surely all over now, with the publication, in 1973 and 1975, of the first two volumes of *The Gulag Archipelago*. Upstairs, in the literary department, we had published a review of Volume Two, by V. S. Pritchett, beautifully and (to me) unforgettably entitled 'When We Dead Awaken'. Pritchett's piece ended: '[Solzhenitsyn] is not a political; he is without rhetoric or doublethink; he is an awakener.' When We Dead Awaken: yes, I thought. That is the next thing now . . . And it hasn't happened. In the general consciousness the Russian dead sleep on.

Hitchens and I used to argue about Communism in the corridors, sporadically, semi-seriously. The fascist novelist John Braine (proletarian, northern, monotonously drunken, and ridiculously influential, socioculturally but not politically, for at least a generation) used to say to left-wingers: 'Why do you *love* despotism? Why do you *yearn* for tyranny?' And this was more or less the question I put to the Hitch:

'Rule by yobs. That's what you want. Why?'

'Yup. Rule by yobs. What I want is the berks in the saddle. Rule by yobs.'

These exchanges took place in a spirit of humorous appraisal, mutual appraisal. We were not quite yet the best friends we would become, and politics was part of the distance between us. Rule by yobs, incidentally, or the dictatorship of the proletariat (an outcome only academically entertained by the Bolsheviks), provided the flavour of the superficial and temporary rearrangement taking place in England then: the transfer of wealth, as the Labour Party put it, to the working classes and their families. I was partly going with the culture, perhaps, but this idea (with 99 per cent income tax in the top bracket, etc.) so little offended me that I too voted for the continuation of Labour policies. Or I tried. On General Election day in 1978 my brother and I (Labour) agreed, in the fascist mansion, to stay at home and swap votes with two *in situ* Conservatives. The Conservatives (we felt) pretended to misunderstand this arrangement and drove off to vote in my step-uncle's car: a fascist Jaguar. ('That's *four* votes you cheated us out of,' I said with some heat to my step-uncle. 'No. Two votes,' he corrected.) Meanwhile, the social effect of trade-union – they used to say trades-union – ascendancy was everywhere apparent. And profound and retroactive. It made me believe that the people of these islands had always hated each other. And this isn't true. The hatred, the universal disobligingness, was a political deformation, and it didn't last.

James Fenton said little during these semi-serious disputes, although they often took place in his office (which was always incredibly tidy, with no more than a lone paper clip on the whole sweep of the desk. Julian's desk was incredibly tidy, also featuring the lone paper clip. My desk was a haystack. Christopher's desk was a haystack. 'You and Christopher ought to get married,' said James resignedly. He was best friends with Christopher, too. And they shared the politics.) James said little during these disputes. Like Christopher, he saw no hope in the 'actually existing' socialism of the USSR, and actively opposed it. Very roughly, their political faith imagined a return to the well of revolutionary energy through the figure of Trotsky, that great eidolon of thwarted possibility. James had had his counter-experiences in Vietnam and Cambodia. But I wondered how he felt, qua poet, about the place of art in a socialist state; and, I thought, he must hate the *language*, the metallic clichés, the formulas and euphemisms, the supposedly futuristic and time-thrifty acronyms and condensations.* Once, when we had a solemn lunch together, James formulated his (local) position as follows: 'I want a Labour government that is weak against the trade unions.' And England, I unelegiacally thought, was going to get that kind of government. This was the future, and it was Left.

So on the phone, the other day, I said to Christopher, 'We'll have to have a long talk about this.'

'A long talk.'

*What Nabokov characterizes as the Com-pom-poms – Sovnarkom and Narkomindel, and so on; the state liquor monopoly was called Soyuzsprit; the agency shunting the Mandelstams around in the early 1920s was unencouragingly known as Centroevac.

'Because I'm wondering about the distance between Stalin's Russia and Hitler's Germany.'

'Oh don't fall for that, Mart. Don't fall for moral equivalence.'

'Why not?'

'Lenin was . . . a great man.'

'Oh no he wasn't.'

'This will be a *long* talk.'

'A *long* talk.'

But progress has already been made. The argument, now, is about whether Bolshevik Russia was 'better' than Nazi Germany. In the days when the New Left dawned, the argument was about whether Bolshevik Russia was better than America.

Ten Theses on Ilyich

(i.)

In his letter to Maxim Gorky about the fate of the country's intellectuals ('they're not its brains. They're its shit'), Lenin wrote (15 September 1922):

> [The writer Vladimir Korolenko] is a pitiful philistine, trapped in bourgeois prejudices! For gentlemen such as this ten million dead in the imperialist war is something worth supporting . . . while the death of hundreds of thousands in a *just* civil war against the landowners and capitalists makes them oh! and ah! and sigh and go into hysterics.

This is the usual figure for military losses in World War I (all belligerent nations): *c.* 7,800,000. This is the usual figure for military losses in the Civil War: *c.* 1,000,000. But then, in the

Russian case, there were a further 12 million civilian losses. '[T]hese figures tell only half the story, since obviously, under normal conditions, the population would not have remained stationary but grown,' writes Richard Pipes in *Russia Under the Bolshevik Regime*. By this calculation the number goes up to 23 million. And there is, I think, a good case for including the birth deficit. Because the Russian experiment wasn't conducted for the betterment of the poor wretches who happened to be alive at the time; it was conducted in the name of their children and their children's children . . . Was the, or a, Civil War inevitable? Was there so much bad blood that the census was foredoomed to its astronomical minus? Well, the Civil War became inevitable when Lenin took power. There are dozens of quotations, slogans, rallying cries attesting to his enthusiasm for civil war. The same is true of Trotsky. Civil war was a cornerstone of Bolshevik policy.

(ii.)

Lenin suffered his first stroke in May 1922. In September he wrote the ferocious letter to Gorky. In the intervening July he was drawing up his many lists of intellectuals for arrest and deportation or internal exile. A month earlier Lenin's doctors had asked him to multiply 12 by 7. Three hours later he solved the problem by addition: $12 + 12 = 24$, $24 + 12 = 36$ . . . The ex-believer Dmitri Volkogonov comments in his *Lenin: A New Biography*:

> He had covered a twenty-one-page notepad with childish scrawls . . . The future of an entire generation of the flower of the Russian intelligentsia was being decided by a man who could barely cope with an arithmetical problem for a seven-year-old.

There were further strokes. Later, Lenin's wife Krupskaya taught him to repeat (and it only worked under direct prompting) the words 'peasant', 'worker', 'people' and 'revolution' . . . Adam Ulam has described the nihilism of the Russian revolutionary tradition as 'at once childish and nightmarish'. The dying Lenin – and, frequently, the living Lenin, too – was childish and nightmarish. In his last ten months he was reduced to monosyllables. But at least they were political monosyllables: *vot-vot* (here-here) and *sezd-sezd* (congress-congress).

(iii.)

It fills you with extraordinary torpor to learn that Lenin read Nikolai Chernyshevsky's insuperably talentless novel *What Is To Be Done?* (1863) *five times* in one summer. To read this book once in five summers would defeat most of us; but Lenin persisted. 'It completely reshaped me,' he said in 1904. 'This is a book that changes one for a whole lifetime.' Its greatest merit, he stressed, was that it showed you 'what a revolutionary *must be like*'. Humiliating though it may feel, we are obliged to conclude that *What Is To Be Done?* is the most influential novel of all time. With its didactic portrait of the revolutionary New Man, its 'russification' of current radical themes, and its contempt for ordinary people, 'Chernyshevsky's novel, far more than Marx's *Capital*, supplied the emotional dynamic that eventually went to make the Russian Revolution' (Joseph Frank). I am reminded of a recent aside by a Russian writer (Victor Erofeyev) who was trying to account for the cult of Rasputin. There are 'some grounds for saying,' he wrote, that 'deep down, Russia has nothing in common with the West'.

(iv.)

In championing the 'unprecedentedly shameful peace' with Imperial Germany (the Treaty of Brest-Litovsk), Lenin temporarily lost ground within the Party. On economic policy he was now stampeded by the visionaries, notably Bukharin. This is Trotsky:

> In Lenin's 'Theses on the Peace', written in early 1918, it says that 'the triumph of socialism in Russia [required] a certain interval of time, *no less than a few months*'. At present [1924] such words seem completely incomprehensible: was not this a slip of the pen, did he not mean to speak of a few years or decades? But no . . . I recall very clearly that in the first period, at Smolny, at meetings of the Council of People's Commissars, Lenin invariably repeated that we shall have socialism in half a year and become the mightiest state.

Thus the regime moved to eliminate a) law, b) foreign relations, c) private property, d) commerce, and e) money. The means chosen to eliminate money was state-driven hyperinflation. In 'the second half of 1919, "treasury operations" – in other words, the printing of money – consumed between 45 and 60 per cent of budgetary expenditures' (Richard Pipes, *The Russian Revolution*). During the attempted invasion of Poland in 1920, Lenin sent the following instruction to a Red Army commissar:

> A beautiful plan. Finish it off with Dzerzhinsky. Under the guise of 'Greens'* (and we will pin it on them later) we shall go forward for ten-twenty versts and hang the kulaks, priests and landowners. Bounty: 100,000 rubles for each man hanged.

*The insurrectionary armies of the Peasant War (1918–22). Lenin, with justice, thought the Greens a greater threat to the regime's survival than the Whites.

By 1921, 100,000 rubles was worth two prewar kopeks.* At this time the set of policies retrospectively labelled War Communism was being abandoned in favour of the New Economic Policy (NEP), which, in effect, legalized the black market that was feeding the cities – with difficulty. The net result of War Communism was the obliteration of the industrial base and the worst famine in European history.

(v.)

Lenin (19 March 1922):

> It is now and only now, when in the regions afflicted by the famine there is cannibalism and the roads are littered with hundreds if not thousands of corpses, that we can (and there-fore must) pursue the acquisition of [church] valuables with the most ferocious and merciless energy, stopping at nothing in suppressing all resistance . . . [N]o other moment except that of desperate hunger will offer us such a mood among the broad peasant masses, which will either assure us of their sympathy, or, at any rate, their neutrality . . . [W]e must now give the most decisive and merciless battle to the [clergy] and subdue its resistance with such brutality that they will not forget it for decades to come . . . The greater the number of the representatives of the reactionary bourgeoisie and reac-tionary clergy that we will manage to execute in this affair, the better.

Church records show that 2,691 priests, 1,962 monks and 3,447 nuns were killed that year. During an earlier Russian famine, that of 1891, in which half a million died, famine relief was a national

---

*Between 1 January 1917, and 1 January 1923, the price of goods increased by a factor of 100 million.

priority. In the regional capital of Samara only one intellectual, a twenty-two-year-old lawyer, refused to participate in the effort – and, indeed, publicly denounced it. This was Lenin. He 'had the courage', as a friend put it,

> to come out and say openly that famine would have numerous positive results . . . Famine, he explained, in destroying the outdated peasant economy, would . . . usher in socialism . . . Famine would also destroy faith not only in the tsar, but in God too.

Famine belongs to the Communist tetrarchy – the other three elements being terror, slavery and, of course, failure, monotonous and incorrigible failure.

(vi.)

It has often been said that the Bolsheviks ruled as if conducting a war against their own people.* But you could go further and say that the Bolsheviks were conducting a war against human nature. Lenin to Gorky:

> Every religious idea, every idea of God . . . is unutterable vileness . . . of the most dangerous kind, 'contagion' of the most abominable kind. Millions of sins, filthy deeds, acts of violence and physical contagions . . . are far less dangerous than the

---

*This made sense doctrinally, too. The Bolsheviks were internationalists; the Soviet Union was no more than the headquarters of Communism while it waited for planetary revolution. As he advanced on Warsaw in July 1920, Marshal Tukhachevsky repeated the official line: 'Over the corpse of White Poland lies the path to world conflagration.' (After the Red Army – largely thanks, it seems, to Stalin – was defeated, the Bolsheviks began to suspect that the fraternal revolutions weren't going to materialize.) As for the Russians themselves, Lenin was frankly racist in his settled dislike for them. They were fools and bunglers, and 'too soft' to run an efficient police state. He made no secret of his preference for the Germans.

subtle, spiritual idea of God decked out in the smartest 'ideological' costumes . . .

Religion is reaction, certainly (and wasn't the Tsar meant to be
divine?). But religion is also human nature. One recalls John
Updike's argument: the only evidence for the existence of God is
the collective human yearning that it should be so. The war against
religion was part of the war against human nature, which was
prosecuted on many other fronts.

(vii.)

Lenin's famine of 1921–22 (*c.* 5 million dead) was not in origin
terroristic. Weather played a part; but so did the Bolshevik policy
of requisitioning – of taking the peasants' grain without paying
for it. Deprived of incentive, the peasants practised circumven-
tion; and the regime, as always, responded with a crescendo of
force, whose climax was the weapon of hunger. Unlike Stalin's
famine of 1933, Lenin's famine was officially recognized as such.*
In July 1921 Maxim Gorky was given permission to form a relief
committee (consisting mostly of intellectuals) and to launch an
international appeal. Socialism, far from catapulting Russia into
planetary prepotence, had reduced her to beggary. Lenin felt
himself heckled by a reality now known all over the world, and
the humiliation expressed itself in a bitterly defensive xenophobia.
He did no more than harry and obstruct the American Relief
Administration. But when the crisis was over he went after
Gorky's committee. First there was a campaign of vilification in

*Though very tardily: the future US president Herbert Hoover had been
agitating for a food campaign in the USSR since 1919. Lenin also continued to
export grain throughout this period (and continued, of course, to commit vast
sums to the fomentation of revolutions elsewhere).

the press, claiming that the ARA was, of all things, 'counter-revolutionary'. This is from *The Harvest of Sorrow:*

> . . . the non-Communist Russian relief representatives in
> Moscow were arrested in the autumn of 1921 (at a time when
> Maxim Gorky was out of the country). Intervention by
> [Herbert] Hoover personally resulted in the commutation of
> death sentences . . .

(viii.)

To be clear: Lenin bequeathed to his successors a fully functioning police state. The independence of the press was destroyed within days of the October coup d'état. The penal code was rewritten in November/December (and already we see the elastic category, 'enemy of the people': 'All individuals suspected [*sic*] of sabotage, speculation, and opportunism are now liable to be arrested immediately'). Forced food-requisitioning began in November. The Cheka (or secret police) was in place by December. Concentration camps were established in early 1918 (and so was the use of psychiatric hospitals as places of detention). Then came fulminant terror: executions by quota; 'collective responsibility', whereby the families and even the neighbours of enemies of the people, or suspected enemies of the people, were taken hostage; and the extermination not only of political opponents but also of social and ethnic groups – the kulaks, or better-off peasants, for example, and the Cossacks ('de-Cossackization'). The differences between the regimes of Lenin and Stalin were quantitative, not qualitative. Stalin's one true novelty was the discovery of another stratum of society in need of purgation: Bolsheviks.

(ix.)

Unlike Stalin, Lenin could plead mitigation – though, like Stalin, he would not have so pleaded.* In March 1887 Lenin's older brother Alexander was arrested for conspiring to murder his namesake, Tsar Alexander III; a plea for clemency would have reduced his sentence to hard labour, but Alexander was possessed of the courage of youth and, two months later, was duly hanged. He was twenty-one. Vladimir Ilyich was seventeen. And their father had died the previous year. Clearly the consequences of these events are entitled to be boundless. My sense of it is that Lenin's moral faculties stopped developing thereafter. Hence his foul-mouthed tantrums, his studied amorality, his flirtatious nihilism, his positively giggly response to violence: his nightmarish child-ishness. How terrible it is to read the verdict of the Australian historian Manning Clark, who found Lenin 'Christ-like, at least in his compassion' and 'as excited and lovable as a little child'.

(x.)

The trouble with Lenin was that he thought you could achieve things by coercion and terror and murder. 'The dictatorship – and take this into account once and for all – means unrestricted power based on force, not on law' (January 1918). 'It is a great mistake to think that the NEP put an end to terror. We shall return to terror and to economic terror' (March 1922). And so on – again, there are dozens of such statements. On his first day

*'There is no hint in any of the vast array of archival material to suggest that [Lenin] was troubled by his conscience about any of the long list of destructive measures he took' (Volkogonov, *Lenin: A New Biography*). 'Nothing in the notes, remarks and resolutions of [Stalin's] last years suggests anything but unfailing confidence that his life's work was eternal' (Volkogonov, *The Rise and Fall of the Soviet Empire*).

in office Lenin was looking the other way when the Second Congress of Soviets abolished the death penalty.* 'Nonsense,' said Lenin: 'how can you make a revolution without executions?' To think otherwise was 'impermissible weakness', 'pacifist illusion', and so on. You needed capital punishment, or it wouldn't be a 'real' revolution – like the French Revolution (and unlike the English Revolution or the American Revolution or, indeed, the Russian Revolution of February 1917). Lenin wanted executions; he had his heart set on executions. And he got them. The possibility has been suggested that in the period 1917–24 more people were murdered by the secret police than were killed in all the battles of the Civil War.[†]

It can be tersely stated: under Lenin, the 'value of human life collapsed', as Alain Brossat put it. And that was the end of the matter, for the next thirty-five years.

Vasily Grossman:

> 'Everything inhuman is senseless and worthless' . . . Amid the total triumph of inhumanity, it has become self-evident that everything effected by violence is senseless and worthless, and that it has no future and will disappear without trace.

Who-Whom?

Who, here, is describing whom?

> In the course of those five February days when the revolutionary fight was being waged in the cold streets of the capital,

---

*Which the Provisional Government under Kerensky had reinstated as a punishment for front-line desertion. The Bolsheviks had earlier campaigned with the slogan, 'Down with capital punishment, reinstated by Kerensky.'
[†]Orlando Figes, *A People's Tragedy: The Russian Revolution 1891–1924.*

there flitted before us several times like a shadow the figure of a liberal of noble family, the son of a former tsarist minister, ******* – almost symbolic in his self-satisfied correctness and dry egotism . . . He now became General Administrator of the Provisional Government . . . In his Berlin exile where he was finally killed by the stray bullet of a White Guard, he left memoirs of the Provisional Government which are not without interest. Let us place that to his credit.

The whom is Vladimir Nabokov (the father) and the who is Leon Trotsky: *History of the Russian Revolution* (1932, and written in exile). How translucently bloodthirsty is the phrase 'he was finally killed . . .' Because Trotsky counted Nabokov among those he wanted killed, and someone 'finally' killed him. Trotsky was not accustomed to waiting so long. He joins Lenin as guilty of the basic charge, although he typically stated the case with more revolutionary 'elan': 'We must put an end once and for all to the papist-Quaker babble about the sanctity of human life.' A considerable severance. Trotsky was not without literary talent, literary expressiveness. But Edmund Wilson, in *To the Finland Station* (1940), is ridiculous when he talks about Trotsky's stuff as being 'part of our permanent literature'. Trotsky's *History* is a valuable historical document, but it is worthless as history, as historiography, as *writing*; truth, like all other human values, is indefinitely postponable. After a while the reader is physically oppressed by the dishonesty of his prose. In any case, Trotsky's final pages, for all their massive, inordinate – indeed, world-historical – complacency, are also quietly ironic when you consider the fate of their author. The *History* runs to three volumes, so these quotes are effectively from pages 1,258–59:

> Enemies are gleeful that fifteen years after the revolution the Soviet country is still but little like a kingdom of universal

well-being . . . Capitalism required a hundred years to elevate science and technique to the heights and plunge humanity into the hell of war and crisis. To socialism its enemies allow only fifteen years to create and furnish a terrestrial paradise . . .

The language of the civilized nations has clearly marked off two epochs in the development of Russia. Where the aristocratic culture introduced into world parlance such barbarisms as *tsar, progrom, knout,* October has internationalized such words as *Bolshevik, soviet* and *piatiletka.* This alone justifies the proletarian revolution, if you imagine that it needs justification.

THE END

Which leaves you wondering if *piatiletka* is Russian for 'summary execution', perhaps, or 'slave camp'.* 'Fifteen years after the revolution': 1932. Stalin, Trotsky's enemy and eventual murderer, was immovably emplaced, and 6 million people were being systematically starved to death. The Ukraine, in Conquest's phrase, was becoming 'one vast Belsen' . . .

Vladimir Nabokov (the son) met Edmund Wilson in 1940, just after the appearance of *To the Finland Station*; and they became good enough friends to produce an inspiring correspondence: *The Nabokov-Wilson Letters 1940–1971.* As the editor, Simon Karlinsky, says in his introduction, Wilson acted, to begin with, as Nabokov's 'unpaid literary agent'. This spontaneous donation of energy was received with desperate gratitude by Nabokov, who would remain grossly overworked and more or less 'penniless' until *Lolita* (1955). He had just fled with his Jewish wife, Véra, and their son, Dmitri, from France, which was then collapsing to

---

*I searched without success for *piatiletka* in five end-of-monograph glossaries. Its clinching 'internationalization', then, didn't last (although Hitler, and later Mao, took it up). *Piatiletka* means 'five-year plan'.

the Germans. Next, going backwards in time, Hitlerian and Weimar Berlin, where Nabokov incorporated into a novel (*The Gift*, 1937–38) an erudite but also brilliantly impressionistic biography of Nikolai Chernyshevsky – whose revolutionary primer (Nabokov translates it as *What to Do?*) was Lenin's looking-glass.* Then, going further back in time, the flight from revolutionary Russia. Cowed, perhaps, by Nabokov's strictures on art and 'ideas', we neglect the political pulse in him and in his fiction. He wrote two novels about totalitarian states (*Bend Sinister* and *Invitation to a Beheading*); these were imaginary, but the totalitarian states Nabokov had experienced were real: Lenin's and Hitler's. And, as Trotsky contentedly noted, Vladimir Nabokov (the father) was assassinated in Berlin in 1922, when Vladimir Nabokov (the son: in *Speak, Memory* he refers to the assailants as 'two Russian Fascists') was turning twenty-three; that night – 'Father is no more' – was the crux of his life. So, yes, there would be a political pulse. And this is partly why Nabokov, in all his fiction, writes with incomparable penetration about delusion and coercion, about cruelty and lies. Even *Lolita*, especially *Lolita*, is a study in tyranny.

Wilson and Nabokov fell out. Their first enduring disagreement had to do with the Russian Revolution. Their second had to do with Russian prosody, and it was this, quaintly but intelligibly, that foreclosed their friendship, together with Wilson's cold words about *Lolita*. As I regretfully see it, Bunny (Bunny was the nickname Volodya was soon using) began to pick fights with his friend at just about the point where Nabokov's reputation was

---

*It would not have escaped Nabokov's notice that Chernyshevsky's centennial (1928) was the occasion of much lugubrious ceremony in the Soviet Union. Chernyshevsky was saluted as the grandsire of the 'Socialist Realism' that Stalin intended to impose on the country's remaining writers.

eclipsing his own. The friendship plummeted in 1966, when Wilson went into print with a hostile (and ignorant) review of Nabokov's translation of *Eugene Onegin* – and gave its last flicker, palely and politely, five years later.

In *To the Finland Station* Wilson had written about Lenin romantically: Lenin the warrior-poet, the quiet man of destiny, with something of the instinctive grace of the noble savage – Lenin, the savage *savant*. When the book was reissued in 1971 Wilson added a new introduction:

> I have also been charged with having given a much too amiable picture of Lenin, and I believe that this criticism has been made not without some justification . . . one can see the point of Lenin's being short with the temporizing and arguing Russians but one cannot be surprised that he gave offense and did not show himself so benevolent as I perhaps tend to make him.

Lenin, we note, is still being assessed merely as a social or collegiate being. As for Trotsky, 'I have not found anything which obliges me to make any rectifications,' writes Wilson, having read Isaac Deutscher's (notoriously mythopoeic) biography. So this stands, among much else: '[I]t is as a hero of the faith in Reason that Trotsky must figure for us.'

Wilson was not lastingly gulled by Stalin, but he could never give up on the essential purity of October. So he played his part in the great intellectual abasement. To explain this abasement certain historical conditions are often adduced. They are: the generational wound of World War I (a war successfully branded as 'imperialist' and therefore capitalist), the Great Depression of 1929–34, the rise of fascism and then Nazism (and their combined involvement in the Spanish Civil War), and, later, the moral force of the Russian losses in World War II. But the fact remains that despite 'more and more voluminous and unignorable evidence' to the contrary (as my father put it, writing of the mid-1950s), the USSR continued to be regarded as fundamentally progressive and benign; and the misconception endured until the mid-1970s. What *was* it? From our vantage it looks like a contagion of selective incuriosity, a mindgame begun in self-hypnosis and maintained by mass hysteria. And although the aberration was of serious political utility to Moscow, we still tend to regard it as a bizarre and embarrassing sideshow to the main events. We must hope to find a more structural connection.

In 1935 Wilson journeyed to the USSR and wrote about it in *Travels in Two Democracies* (1956), which, as Professor Karlinsky puts it,

> is an affecting mixture of his own naive expectations and the harsh realities he does his best to explain away . . . Unlike such Western travelers as G. B. Shaw, who visited the USSR at the height of the post-collectivization famine and declared after his return that Soviet citizens were the best-fed people in Europe, Wilson perceived enough of Soviet realities to make him see that this was not the free and idealistic utopia, run by workers and peasants, which he had hoped to find.

Now: let us consider this utopia, the fully achieved utopia that Wilson hoped to find. Ten seconds of sober thought will decisively inform you that such a place is not heaven but a species of hell; that such a place is alien to us; that such a place is non-human. The 'Potemkin villages' occasionally rigged up to deceive foreign VIPs, with the appearances of plenitude trucked in from the cities, and labourers and cowgirls impersonated by the secret police, and imported trees wedged into slots on the road-side:

such a setting is an appropriate figure for utopia, any utopia, because it is farce, because it is travesty.

Wilson shepherded his illusions into his grave (1972). I want to quote some extracts from Nabokov's great letter of 23 February 1948: 1948. In its opening sentences you can hear Nabokov rolling his sleeves up, and you can feel the prose moving a notch towards his high style:

> Dear Bunny,
>   You naively compare my (and the 'old Liberals'') attitude towards the Soviet regime (*sensu lato* [broadly]) to that of a 'ruined and humiliated' American Southerner towards the 'wicked' North. You must know me and 'Russian Liberals' very little if you fail to realize the amusement and contempt with which I regard Russian émigrés whose 'hatred' of the Bolsheviks is based on a sense of financial loss or class *degringolade*. It is preposterous (though quite in line with Soviet writings on the subject) to postulate any material interest at the bottom of a Russian Liberal's (or Democrat's or Socialist's) rejection of the Soviet regime.

Despite his palpable warmth of feeling, Nabokov is here showing restraint. For Wilson has clearly delivered a gross injury to his friend and to their friendship. Nabokov is bearing in mind that Wilson, not understanding the Bolshevik reality, does not understand the insult, either.

Ominously gathering force, the letter continues. Nabokov reminds, or informs, Wilson that the opposition to Bolshevism was and is pluralistic. There follows a comparatively playful elucidation ('[i]ncidental but very important') on the exact constituency of the Russian 'intelligentsia' (they were, definingly, professionals: 'In fact a typical Russian *intelligent* would look askance at an avant-garde poet'); Nabokov lists their strengths and virtues (we feel VN Senior as a powerful exemplum here), and firmly proceeds:

> But of course people who read Trotsky for information anent Russian culture cannot be expected to know all this. I have also a hunch that the general idea that avant-garde literature and art were having a wonderful time under Lenin and Trotsky is mainly due to Eisenstadt [Eisenstein] films – 'montage' – things like that – and great big drops of sweat rolling down rough cheeks. The fact that pre-Revolution Futurists joined the party has also contributed to the kind of (quite false) avantgarde atmosphere which the American intellectual associates with the Bolshevik Revolution.

Nabokov starts a new paragraph. This letter impresses me further every time I read it. I like the even cadences, now, as the writer reasserts the decorum of friendship: 'I do not want to be personal, but here is how I explain your attitude . . .' There follows a perceptive and generous and near-universal analysis (one I will hope to add something to) of the kind of conditions that would facilitate such a severe cognitive dissonance. In 1917 Wilson was twenty-two; the Russian 'experiment' – remote and largely obscure – spoke to his natural ardour.

> Your concept of pre-Soviet Russia came to you through a pro-Soviet prism. When later on (i.e., at a time coinciding with Stalin's ascension) improved information, a more mature judgment and the pressure of inescapable facts dampened your enthusiasm and dried your sympathy, you somehow did not bother to check your preconceived notions in regard to old Russia while, on the other hand, the glamor of Lenin's reign retained for you the emotional iridescence which your optimism, idealism and youth had provided . . .

> The thunderclap of administrative purges [1937–38] woke
> you up (something that the moans of Solovki or at the
> Lubianka had not been able to do) since they affected men
> on whose shoulders St Lenin's hand had lain.

Solovki: cradle of the gulag (and established under Lenin). The
Lubyanka was the Cheka's headquarters in Moscow; its dates are
1918–91.

'I am now going to state a few things,' writes Nabokov,
winding up, 'which I think are true and I don't think you can
refute.' The letter ends with two encapsulations. Pre-1917:

> Under the Tsars (despite the inept and barbarous character
> of their rule) a freedom-loving Russian had incomparably
> more possibility and means of expressing himself than at
> any time during Lenin's and Stalin's regime. He was
> protected by law. There were fearless and independent judges
> in Russia. The Russian *sud* [legal system] after the Alexander
> reforms was a magnificent institution, not only on paper.
> Periodicals of various tendencies and political parties of all
> possible kinds, legally or illegally, flourished and all parties
> were represented in the Duma. Public opinion was always
> liberal and progressive.

Post-1917:

> Under the Soviets, from the very start, the only protection a
> dissenter could hope for was dependent on governmental
> whims, not laws. No parties except the one in power could
> exist. Your Alymovs [Sergei Alymov was a showcase hack
> poet] are specters bobbing in the wake of a foreign tourist.
> Bureaucracy, a direct descendant of party discipline, took
> over immediately. Public opinion disintegrated. The intelli-
> gentsia ceased to exist. Any changes that took place between
> November [1917] and now have been changes in the decor

which more or less screens an unchanging black abyss of oppression and terror.

'Intellectual' is a word commonly applied to the Bolshevik leaders (and it is often said that Stalin was 'the only non-intellectual' among them). They qualified, one supposes, as intellectuals of the radical fringe, in that they were half-educated in history and political economy, and in nothing else. As Nabokov has just explained, however, a Russian intellectual is a professional; and it was a rare Old Bolshevik who ever presented himself for gainful employment (though Lenin, earlier, lost a couple of cases as a lawyer). We have seen, too, that the revolutionary vanguard developed an abnormal aversion to the intellectuals, who were, as Lenin said, 'shit'. And in 1922 Lenin threw himself into the business of what Solzhenitsyn, establishing a metaphor for the gulag, calls 'sewage disposal'. Some were executed or internally exiled, and scores of thousands were deported. American commentators 'saw us', writes Nabokov, 'merely as villainous generals, oil magnates, and gaunt ladies with lorgnettes', but the émigrés were very broadly the intelligentsia. They were the civil society.

In another sense, of course, the revolutionaries *were* professionals: avowedly and disastrously, they were 'professional revolutionaries', just as Chernyshevsky had enjoined them to be, 'fulltime revolutionaries', with their leather jackets, revolvers, hideouts, trysts, schisms, conspiracies, passwords, false beards, false names.* Watched, trailed, shadowed, menaced, detained,

---

*'Lenin' is thought to derive from the River Lena. 'Stalin': man of steel. 'Kamenev': man of stone. 'Molotov': the hammer. 'Trotsky' (*né* Lev Bronstein) was the name on one of his false passports; it stuck.

searched, infiltrated, provoked, arrested, imprisoned, interrogated, tried, sentenced: when, in the course of a single evening, these undergrounders found themselves at the commanding heights, how could it be otherwise than *who-whom?* (in Lenin's famous question)? Who will vanquish whom? Who will destroy whom?

Nabokov's 'Life of Chernyshevsky', which comprises about a hundred pages of *The Gift*, is serious (and comic) and scholarly, and based on deep reading. And poor Nikolai Gavrilovich, of course, emerges as a Gogolian grotesque (obsessed by perpetual-motion machines and encyclopedias), a shambling cuckold, and a literary anti-talent (who, with his 'agonisingly circumstantial' style, was 'a person ridiculously alien to artistic creation'). The following lines take on wide application, if we regard Chernyshevsky as the tutelary spirit, the jinx or genius of Bolshevism and its transformative dream:

> In the descriptions of his absurd experiments and in his commentaries on them, in this mixture of ignorance and ratiocination, one can already detect that barely perceptible flaw which gave his later utterances something like a hint of quackery . . . Such was the fate of Chernyshevsky that everything turned against him: no matter what subject he touched there would come to light – insidiously, and with the most taunting inevitability – something that was completely opposed to his conception of it . . . Everything he touches falls to pieces. It is sad to read in his diaries about the appliances of which he tries to make use – scale-arms, bobs, corks, basins – and nothing revolves, or if it does, then according to unwelcome laws, in the reverse direction to what he wants: an eternal motor going in reverse – why, this is an absolute nightmare, the abstraction to end all abstractions, infinity with a minus sign, plus a broken

jug into the bargain . . . it is amazing how everything bitter and heroic which life manufactured for Chernyshevsky was invariably accompanied by a flavouring of vile farce.

But now we feel a freedom, do we not – a freedom from *who-whom*? Edmund Wilson, in his trundling way, might have expected Nabokov to harbour some distaste for his dispossessor and deracinator. And it isn't so. Nabokov writes about Chernyshevsky with pity, with reverence, with artistic love. And I'm afraid that this is as far as we are ever going to get with the utopia and the earthly paradise. Only in art will the lion lie down with the lamb, and the rose grow without thorn.

Insecure: More Background

Considering that Trotsky
Did *not* ski,
It was a bit thick
To fricassee his brains with an ice-pick.

You could always joke about it. This was a contribution by Robin Ravensbourne to a clerihew competition in the *New Statesman* (another notable winner was Basil Ransome's 'Karl Marx / Provided the clerks / With a dialectical reason / For their treason'). A month later there was a Weekend Comp. where you had to think up the names of organizations whose acronyms mocked and betrayed them: Barnaby Rudge and Oliver Twist Hostel for Elderly Ladies, for example. Robert Conquest won first prize with, among others, Teachers' Organization for Aiding Disoriented Youth, and Sailors', Yachtsmen's and Pilots' Health Institute for Long Island Sound. (And I also admired Mr Ransome's post-modernist Professional Institute of Registered Newspaper

Typesetters.) But my father took the bays with the following: Institute of *New Statesman* Editors and Contributors for Underwriting the Russian Experiment. And once a month or so, upstairs, there was another Russian connection: our ballet critic, Oleg Kerensky, was the nephew of Alexander Kerensky, that 'buffoon, charlatan and nincompoop', as a contemporary relevantly described him, who headed the Provisional Government of 1917. An additional ten IQ points in Kerensky might have saved Russia from Lenin; and a similar elevation in Tsar Nicholas II might have saved Russia from Kerensky. It is now 1975, and Kerensky is not long dead, over in New York. And his nephew, Oleg (a homosexual of a familiar type: warm, courteous, and passionate about the arts), looks in once a month with his ballet column.

Insecure. When you can joke about something, you're meant to feel secure about it. And you could always joke about the USSR. Christopher Hitchens joked about the USSR. For instance . . . Two comrades are discussing the inexplicable failure of a luxurious, state-run, Western-style cocktail lounge, recently opened in Moscow. The place is going under, despite all the gimmicks: rock music, light shows, skimpily clad waitresses. Why? Is it the furnishings? No, it can't be the furnishings: they were all imported from Milan, at startling cost. Is it the cocktails? No, it can't be the cocktails: the booze is of the finest, and the bartenders are all from the London Savoy. Is it the waitresses, in their bustiers and cupless brassieres, their thongs, their G-strings? No, it can't be the waitresses ('The chicks it's not,' I remember Christopher saying). It can't be the waitresses: they've all been loyal party members for at least forty-five years.

This is a joke with a limited constituency (women are seldom

amused by it), but it does point to one of the Bolsheviks' most
promethean projects. They intended to break the peasantry; they
intended to break the church; they intended to break all opposition and dissent. And they also intended (as Conquest, writing
of Stalin, put it) 'to break the truth'.

Sometimes, in our casual office arguments, I saw an acknowl-
edgment of this in Christopher's eyes. He could joke about it.
But he wasn't secure. How could he have been? Still, the truth,
like much else, was postponable; there were things that, for now,
were more important.* Although I always liked Christopher's
journalism, there seemed to me to be something wrong with it,
something faintly but pervasively self-limiting: the sense that the
truth could be postponed. This flaw disappeared in 1989, and his
prose made immense gains in burnish and authority. I used to
attribute the change to the death of Christopher's father, in late
1988, and to subsequent convulsions in his life. It had little or
nothing to do with that, I now see. It had to do with the demise
of the socialist possibility. The residue of a tiring aspiration had
evaporated.

We will all go on joking about it because there's something
in Bolshevism that is painfully, unshirkably comic. This became
palpable when the Russian experiment entered its decadent phase:
the vanity and high-bourgeois kleptomania of Brezhnev, the truly
pitiful figure of Chernenko (an old janitor with barely enough

---

*I would like to emphasize that Christopher (like James Fenton, and all other
Trotskyists known to me) was, of course, strenuously anti-Stalinist. But as a socialist
he needed to feel that October had not been an instantaneous – or indeed an
intrinsic – disaster. Even in 1975 it was considered tasteless or mean-spirited to be
too hard on the Soviet Union. No one wanted to be seen as a 'red-baiter' – or no
one except my father.

strength to honour himself as a Hero of Socialist Labour). Both
these men, and Andropov (the KGB highbrow), whom they
flanked, presided over a great landmass of suffering. The country
was living at African levels of poverty, malnutrition, disease and
child mortality. (And Afghanistan, meanwhile, was having its next
census slashed – indeed, almost halved.)*

Throughout this period the Russian people heard nothing
from their leaders but a drone of self-congratulation. And the
truth, no longer postponable by the standard Bolshevik means
(violence), screamed with laughter at what it saw. Napoleon said
that power is never ridiculous (and despotic power is presumably doubly unsmiling); but Bolshevism, by this stage, was ridiculous. *Glasnost*, which was a euphemism for not lying, laughed the
Bolsheviks off the stage. The poets had talked about the inhuman
power of the lie – but there is an antithesis to that: the human
power of the truth. Lying could no longer be enforced, and the
regime fell. And the leaders had become too evolved, and were
incapable of the necessary cruelty – the cruelty of Lenin and
Stalin, which was not medieval so much as ancient in its severity.

In *Lenin's Tomb* David Remnick addresses himself to the
squalid comedy of the Bolshevik disintegration:

> The exhibition of Economic Achievements, a kind of vast
> Stalinist Epcot Centre near the Moscow television tower, had
> for years put on displays of Soviet triumphs in the sciences,

---

*Sylvain Boulouque in *The Black Book of Communism*: 'Out of a population
of approximately 15.5 million, more than 5 million inhabitants have left for Pakistan
and Iran, where they now live in miserable conditions . . . [M]ost observers agree
that the war took between 1.5 million and 2 million lives, 90 per cent of whom
were civilians. Between 2 million and 4 million were wounded.' These figures are
due for revision, post-2001.

engineering, and space in huge neo-Hellenic halls. Vera Mukhina's gigantic statue *Worker and the Collective Farm Girl* (jutting breasts and biceps, bulging eyes) presided at the entrance, providing citizens with a sense that they were now part of a socially and genetically engineered breed of muscular proletarians. But with glasnost, the directors grew humble and put up an astonishingly frank display, 'The Exhibit of Poor-Quality Goods.'

At the exhibit, a long line of Soviets solemnly shuffled past a dazzling display of stunning underachievement: putrid lettuce, ruptured shoes, rusted samovars, chipped stew pots, unravelled shuttlecocks, crushed cans of fish, and, the show-stopper, a bottle of mineral water with a tiny dead mouse floating inside. All the items had been purchased in neighbourhood stores.

There is also something horribly comic in Remnick's remark that the 'leading cause of house fires in the Soviet Union was television sets that exploded spontaneously'. But the facts are of course intense. As the economist Anatoly Deryabin wrote in the official journal *Molodoi Kommunist*: 'Only 2.3 per cent of all Soviet families can be called wealthy, and about 0.7 of these have earned that income lawfully . . . About 11.2 per cent can be called middle-class or well-to-do. The rest, 86.5 per cent, are simply poor.' Towards the end of this chapter ('Poor Folk') Remnick visits a ghost village of the Collectivization in the Volgoda region, once a prosperous community, and now 'little more than a few collapsed cabins, a graveyard, and wheel ruts in the mud'. An old woman told him: 'The collective farms are a disaster. There's nothing left. It's all lost.' And a neighbour adds:

We were all supposed to be one big family after collectivization. But everyone was pitted against everyone else, everyone

suspicious of everyone else. Now look at us, a big stinking ruin.
Now everyone lives for himself . . . What a laugh, what a big
goddam laugh.

Back at the *New Statesman*, towards the end of 1975, V. S. Pritchett might have passed Oleg Kerensky on the stairs when he delivered his review of the second volume of *The Gulag Archipelago*. The laughter should have stopped around then. Why didn't it?

The Collapse of the Value of Human Life in Practice – 1*

Sir C. Eliot to Earl Curzon. – (Received 23 February.)
(Telegraphic.)   *Vladivostok,* 22 *February* 1919.
'Following report of 71 Bolshevik victims [that is, victims of Bolsheviks] received from consular office at Ekaterinburg, dated 19th February:—

'"Nos. 1 to 18 Ekaterinburg citizens (first three personally known to me) were imprisoned without any accusation being made against them, and at four in the morning of 29th June were taken (with another, making 19 altogether) to Ekaterinburg sewage dump, half mile from Ekaterinburg, and ordered to stand in line alongside of newly-dug ditch. Forty armed men in civil clothes, believed to be Communist militia, and giving impression of semi-intelligent people, opened fire, killing 18. The 19th, Mr Chistorserdow, miraculously escaped in general confusion. I, together with other consuls at Ekaterinburg, protested to Bolsheviks against brutality, to which Bolsheviks replied, advising us to mind our own business, stating that they had shot these people to avenge death

*All this is taken from *The Russian Revolution, 1917* in the always-fascinating 'Uncovered Editions' series. I have followed punctuation and house style. And I confront the reader with what follows not for its detail but for its overall effect.

of their comrade, Malishev, killed at front, against Czechs.

'"Nos. 19 and 20 are 2 of twelve labourers arrested for refusing to support Bolshevik Government, and on 12th July thrown alive into hole into which hot slag deposits from works at Verhisetski near Ekaterinburg. Bodies were identified by fellow labourers.

'"Nos. 21 to 26 were taken as hostages and shot at Kamishlof on 20th July.

'"Nos. 27 to 33, accused of plotting against Bolshevik Government, arrested 16th December at village of Troitsk, Perm Government. Taken 17th December to station Silva, Perm railway, and all decapitated by sword. Evidence shows that victims had their necks half cut through from behind, head of No. 29 only hanging on small piece of skin.

'"Nos. 34 to 36, taken with 8 others beginning of July from camp, where they were undergoing trench-digging service for Bolsheviks to spot near Oufalay, about 80 versts from Ekaterinburg, and murdered by Red Guards with guns and bayonets.

'"Nos. 37 to 58, held in prison in Irbit as hostages, and 26th July murdered by gunshot, those not killed outright being finished off by bayonet. These people were shot in small groups, and murder was conducted by sailors and carried out by Letts, all of whom were drunk. After murder, Bolsheviks continued to take ransom money from relatives of victims, from whom they concealed crime.

'"No. 59 was shot at village Klevenkinski, Verhotury district, 6th August, being accused of agitation against Bolsheviks.

'"No. 60, after being forced to dig his own grave, was shot by Bolsheviks at village Mercoushinski, Verhotury district, 13th July.

'"No. 61 murdered middle of July at Kamenski works for allowing church bells to be sounded contrary to Bolshevik orders, body afterwards found with others in hole with half head cut off.

'"No. 62 arrested without accusation, 8th July, at village Ooetski, Kamishlov district. Body afterwards found covered with straw and dung, beard torn from face with flesh, palms of hands cut out, and skin incised on forehead.

'"No. 63 was killed after much torture (details not given), 27th July, at station Anthracite.

'"No. 67 murdered, 13th August, near village of Mironoffski.

'"No. 68 shot by Bolsheviks before his church at village of Korouffski, Kamishlov district, before eyes of villagers, his daughters and son, date not stated.

'"Nos. 69 to 71, killed at Kaslingski works near Kishtin, 4th June, together with 27 other civilians. No. 70 had head smashed in, exposing brains. No. 71 had head smashed in, arms and legs broken, and two bayonet wounds.

'"Dates in this telegram are 1918."'

Sir C. Eliot to Earl Curzon. – (Received 25 February.)
(Telegraphic.)   *Vladivostok, 24 February* 1919.
'My telegram of 22nd February.
'Following from consul at Ekaterinburg:

'"Nos. 72 to 103 examined, 32 civilians incarcerated and taken away by Bolsheviks with 19 others at various dates between 9th July, 7th August, 27th July, all 51 having been declared outlaws. Official medical examination of 52 bodies (of which 32 examined, Nos. 72 to 103 not identified), found in several holes; 3 from Kamishlof revealed that all had been killed by bayonet, sword, and bullet wounds. Following cases being typical: No. 76 had 20 light bayonet wounds in back; No. 78 had 15 bayonet wounds in back, 3 in chest; No. 80, bayonet wounds in back, broken jaw and skull; No. 84, face smashed and wrist hacked; No. 89 had 2 fingers cut off and bayonet wounds; No. 90, both hands cut off at wrist, upper jaw hacked, mouth slit both sides, bayonet wound shoulder;

No. 98, little finger off left hand and 4 fingers off right hand, head smashed; No. 99 had 12 bayonet wounds; No. 101 had 4 sword and 6 bayonet wounds.

'"These victims are distinct from 66 Kamishlof hostage children shot by machine guns near Ekaterinburg beginning of July, names not obtainable."'

Nicholas the Last

Charles I and Louis XVI were publicly executed after open trials. Nicholas II was secretly shot in a provincial basement along with his immediate family (and four members of his staff). It was a small room and it contained eleven victims and eleven killers. They were supposed to concentrate on one victim each, but the killers were soon firing at random. Those still alive when the gunsmoke cleared were disposed of by bayonet or further shots to the head. The bodies were transported by truck to a disused goldmine; sulphuric acid was poured on their faces before burial elsewhere – to make the Romanovs harder to identify.

In his 'Introduction, 1971', as we have seen, Edmund Wilson was forced to give ground on the question of Lenin's amiability and benevolence (his words). It may seem sadistic to go on quoting him, but Wilson was distinguished and representative and by no means the worst offender (he is by now allowing that he 'had no premonition that the Soviet Union was to become one of the most hideous tyrannies that the world had ever known, and Stalin the most cruel and unscrupulous of the merciless Russian tsars'). Towards the end of the piece, however, Wilson is still trying to account for Lenin's bad manners. Were they attributable, perhaps, to the poor breeding of Lenin's father? 'Lenin himself, although his mother came from a somewhat superior stratum, and though Lenin distinguished himself as a scholar, had always rude and rather vulgar traits.' Wilson regretfully adds:

> . . . I have found that it was not true, as I had been led to suppose – this matter was hushed up in the Soviet Union – that Lenin knew nothing about and had not approved the execution of the royal family. Trotsky – and, one imagines, also Lenin – were both extremely cold-blooded about this . . .

He then quotes, without comment, Trotsky's page-long rationalization of the murders. Indeed, Wilson writes as if regicide – and bad manners – were Lenin's only blemishes; and maybe he was 'led to believe' that there were no others. It is a bizarre emphasis. The clouds of ignorance part, revealing the solar fire of archaic snobbery.

Trotsky had half a point when he said (elsewhere) that the Romanov children paid the price for the monarchical principle of succession. This would certainly apply to the Tsarevich, Alexis; but the four girls could expect no such inheritance – and neither could the doctor, the valet, the maid, the cook, or the dog.* Wilson quotes Trotsky's *Diary in Exile* (1935):

> The execution of the Tsar's family was needed not only to frighten, horrify and dishearten the enemy, but also in order to shake up our own ranks, to show them that there was no turning back, that ahead lay either complete victory or complete ruin. In the intellectual circles of the Party there probably were misgivings and shakings of heads. But the masses of workers and soldiers had not a minute's doubt. They would

---

*It seems that the Romanovs had two dogs with them in Ekaterinburg. One of them, Jemmy, was killed in the basement. The other, Joy, survived, despite her breed: she was a King Charles spaniel.

not have understood and would not have accepted any other decision. *This* Lenin sensed well.

But Trotsky is lying. The masses of workers and soldiers were not told of the 'decision' to execute the entire family; for almost a decade they were told, instead, that the Tsarina and her children were in 'a place of security'.* Nor was it proclaimed, as an additional morale-stiffener, that the Cheka had simultaneously murdered Grand Duchess Yelizaveta Feodorovna, Grand Duke Sergei Mikhailovich, Prince Ivan Konstantinovich, Prince Konstantin Konstantinovich, Prince Igor Konstantinovich and Count Vladimir Paley. This group was recreationally tortured, ante mortem. Grand Duke Sergei was dead on arrival, but the rest were thrown alive into the mine shaft where their bodies were eventually found.

The murder of the Romanovs seems to me fractionally *less* odious than, say, the murder of a Cossack family of equivalent size. The Tsar, at least, was guilty of real crimes (the encouragement of pogroms, for example). His end provoked, among the masses, little comment and no protest. The murder of the Tsarina and the five children was clearly seen by the Bolsheviks as a political deficit. It was therefore an irrational act, an expression of anger and hatred, though you can imagine how it was parlayed into an assertion of Bolshevik mercilessness, of 'stopping at nothing'. The ancillary killings sent no message to the Red Army or to the Party rump (except as a rumour). It sent a

---

*Reading Trotsky, one is often impressed by how much dishonesty he can pack into a paragraph. As to the details of the murders: 'I was never curious about *how* the sentence [*sic*] was carried out and, frankly, do not understand such curiosity.' Well, the Bolshevik leadership was certainly curious about the *how*: hence the secrecy, the eight-year cover-up; hence the sulphuric acid.

message to the Politburo, and the message said: we will have to
win now, because we at last deserve anything they care to do to
us if we fail. The Romanovs were murdered in mid-July 1918.
By this time the regime had lost much of its pre-October
support, and was responding with hysterical insecurity – that
is, with violence. On 3 and 5 September came the decrees legit-
imizing the Red Terror.

There are several accounts, written or deposed, by the guards,
executioners and inhumers of the Romanovs. One of the inhumers said that he could 'die in peace because he had squeezed
the Empress's—'.* Imagining this, we arrive at a representative
image of the gnarled hand of October. One executioner wrote
(and he is quoted here for the dullness of his moral tone):

> I know all about it. The shooting was all over the place. I know
> that . . . Medvedev took aim at Nicholas. He just shot at Nicho-
> las . . . Anyway, it was just another sentence that had to be
> carried out, we looked on it as just another chore.[†] . . . Of
> course, you start to think about its historical importance . . .
> In fact, the whole thing was badly organized. Take Alexei, it
> took a lot of bullets before he died. He was a tough kid.

Yes, an imposing enemy: a thirteen-year-old haemophiliac. The
Tsarevich outlived Nicholas II (deservedly renamed Nicholas the
Last by Orlando Figes). In those final seconds, then, the child was
Alexis II. Or Alexis the Last – but undeservedly.

---

*Pipes's note reads: 'Deposition by P. V. Kukhtenko in Solokov Dossier I, dated
8 September 1918; omission in the original.'

[†]'This group had not long before executed Prince Dolgorukov, General
Tatishchev, Countess Gendrikova and Yekaterina Schneider, who had been accom-
panying the Romanovs' (Volkogonov, *Lenin*).

The Collapse of the Value of Human Life in Practice – 2

Stalin famously said: 'Death solves all problems. No man, no problem.' After the death there would be no man and no problem; but there would indisputably be a corpse.

Corpse-disposal was a national tribulation throughout the period of hard Bolshevism, which ended in 1953. By December 1918, when the regime, responding to the crisis, announced its monopoly of the funeral industry, there were stacks of corpses (and packs of sated dogs) outside the cemeteries of every major city, and you could smell a hospital from a distance of several streets; annual epidemics came with the spring thaw. 'To die in Russia in these times is easy,' writes a diarist, 'but to be buried is very difficult.' After the nationalization of the graveyards, burial depended on bribery, a process surrealized by hyper-inflation:

> Ninotchka's funeral in November 1919 cost 30,000 [writes another diarist]; Uncle Edward's funeral in December 1921 was 5,000,000; M. M.'s funeral in March 1922 was 33,000,000.

Cremation was attractive to the regime. For one thing it undermined the Orthodox Church, which expressly prescribed interment. Cremation was also modern, 'a new, industrialised and scientific world of flame and ash'.* After many ponderous experiments the first crematorium was opened in December 1920 in Petrograd. It could manage barely 120 bodies a month, and, in February 1921, cremated itself when the wooden roof caught fire. Another solution, of course, was the mass grave. The pits

---

*From Catherine Merridale's *Night of Stone: Death and Memory in Russia*. In this section I am gratefully dependent on her striking chapter, 'Common and Uncommon Graves'.

at Butovo, near Moscow, are thought to hold 100,000 bodies; another Stalin-era necropolis, at Bykovna in the Ukraine, is thought to hold 200,000.

In 1919, as part of a further move against religion, the coffins of medieval 'saints' were opened up and exposed to scientific scrutiny. The sweet-smelling, tear-shedding, eternally fresh dead bodies of church doctrine were revealed as little bundles of bone and dust. 'The cult of dead bodies and of these dolls must end,' read the Justice Department's instruction. The policy ceased to apply when, in January 1924, Lenin had his last stroke. A powerful refrigerator was imported from Germany, and the Immortalization Commission worked flat out for six months, anxiously monitoring the mould on Lenin's nose and fingers. The corpse was rendered incorruptible, by science, and enshrined as an icon.

After the war, in Kolyma, Stalin's Arctic Auschwitz, natural erosion brought about a strange discovery: 'A grave, a mass prisoner grave, a stone pit stuffed full with undecaying corpses from 1938 was sliding down the side of the hill, revealing the secret of Kolyma.' The bodies were transferred to a new mass grave by bulldozer. Varlam Shalamov* was there:

> The bulldozer scraped up the frozen bodies, thousands of bodies of thousands of skeleton-like corpses. Nothing had decayed: the twisted fingers, the pus-filled toes which were reduced to mere stumps after frostbite, the dry skin scratched bloody and eyes burning with a hungry gleam . . .

> And then I remembered the greedy blaze of the fireweed, the furious blossoming of the taiga in summer when it tried to

*See also pp. 154–58.

hide in the grass and foliage any deed of man – good or bad.
And if I forget, the grass will forget. But the permafrost and
stone will not forget.

Getting to the Other Planet

Your chair is never softer, your study never warmer, your prospect
of the evening meal never more secure than when you read about
the gulag: the epic agony of the gulag. And your lecteurial love
for Aleksandr Solzhenitsyn (at such moments you are tempted
to reach for Aleksandr Isayevich) never more intense. 'How much
does the Soviet Union weigh?' Stalin once rhetorically asked a
team of interrogators who were having difficulty in breaking a
suspect (Kamenev). He meant that no individual could with-
stand the concerted mass of the state. In February 1974 the
Moscow Cheka served Solzhenitsyn with a summons. Instead of
signing the receipt, he returned the envelope with a statement
that began:

> In the circumstances created by the universal and unrelieved
> illegality enthroned for many years in our country . . . I refuse
> to acknowledge the legality of your summons and shall not
> report for questioning to any agency of the state.

And, for that moment, the Soviet Union and Aleksandr
Solzhenitsyn weighed about the same.

Exertions of the imagination are now called for. The Christmas before last, when she came to stay, my mother revealed an
interest in Russian 'witness' literature. I slipped her a paperback
called *Man Is Wolf to Man: Surviving the Gulag*. She accepted it
gratefully but responsibly. 'Didn't they have terrible times,' she
asked me (and there was no question mark). 'Yes,' I said. 'Didn't

they.' '*Terrible* times,' she said. The experience of the gulag was like a nightmare that ever worsened. It was a torment as lavish as any divinity could devise; and we are only on page 94 of Eugenia Semyonovna Ginzburg's *Into the Whirlwind* when we hear the words of Job (these words are repeatedly whispered in her ear): 'For the thing which I greatly feared is come upon me, and that which I was afraid of is come unto me' . . .

They had terrible times: unbelievably terrible times. And the camps of the gulag were just the last and longest stop on an unbelievably terrible road. First, arrest (almost always at night).* Solzhenitsyn describes the body chemistry of the arrested in terms of sudden heat – you are burning, boiling. 'Arrest is an instantaneous, shattering thrust, expulsion, somersault from one state into another . . . That's what arrest is: it's . . . a blow which shifts the present into the past and the impossible into omnipotent actuality.' In this instant, a poet wrote, 'you tire as in a lifetime'. Thus you were taken from your world and you entered . . . You entered what? One must bear in mind Martin Malia's more general warning: it is not the work of a moment to '[grasp] the extraordinary combination of dynamism and horror that characterized the Soviet experiment'.

Next, imprisonment and interrogation: this period normally lasted for about three months. In the chapter called 'The Interrogation' Solzhenitsyn tabulates thirty-one forms of psycho-

---

*This presented a logistical challenge in oft-purged Petrograd/Leningrad during the long days of arctic summer. Witnesses describe the two or three hours of darkness as something like a Monte Carlo Rally of black marias. The Cheka preferred the night, but they needed you to know that you were never safe. They could come for you at any time, in any place: on the street, in hospital, at the office or the opera.

logical and physical torture (the use of the latter became official policy in 1937). Red Terror torture was competitive and hysterical and baroque. Stalin-era torture could be all that too, but here, in the prisons of the cities, its setting was bureaucratic and cost-efficient. The interrogators needed confessions. It is important to understand that those accused of political crimes were almost invariably innocent. The interrogators needed confessions because these had been demanded from above *by quota* – that cornerstone of Bolshevik methodology. The apparatus was now immovably plugged into the Stalin psychodrama, and responded accordingly to his spasms of fear and rage, and his simpler need to exert power by mere intensification.

The tortures described by Solzhenitsyn are unendurable. This reader has endured none of them; and I will proceed with caution and unease. It feels necessary because torture, among its other applications, was part of Stalin's war against the truth. He tortured, not to force you to reveal a fact, but to force you to collude in a fiction. This is Solzhenitsyn's description of 'the swan-dive':

> A long piece of rough towelling was inserted between the prisoner's jaws like a bridle; the ends were then pulled back over his shoulders and tied to his heels. Just try lying on your stomach like a wheel, with your spine breaking – and without water and food for two days . . .

Another method was to confine the prisoner in a dark wooden closet where

> hundreds, maybe even thousands, of bedbugs had been allowed to multiply. The guards removed the prisoner's jacket or field shirt, and immediately the hungry bedbugs assaulted him,

crawling onto him from the walls or falling off the ceiling. At first he waged war with them strenuously, crushing them on his body and on the walls, suffocated by their stink. But after several hours he weakened and let them drink his blood without a murmur.

Yet even here, in his representations of obliterating defeat, Solzhenitsyn is quietly adding to our knowledge of what it is to be human. He does this again and again:

> *Beatings* – of a kind that leave no marks. They use rubber truncheons and wooden mallets and small sandbags. They beat Brigade Commander Karpunich-Braven for twenty-one days in a row. And today he says: 'Even after thirty years all my bones ache – and my head too.'

> *Starvation* has already been mentioned in combination with other methods . . . Chulpenyev was kept for a month on three and a half ounces of bread, after which – when he had just been brought in from the pit [a deep grave in which the half-stripped suspect lay open day and night to the elements] – the interrogator Sokol placed in front of him a pot of thick borscht, and half a loaf of white bread sliced diagonally. (What does it matter, one might ask, how it was sliced? But Chulpenyev even today will insist that it was really sliced very attractively.) However, he was not given a thing to eat.

And all this was superimposed on a regimen of unimaginable overcrowding ('crammed into GPU cells in numbers no one had considered possible up to then')* and chronic, depersonalizing sleeplessness: 'In all the interrogation prisons the prisoners were

---

*Conquest notes the case of an eight-man cell at Zhitomir prison containing 160 inmates. 'Five or six died every day,' wrote a survivor. The bodies 'continued to stand up because there was no room to fall down'. It was known as 'cell torture'.

forbidden to sleep even one minute from reveille to taps.' *Taps* means the bugle call for lights-out; but here the lights burned all night, both in the heaving cells and in the interrogation rooms. The overall process was known as 'the Conveyor', because the enemy, who never slept either, came at you in relays for as long as it took. Once in a blue moon we read about people (were *they* human?) who withstood the attrition and refused to confess, which was nearly always fatal. The confession was in any case merely part of a more or less inevitable process. When it was their turn to be purged, former interrogators (and all other Chekists) immediately called with a flourish for the pen and the dotted line.

Three months of that and then the prisoners faced the journey to their islands in the archipelago. The descriptions of these train rides match anything in the literature of the Shoah. I thought for a moment that there might be a qualitative difference: the absence of children, or at least the absence of their ubiquity. But the entire families of the 'kulaks', the targeted peasants, were deported and encamped in their millions during the early 1930s alone; and entire nations were deported and encamped during and after the war.* No, the children were there, as victims, and not just on the transports. About 1 million children died in

---

*These 'specially displaced' people were usually led to some crag or snowfield with a peg sticking out of it (bearing a number) and nothing else. Jonathan Glover in his recent book *Humanity: A Moral History of the Twentieth Century* succinctly passes on the following case: 'In 1930, 10,000 families were sent on a journey over the ice of the Vasyugan river. Many, especially children, died on the journey. The survivors were left, with no food or tools, on bits of land in the middle of the marshes. The paths back were guarded with machine-guns. Everyone died.'

the Holocaust. About 3 million children died in the Terror-Famine of 1933.

It is the journey we have all read about in Primo Levi and elsewhere, but there were also some Russian refinements. The journey would tend to be much longer (and much colder: Stalin, as we shall see, had things that Hitler didn't have) – a month, six weeks. The prisoners' diet – sometimes a combination of heavily salted Sea of Azov anchovies plus no water-ration – has a Russian feel to it. And there is the unshirkable question of Russian stoicism and humour, and of Russian obedience to the herd.

Eugenia Ginzburg had already been in prison for two years when she was transported to Vladivostok, sharing 'van 7' with seventy-six others. At a stop in the neighbourhood of Irkutsk a further consignment of prisoners was wedged on board. All the women in van 7 were half dead with starvation and disease, but there was something about the physical appearance of the newcomers that caused universal dismay: their heads had been shaved. It is difficult, at first, for the male reader to grasp this 'supreme insult to womanhood' (Solzhenitsyn notes that among the men head-shaving bothered nobody): '[The newcomers] viewed our dusty, greying, dishevelled plaits and curls with envious admiration ... "They might do the same to us tomorrow." I ran my fingers through my hair. No, that is something I thought I would hardly survive.' There follows a scene of passionate commiseration. Then:

> From the corner in which the orthodox Marxists had ensconced themselves (they hadn't given up a centimetre of space to the newcomers) came a voice of dissent:
>
>   'Did it not occur to you that the order to shave your heads

might have been motivated by reasons of hygiene?' . . .

The women from Suzdal, who had considered this possibility long ago, had one and all rejected it.

'. . . No, it had nothing to do with hygiene, they just wanted to humiliate us.'

'Well, simply to crop someone's hair is hardly an insult. It was very different in the Tsarist prisons, where they shaved only one half of your head!'

This was more than Tanya Stankovskaya [who is dying of scurvy] could bear. By some miracle she found the strength to scream out so loud that the whole van could hear her:

'That's the spirit, girls! A vote of thanks to Comrade Stalin . . . One's no longer shaved on only one side but on both. Thanks, father, leader, creator of our happiness!'

And Ginzburg herself, in the epilogue of her stoical and humorous – and, in every sense, devastating – book, after eighteen years of graphic torment, astonishingly concludes: 'How good that . . . the great Leninist truth has prevailed in our country and party . . . Here they are, then – the memories of a rank-and-file communist, a chronicle of the times of the cult of personality.'* Reading this, Solzhenitsyn, with his national-historical grasp, must have given a long low whistle.

There was another Soviet innovation: slave ships. But first, at the Vladivostok terminus, the transit camps – and the Tolstoyan scale of the operation, with vast landscapes traversed, it seemed, by entire populations. 'As far as the eye could see there were

---

*These words could hardly be an attempt to placate Moscow. Ginzburg's *Into the Whirlwind* (London: Harvill Press, 1967), a much more harrowing book than Solzhenitsyn's *One Day in the Life of Ivan Denisovich* (*Novy mir*, 1962: under Khrushchev), had no chance whatever of being published in the Soviet Union.

columns of prisoners marching in one direction or another like armies on a battlefield,' writes the Romanian witness Michael Solomon. 'One could see endless columns of women, of cripples, of old men and even teenagers . . . directed by whistles and flags.' At Vanino, en route to Kolyma, the prisoners entered what was in effect a slave market, where they were prodded and graded and assigned. Political prisoners, unlike the honest embezzlers and speculators, were detailed for the hardest labour, and for this they needed a first-class health clearance. Blind and skeletal from scurvy, Tanya Stankovskaya ('That's the spirit, girls!') was given a first-class health clearance. She died four hours later. On the planet Earth, we are told, for every human being there are a million insects. The transit prisoners at Vanino seemed to have experienced this as an immediate truth. 'The bugs were so legendary, even by camp standards, that they are reported in almost all the prisoners' accounts as provoking every night a struggle which would last till dawn' (Conquest, *Kolyma: The Arctic Death Camps*). But not even the insects would approach Tanya Stankovskaya.

For the fantastic sordor of the slave ships we again rely on Michael Solomon:

> . . . my eyes beheld a scene which neither Goya nor Gustave Doré could ever have imagined. In that immense, cavernous, murky hold were crammed more than two thousand women. From the floor to the ceiling, as in a gigantic poultry farm, they were cooped up in open cages, five of them in each nine-foot-square space. The floor was covered with more women. Because of the heat and humidity, most of them were only scantily dressed; some had even stripped down to nothing. The lack of washing facilities and the relentless heat had covered their bodies with ugly red spots, boils and blisters. The majority

were suffering from some form of skin disease or other, apart from stomach ailments and dysentery.

At the bottom of the stairway . . . stood a giant cask, on the edges of which, in full view of the soldiers standing guard above, women were perched like birds, and in the most incredible positions.* There was no shame, no prudery, as they crouched there to urinate or to empty their bowels. One had the impression that they were some half-human, half-bird creatures which belonged to a different world and a different age. Yet seeing a man coming down the stairs . . . many of them began to smile and some even tried to comb their hair.

The biggest ship in the fleet (grossing 9,180 tons) was called the *Nikolai Yezhov*, after the Cheka chief who presided over the Great Terror; when Yezhov was himself purged, in 1939, the *Nikolai Yezhov* became the *Feliks Dzerzhinsky*, honouring the Cheka's ferocious founder. Eugenia Ginzburg's ship, the *Dzhurma*, 'stank intolerably' from a fire in which many prisoners, hosed down with freezing bilge during a riot, were boiled alive. In 1933 the *Dzhurma* sailed too late in the year and was trapped in the ice near Wrangel Island: all winter. She was carrying 12,000 prisoners. Everyone died.

It was on board the ships that the 'politicals' – a.k.a. 'the 58s' (after Article 58 of the Criminal Codex), 'the counters' (counter-revolutionaries), and 'the fascists' – would usually receive their introduction to another integral feature of the archipelago: the *urkas*. Like so many elements in the story of the gulag, the *urkas* constituted a torment within a torment. Mrs Ginzburg sits in the floating dungeon of the *Dzhurma*: 'When it seemed as though

---

*For what prison life was like *without* a latrine bucket see *The Gulag Archipelago*, Volume One, page 540 ff.

there was no room left for even a kitten, down through the hatchway poured another few hundred human beings . . . [a] half-naked, tattooed, apelike horde . . .' And they were only the women. The *urkas*: this class, or caste, a highly developed underground culture, 'had survived,' writes Conquest, 'with its own traditions and laws, since the Time of Troubles at the beginning of the seventeenth century, and had greatly increased in numbers by recruiting orphans and broken men of the revolutionary and collectivization periods.' Individually grotesque, and, en masse, an utterly lethal force, the *urkas* were circus cut-throats devoted to gambling, plunder, mutilation and rape.

In the gulag, as a matter of policy, the *urkas* were accorded the status of trusties, and they had complete power over the politicals, the fascists – always the most scorned and defenceless population in the camp system. The 58s were permanently exposed to the *urkas* on principle, to increase their pain. And one can see, also, that the policy looked good ideologically. It would be very *Leninist* to have one class exterminating another, higher class. How Lenin had longed for the poorer peasants to start lynching all the kulaks . . . Imprisoned thieves were amnestied under Lenin, as part of his 'loot the looters' campaign in the period of War Communism. As Solzhenitsyn says, the theft of state property became and remained a capital crime, while *urka*-bourgeois theft became and remained little more than a misdemeanour. Apart from the new privilegentsia and a few 'hereditary proletarians', the *urkas* were the only class to benefit from Bolshevik policies. The *urkas*, who played cards for each other's eyes, who tattooed themselves with images of masturbating monkeys, who had their women assist them in their rapes of nuns and politicals. In *Life and Fate* Vasily Grossman writes almost casually of an *urka* 'who had once knifed a family of six'. The gulag officially designated the *urkas* as Socially Friendly Elements.

In the case of Kolyma another strange cruelty was provided by topography. It is not clear to me how they built up their sense of it (the guards seemed to disappear and prisoners were seldom taken from the squirming hold), but there was a near-universal feeling that the ship was disappearing over the shoulder of the world. 'And so, finally,' writes Conquest,

> the columns wound down to the boats. It was for the great majority of the prisoners their first sight of the open sea, for almost all of them their first sea voyage. On the Russians, in particular, the effect of the long cruise northward over the open ocean greatly enhanced the feeling already common to prisoners that they had been removed from the ordinary world. It seemed not merely a transportation from the 'mainland' (as the prisoners always referred to the rest of the country) to some distant penal island, but even to another 'planet', as Kolyma was always called in songs and sayings.

The Epic Agony of the Gulag

The shoes: sections of old car tyre, secured with a wire or an electrical cord.

Made from buckwheat, the thin porridge is found by one inmate (P. Yakubovich) to be 'inexpressibly repulsive to the taste'.

In the Arctic camps the prisoners were not supposed to work outside when the temperature fell below minus fifty – or at any rate sixty – degrees Fahrenheit. At fifty below it starts to be difficult to breathe. It was forbidden to build fires.

A group of prisoners at Kolyma were hungry enough to eat

a horse that had been dead for more than a week (despite the stench and the infestation of flies and maggots).

Scurvy makes the bones brittle; but then, 'Every prisoner welcomes a broken arm or leg.' Extra-large scurvy boils were 'particularly envied'. Admission to hospital was managed by quota. To get in with diarrhoea, you had to be evacuating (bloodily) every half an hour. The hospitals were themselves deathtraps, but inert deathtraps. A man chopped off half his foot to get in there. And prisoners cultivated infections, feeding saliva, pus or kerosene to their wounds.

Goldmining could break a strong man's health forever in three weeks. A three-week logging term was likewise known as a 'dry execution'. Solzhenitsyn: '[Varlam] Shalamov cites examples in which the whole membership of the brigade died several times over in the course of one gold-washing season on the Kolyma but the brigadier remained the same.' And the brigadier, typically, was an *urka*.

At Serpantinka, the *anus mundi* of the gulag, prisoners were crammed upright into a shed so tightly that they were denied the use of their arms. They had to catch the pieces of ice thrown in to them with their mouths, like penguins. The men were in there for 'several days'; and they were waiting to be shot.

According to Solzhenitsyn, almost all women prisoners – many of them wives and mothers – would sooner or later find themselves walking up and down the corridors between the men's bunks saying, 'Half a kilo. Half a kilo': 'A multiple bunk curtained off with rags from the neighbouring women,' he writes, 'was a classic camp scene.'

During the early 1930s every non-apparatchik in the USSR was hungry, and the peasants were starving in their millions. The zeks of the gulag, from 1918 to 1956, were always somewhere in between.

The mature gulag ran on food and the deprivation of food. Illuminatingly, the history of Communism keeps bringing us back to this: the scarcity or absence of food.

In 1929 Stalin made the acquaintance of a talented maniac called Naftaly Frenkel. Notice Solzhenitsyn's tone:

> Here once again the crimson star of Naftaly Frenkel describes its intricate loop in the heavens of the Archipelago . . . [He] did not weary of thirsting for the one true service, nor did the Wise Teacher weary of seeking out this service.

The style is mock-epic, and it is appropriate, because Frenkel is a figure so freakish in his severity. It seems he had no ideology (he wanted only money and power), but in his literalism, his scientism, and his natural indifference to all human suffering Frenkel was an excellent Bolshevik. It was he who advised Stalin to run the gulag on the steady deprivation of food.

Again they used norms and quotas:

for the full norm: 700 grams of bread, plus soup and buck-
    wheat
for those not attaining the norm: 400 grams of bread, plus
    soup

The 'full norm' was near-unachievable (sometimes more than 200 times higher than the Tsarist equivalent). A socialist-realist superman might manage it, for a time. But you were not meant to manage it. As the zek increasingly fell further behind the norm, he weakened further too, and his ration would soon be demoted to 'punitive' (300 grams). As for the rations, Conquest cites those of the Japanese POW camps on the River Kwai (Tha Makham): 'There, prisoners got a daily ration norm of 700 grams of rice, 600 of vegetables, 100 of meat, 20 of sugar, 20 of salt, and 5 of oil . . .'; all these items were, of course, great rarities and delicacies in the archipelago. Solzhenitsyn describes a seven-ounce loaf (218 grams): 'sticky as clay, a piece little bigger than a matchbox . . .'

Marx dismissed slavery as unproductive by definition. But Frenkel argued that it could work economically – so long as the slaves died very quickly. Solzhenitsyn seems to be quoting Frenkel here: '"We have to squeeze everything out of a prisoner in the first three months – after that we don't need him any more."' Three months: you can read a whole scholarly monograph on world slavery without once seeing an expectancy as low as three months. Three months. The photographs on the walls of the Auschwitz Museum commemorating a few score victims who were not killed immediately give the date of arrival and the date of death. The median period is three months. That is evidently how long the worked human body lasts without solace or sustenance or, finally, hope.

What made the difference between succumbing and surviving? Easily the most powerful force in the cosmos of the gulag was chance, was luck; but you had to make yourself a candidate for luck. One reads of two Bulgarians, two brothers, who hanged themselves with their scarves on the first *day*; and part of you concedes that this was an entirely reasonable act. Others were able to absorb something of the gulag into themselves, and take inner strength from it. In a place dedicated to death, what you needed in your self was force of life: force of life. Our witnesses are unrepresentative – they are professionals, intellectuals. The others' tales, the peasants' tales, for example, remain largely untold, or unwritten. But I am repeatedly struck by the quality of these testimonials, not just in their breadth of soul but in their talent: the expressiveness, the level of perception. And these, too, are subsidiary manifestations of force of life.

'The worst prison is better than the best camp,' formulated Tibor Szamuely (the nephew). 'Prison, and more particularly solitary confinement,' writes Eugenia Ginzburg, 'ennobled and purified human beings and brought to light their most genuine resources.' In one of his more extraordinary strophes Solzhenitsyn insists: 'Prison has wings!' What lies before you is a great project of self-communion and, to begin with at least, a great argument with fear and with despair; then, perhaps, comes the moment when (as Solzhenitsyn puts it), '. . . I had the consciousness that prison was not an abyss for me, but the most important turning point in my life.' Not the conviction but the 'consciousness', the discovery of something in yourself that was already there. After that, a different spiritual state, a different degree of humanity seemed to be achievable. Here are two glimpses of it. First, Solzhenitsyn's (this comes at the end of seven days and nights of solitary and interrogation):

> . . . by the time I arrived, the inhabitants of Cell 67 were already asleep on their metal cots with their hands on top of their blankets.
>
> At the sound of the door opening, all three started and raised their heads for an instant. They, too, were waiting to

learn which of them might be taken to interrogation.

And those three lifted heads, those three unshaven, crumpled pale faces, seemed to me so human, so dear, that I stood there, hugging my mattress, and smiled with happiness. And they smiled. And what a forgotten look that was – after only one week!

And here, again, is Eugenia Ginzburg:

There are no words to describe the feelings of a 'solitary' who, after two years and countless warders, catches sight of her fellow-prisoners [all of them strangers]. People! Human beings! So there you are, my dear ones, my friends whom I thought I should never see.

So human, so dear.*

But the worst prison is better than the best camp. In the camps, such words (*dear, human*) are used facetiously or contemptuously or not at all; the future tense is never heard; and for the zek, more generally, the 'natural desire to share what he has experienced dies in him' (Solzhenitsyn); 'He has forgotten empathy for another's sorrow; he simply does not understand it and does not desire to understand it' (Varlam Shalamov). Thus there was nowhere to turn but inwards. Speculating on the 'astounding rarity' of camp suicides, Solzhenitsyn writes:

If these millions of helpless and pitiful vermin still did not put an end to themselves – this meant that some kind of

---

*The circumstances are of course very different, but one can respectfully infer an interesting sex difference in these two little epiphanies. After a few expressions of gruff solidarity, Solzhenitsyn's cellmates (one of whom, incidentally, was a stoolie) adjured him to silence: 'Tomorrow! Night is for sleeping.' Mrs Ginzburg and her new friends, by contrast, all talked incessantly – and without listening – to the point of clinical exhaustion: '"Yes, it's lovely to be with people, but what a strain!"'

invincible feeling was alive inside them. Some very powerful idea.

This was their feeling of universal innocence.

Because they were all innocent, the politicals. None of them had done anything. On arrest, the invariable response was *Zachto? Why? What for?* When she heard that a friend had been picked up (this was in the early 1930s), Nadezhda Mandelstam said: *Zachto?* Anna Akhmatova lost patience. Don't you understand, she said, that they are now arresting people *for nothing.* Why, what for? That was the question you asked yourself each day in the gulag archipelago. And we must imagine this word carved on the trunk of every tree in the taiga: *Zachto?*

There are several names for what happened in Germany and Poland in the early 1940s. The Holocaust, the Shoah, the Wind of Death. In Romani it is called the *Porreimos* – the Devouring. There are no names for what happened in the Soviet Union between 1917 and 1953 (although Russians refer, totemically, to 'the twenty million', and to the *Stalinshchina* – the time of Stalin's rule). What should we call it? The Decimation, the Fratricide, the Mindslaughter? No. Call it the *Zachto?* Call it the What For?

The Isolator

'By pressing men against each other, totalitarian terror destroys the space between them,' writes Hannah Arendt. This feels profoundly true of life as it was lived under Bolshevism. Does the *size* of Russia (easily the largest country on Earth: a sixth of its land surface) – does the very size of Russia perversely account for its prodigies of overcrowding, of claustrophobic densities, of

cramming, of stacking people up against one another? In the
countryside there were the huddled huts, and, in the cities, there
was a family behind every window. The trams (and the trains)
were always dangerously full; riding them was a physically
bruising experience, and one long-pondered by anyone over fifty.
Then, too, we think of punitive proximities: the men at Stapi-
anka, awaiting death, wedged together, upright, with their arms
stuck to their sides; the men at Kolyma, trussed and stacked like
logs in vans and then driven off for execution; the men in
Zhitomir prison, 160 in a cell for eight, with no room for the
dead to fall or, it seems, even slump. And this form of torture
was no secret for ordinary Russians. It was part of the atmosphere, the rumour, the terror. The old British FO hand, Reader
Bullard, records in his diary entry for 2 April 1934 (in the calm
before the Purge):

> [She] isn't a bad little creature. She had nine months in an
> OGPU* prison without allowing it to break her spirit. She told
> me that it sometimes happens in those crowded prisons that
> one of the prisoners will have a fit of hysteria and begin to
> scream, which spreads to others until perhaps hundreds are
> screaming uncontrollably. [She] says people who live near the
> OGPU place in Moscow have heard the screaming more than
> once, and describe it as terrifying.

In the camps you could feel moments of thrilling solitude –
in the taiga, the steppe, the desert. But solitude, too, has its penal
applications.

Janusz Bardach is not a literary personage, and his book of

---

*The secret police renamed itself seven times: Cheka (1917–22), GPU (1922–23),
OGPU (1923–34), NKVD (1934–43), NKGB (1943–46), MGB (1946–53), MVD
(1953–54), and KGB thereafter.

1998, *Man Is Wolf to Man*, was co-written.* But he has what all the articulate survivors seem to have: force of life, amplitude of soul. His five days and nights in the Isolator are very far from being one of the most painful episodes in gulag literature: Bardach himself had worse times. But in its janitorial gloom, its grasp of a settled, a second-generation thickening of cruelty . . .

This is Kolyma. Note the chilled solidity of the cadences (and the integrity of the memory):

> The isolator was a windowless, grey concrete building with a flat tar roof. I passed twice every day . . . The solitary building was outside the zone and encircled by a double row of barbed wire.
>
> Every time I passed the building I felt disturbed and slightly frightened. I always feared that one day I, too, would be locked inside. The feeling was like a premonition; that in some unknowable way, my fate was connected to the isolator . . .

After a fistfight with a violently anti-Semitic work foreman (an *urka* turned trusty, and so technically a 'bitch'), Bardach gets five days.

Some isolators consisted of split logs thrown together; some

---

*With Kathleen Gleeson (and their names are the same size on the cover of the paperback and hardcover). Bardach worked on his memoir while in his seventies (he is now a resident of Iowa City, and a world-renowned reconstructive surgeon), in itself sufficiently remarkable when you consider that the gulag experience almost always destroyed the faculty of memory. Nadezhda Mandelstam cohabited for three months with the amnestied journalist Kozarnovski (she was hiding him from the Cheka). For three months she systematically questioned him about the fate of her husband. She was not surprised (though she was doubly grieved) when she established that Kozarnovski's 'memory was like a huge, rancid pancake in which fact and fancy from his prison days had been mixed up together and baked into one inseparable mass'.

had no roofs, exposing the prisoner to the elements – and the insects; some were designed to force the prisoner to stand upright (seventy-two hours of this could be enough to cause permanent damage to the knees). Bardach's isolator was windowless, grey, concrete. The prisoner is led into an antechamber; and then *Man Is Wolf to Man* gives us the following: 'A single encaged lightbulb burned through a film of dust, cobwebs, and dead insects.' The lightbulb is 'single' (of course); it is also 'encaged'. Bardach is ordered to strip to his underwear and is steered down a hallway, where another encaged lightbulb illuminates water on the floor of his cell. The water, ice-cold, was 'a permanent feature of the isolator; I could tell by the thickness of the slime on the walls . . .'* The ceiling drips. The furnishings comprise a bucket and a bench of 'soggy raw wood' (with 'soft but pointed splinters') to which the prisoner is permanently confined. A lot of thought has gone into the bench – it is a piece of work. Wedged up against the wall, with its supports sunk into the cement floor (lest the prisoner think of improving its position), the bench was so narrow that 'I could not lie on my back, and when I lay on my side, my legs hung over the edge; I had to keep them bent all the time. It was difficult to decide which way to lie . . . I lay with my back to the wall, preferring a cold, wet back to a face full of mould and mildew.' The silence climbs. Soon Bardach starts chanting, then swearing, then screaming.

*In Bardach's cell the water was ankle-deep. Cf. *Gulag 2* (p. 420). Solzhenitsyn tells of a whole penalty block where the water reached the prisoners' knees: 'In the autumn of 1941 they gave them all 58–14 – economic counterrevolution – and shot them.' Torture preludial to death: this is a persistent theme. Sometimes the torture was, so to speak, situational; sometimes it was vigorous and concerted.

During the second day a rhythm established itself – a strange *pas de deux* of physical and mental distress. There was water in the cell (the bilgey sewage on the floor), but no drinking water. Bardach's thirst was so intense that he considered licking the bacterial slime off the walls: 'My lips became chapped, my tongue stuck to the roof of my mouth, my throat became sticky. I could hardly swallow.' He lay 'as though on a slow-moving river', with his thoughts 'climbing on top of each other'. Sleep, always unutterably precious to the zek (at reveille, writes Solzhenitsyn, you yearned with every atom for another half-second of rest), now became 'a desperately needed harbour'. He was exhausted – exhausted by continual shivering; but sleep would not come. To thirst, hunger, cold, pain, lice and bedbugs (they dropped on him from the ceiling), the isolator now added dysentery. And confinement added fear, too, 'manageable at first but more difficult to conquer as time passed'. His muscles quivered, his teeth chattered, his parched tongue filled his mouth.

Bardach was now obliged to go on a journey within himself and examine the boundaries of his spirit: 'Is this unbearable, or is it something I can survive? I wondered. What is unbearable? How am I to decide what my limit is? . . . What is it like to break down?' He thought of the self-mutilators; he thought of the man 'dragging a partially severed foot as he walked to the guards'. He thought of the *dokhodyagas*, the 'goners', the garbage-eaters: 'Why some and not others? Why some and not all?' And the answer came, inarticulately, from his soul. Somehow, 'hope circled back, though I didn't know how or why.'

Late in the evening of the fifth day the guard released him, and he was reunited with the slave camp and the Kolyma winter.

* * *

The New Men

So where, in this landscape, do we find them, the New Men? Where is *homo Sovieticus*, that new breed of 'fully human' human beings?

Among the professors and ballet dancers hacking with spoons at the permafrost? Among the bitches and *urkas*, among the waddling janitoriat?

Perhaps we shall find them in Elgen ('Elgen is the Yakut word for "dead"'), among the returning workers glimpsed by Eugenia Ginzburg:

> It was the hour of the mid-day break and long lines of workers, surrounded by guards, filed past us on their way to camp . . . All the workers, as though by order, turned their heads to look at us. We, too, shaking off the fatigue and stupor of the journey, gazed intently at the faces of our future companions . . . these creatures in patched breeches, their feet wrapped in torn puttees, their caps pulled low over their eyes, rags covering the lower part of their brick-red frost-bitten faces.

These could, in theory, be the New Men. Because they're women. '[T]hat's where we had got to,' writes Ginzburg. Nobody could tell the difference.

But the best candidates are to be found among the *dokho-dyaga*: the goners. It is easy to miss the goners because (as Bardach says), '[r]ummaging through the garbage, eating rancid scraps of meat, chewing on fish skeletons – such behaviour was so common that no one noticed'. The goners became 'semi-idiots,' writes Vladimir Petrov,* 'whom no amount of beating could drive from the refuse heaps'. Consider that: no amount of

---

* *It Happens in Russia*, published in England in 1951.

beating. If the scraps were thrown into the latrine, then the goners went in after them.

'The name *dokhodyaga* is derived from the verb *dokhodit* which means to arrive or to reach,' writes Petrov:

> At first I could not understand the connection, but it was explained to me: the *dokhodyagas* were '*arrivistes*', those who had arrived at socialism, were the finished type of citizen in the socialist society.

I knew that we would find them, the New Men. There they are, beaten, beaten, and, once again, beaten, down on all fours and growling like dogs, kicking and biting one another for a gout of rotten trash.

There they are.

The Little Moustache and the Big Moustache

In the early pages of *Gulag 3* Solzhenitsyn writes about the punishments meted out to Soviet citizens who went on functioning under German occupation. These included schoolteachers. What were the differences in the classroom under the two regimes? Under Hitler, Solzhenitsyn decides, teachers would spend much less time lying to their students (under Stalin, 'whether you were reading Turgenev to the class or tracing the course of the Dnieper with your ruler, you had to anathematize the poverty-stricken past and hymn our present plenty'). Otherwise the differences were largely symbolic. There would be celebrations at Christmas rather than at New Year; an imperial anniversary would replace that of the October Revolution; and '[p]ictures of the big moustache would have to be taken out of school, and pictures of the little moustache brought in'.

Solzhenitsyn picks up the theme 400 pages later. It is now 1952; he has been released from camp and sentenced to internal exile (a most precarious existence, usually indistinguishable from beggary, and terrorized beggary at that). Solzhenitsyn considered himself improbably blessed: he became a schoolteacher in Kazakhstan. (And his pupils, one feels sure, were also improbably blessed.) Not until years later would he discover

> that sometime during or since the war the Soviet school had died: it no longer existed; there remained only a bloated corpse. In the capital and in the hamlet the schools were dead.

Another casualty: dead schools.

What is the difference between the little moustache and the big moustache (and under the big moustache we ought to subsume the middling moustache of Vladimir Ilyich)?

In 1997, during an interview with *Le Monde*, Robert Conquest was asked whether he found the Holocaust 'worse' than the Stalinist crimes: 'I answered yes, I did, but when the interviewer asked why, I could only answer honestly with "I feel so."' Conquest, anti-Sovietchik number one, feels so. Nabokov, the dispossessed noble, felt so. We feel so. When you read about the war, about the siege of Leningrad – when you read about Stalingrad, about Kursk – your body tells you whose side you are on. You feel so. In attempting to answer the question why, one enters an area saturated with qualms.

(i.)

Figures. Even if we add the total losses of the Second World War (40–50 million) to the losses of the Holocaust (*c.* 6 million), we arrive at a figure which, apparently, Bolshevism can seriously rival.

Civil War, Red Terror, famine; Collectivization accounted for perhaps 11 million, Conquest suggests; Solzhenitsyn gives a figure ('a modest estimate') of 40–50 million who were given long sentences in the gulag from 1917 to 1953 (and many followed after the brief Khrushchev thaw); and then there is the Great Terror, the deportations of peoples in the 1940s and 1950s ('the specially displaced'), Afghanistan . . . The 'twenty million' begins to look more like the forty million. Of course, the figures are still not secure, and they vary dismayingly. But these are not the 'imaginary' zeros of the millennium, and we will certainly need seven of them in our inventory of the Soviet experiment.* We badly need to know the numbers of the dead. More than this, we need to know their names.[†] And the dead, too, need us to know their names.

(ii.)

The exceptional nature of the Nazi genocide has much to do with its 'modernity', its industrial scale and pace. This piercingly

---

*One still encounters the resilient superstition that it is right-wing to give high figures. Conquest and Pipes were Cold Warriors (Conquest advised Thatcher, Pipes advised Reagan); their figures are therefore 'Cold Warrior' figures, inflated for the purposes of propaganda. But Conquest and Pipes are world-renowned historians; they are under oath. When Conquest sent me a copy of his *Kolyma*, he wrote on the dedication page: 'NB Chapter 9 is *obsolete.*' And under the chapter heading itself ('The Death Roll') he added: 'This is now known to be less than these reports indicate.' Conquest's figure for the executions in the Great Terror, on the other hand, has gone up, and is close to a ferocious 2 million for 1937–38 . . . The mass graves now being discovered can present additional difficulties of tabulation. In *Night of Stone* Catherine Merridale writes: 'The bodies, a twisted mass in death, have rotted now, and the skeletons are impossible to separate. It is inadvisable to rely on a skull-count because most of the skulls were damaged, if not shattered, by the executioners' bullets . . . When you have finished, you count the femurs and divide by two. In most cases, the figure will run into thousands.'

†The Memorial Society, an agency of Russian remembrance, prints its lists of the dead in books the size of telephone directories.

offends us, but the disgust, perhaps, is not rigorously moral; it is partly aesthetic. (At Hiroshima approximately 50,000 people died in 120 seconds, most of them instantly. Again, as well as a moral disgust, we feel an aesthetic disgust, a supererogatory affront. But what would you prefer? Of the deaths on such prodigal display, I would choose August 1945; I would become a wall-shadow at the speed of light.) In Nazi circles during the early 1940s there was much frowning talk of the need to streamline the killings, to make them more '*elegant*'; the supposed concern was for the mental health of the executioners. 'Look at the eyes of the men in this *Kommando*,' General Erich von Bach-Zelewski told Himmler at the conclusion of a massacre in 1941. 'These men are finished [*fertig*] for the rest of their lives.' The basic concern was not for the men's sanity so much as for their effectiveness; and the subsequent quest for more 'humane methods' (i.e., gas) was fundamentally a quest for the necessary tempo. But the regime went through the motions – it provided the executioners with 'counselling', and so on. In the USSR there seems to have been little anxiety about the moral and psychological wounds sustained by the Chekists.* 'Find tougher people' was all that Lenin had to say on the question. And Stalin, selecting downwards, as always, evidently *wanted* his men to be finished, morally finished; it bound them to him, and, more than that, it confirmed his unspoken assessment of human nature. He knew that human beings, given certain conditions, can in fact kill all day, and all year. Is there a clear moral difference between the railtracks and smokestacks of Poland, on the one hand, and, on the other, the

*Except at the highest level. We read of an exhausted Dzerzhinsky's costly rest cures in European spas.

huge and unnatural silence that slowly settled on the villages of the Ukraine in 1933? The Holocaust is 'the only example which history offers to date of a deliberate policy aimed at the total physical destruction of every member of an ethnic group,' write Ian Kershaw and Moshe Lewin in *Stalinism and Nazism: Dictatorships in Comparison* – whereas, under Stalin, 'no ethnic group was singled out for total annihilation'. The distinction thus resides in the word 'total', because Lenin pursued genocidal policies (de-Cossackization) and so of course did Stalin (see below). Indeed, most historians agree that if Stalin had lived a year longer his anti-Semitic pogrom would have led to a second catastrophe for Jewry in the mid-1950s. The distinction may be that Nazi terror strove for precision, while Stalinist terror was deliberately random. Everyone was terrorized, all the way up: everyone except Stalin.

(iii.)

Ideology. Orlando Figes summarizes the representative view:

> The Bolshevik programme was based on the ideals of the Enlightenment – it stemmed from Kant as much as from Marx – which makes Western liberals, even in this age of post-modernism, sympathise with it, or at least obliges us to try and understand it, even if we do not share its political goals; whereas the Nazi efforts to 'improve mankind', whether through eugenics or genocide, spat in the face of the Enlightenment and can only fill us with revulsion.

Marxism was the product of the intellectual middle classes; Nazism was yellow, tabloidal, of the gutter. Marxism made wholly unrealistic demands on human nature; Nazism constituted a direct appeal to the reptile brain. And yet both ideologies worked identically on the moral sense. 'The imagination and spiritual strength of Shakespeare's evildoers stopped short at a dozen corpses,' writes Solzhenitsyn.* 'Because they had no *ideology*.' He goes on:

> Physics is aware of phenomena which occur only at *threshold* magnitudes, which do not exist at all until a certain *threshold* encoded by and known to nature has been crossed . . . Evidently evildoing also has a threshold magnitude. Yes, a human being hesitates and bobs back and forth between good and evil all his life . . . But just so long as the threshold of evildoing is not crossed, the possibility of returning remains, and he himself is still within reach of our hope.

Ideology brings about a disastrous fusion: that of violence and righteousness – a savagery without stain. Hitler's ideology was foul, Lenin's fair-seeming. And we remember Figes's simple

---

*This is more or less true of Iago, Claudius and Edmund (to take only the major tragedies). But we are left staring at the fact that Macbeth did *not* stop short – that he was, indeed, a usurping dictator who ruled by terror (and terror, perhaps, is always a confession of illegitimacy). 'Each new morn, / New widows howl, new orphans cry . . .' The fullest evocation of a terrorized society is given to the minor, linking character of Ross; but it has its points:

> Alas, poor country!
> Almost afraid to know itself. It cannot
> Be call'd our mother, but our grave; where nothing,
> But who knows nothing, is once seen to smile;
> Where sighs, and groans, and shrieks that rend the air
> Are made, not mark'd; where violent sorrow seems
> A modern ecstasy [an everyday emotion]: the dead man's knell
> Is there scarce asked for who; and good men's lives
> Expire before the flowers in their caps . . .

Macbeth incidentally contains an annihilating definition of the reality of War Communism (and Lenin's slogan, 'The worse the better'). It consists of seven words and is chanted by the Witches in unison (I.i.11): 'Fair is foul, and foul is fair . . .'

point: the Russian Revolution launched 'an experiment which the human race was bound to make at some point in its evolution, the logical conclusion of humanity's historic striving for social justice and comradeship'. Whereas Hitler's programme stood a fair chance of staying where it belonged – in the dreams of the young artist on his bunk in the *Asyl für Obdachlose*, a shelter for the destitute in Vienna.

(iv.)

Is there a moral difference between the Nazi doctor (the white coat, the black boots, the pellets of Zyklon B) and the blood-bespattered interrogator in the penalty camp of Orotukan? The Nazi doctors participated not only in experiments and 'selections'. They supervised all stages of the killing process. Indeed, the Nazi vision was in essence a biomedical vision. This is from Robert Jay Lifton's classic study, *The Nazi Doctors*:

> Pointing to the chimneys in the distance, [Dr Ella Lingens-Reiner] asked a Nazi doctor, Fritz Klein, 'How can you reconcile that with your oath as a doctor?' His answer was, 'Of course I am a doctor and I want to preserve life. And out of respect for human life, I would remove a gangrenous appendix from a diseased body. The Jew is the gangrenous appendix in the body of mankind.'

This was a capsizal that Bolshevism did not attempt: the concerted use of healers as killers. Lifton writes:

> We may say that the doctor standing at the ramp represented a kind of omega point, a mythical gatekeeper between the worlds of the dead and the living, a final common pathway of the Nazi vision of therapy via mass murder.

*   *   *

(v.)

Nazism did not destroy civil society. Bolshevism did destroy civil society. This is one of the reasons for the 'miracle' of German recovery, and for the continuation of Russian vulnerability and failure. Stalin did not destroy civil society. Lenin destroyed civil society.

(vi.)

The refusal of laughter to absent itself, in the Soviet case, has already been noted (and will be returned to). It seems that the Twenty Million will never command the sepulchral decorum of the Holocaust. This is not, or not only, a symptom of the general 'asymmetry of indulgence' (the phrase is Ferdinand Mount's). It would not be so unless something in the nature of Bolshevism permitted it to be so.

(vii.)

Hitler and Stalin, or their ghosts, might at this point choose to enter a plea of diminished responsibility. Who has the weaker claim? In his essay '"Working Towards the Führer"' Ian Kershaw has to do much shrugging and writhing and coughing behind his hand, but he gets it said in the end:

> Stalin's rule, for all its dynamic radicalism in the brutal collec-tivisation programme, the drive to industrialisation, and the paranoid phase of the purges, was not incompatible with a rational ordering of priorities and attainment of limited and comprehensible goals, even if the methods were barbarous in the extreme and the accompanying inhumanity on a scale de-fying belief. Whether the methods were the most appropriate to attain the goals in view might still be debated, but the

attempt to force industrialisation at breakneck speed on a highly backwards economy and to introduce 'socialism in one country' cannot be seen as irrational or limitless aims.

Well, the case is just about capable of being made; and no one would attempt anything of the kind on behalf of Hitler. When you read Alan Bullock's thousand-page *Hitler and Stalin: Parallel Lives*, in which the protagonists are considered in roughly alternating chapters, you feel like a psychiatric-ward inspector unerringly confronted by the same two patients. The German patient exhibits a florid megalomania of the manic variety. Hitler, indeed, created a whole new style of insanity – in which the simulacrum of preternatural self-assurance is repeatedly dispersed in a squall of saliva. Giving his arguments for an immediate attack on Poland (22 August 1939), Hitler addressed his top brass at the Berghof:

> First of all, two personal factors: my own personality and that of Mussolini. All depends on me, on my existence, because of my political talent. Probably no one will ever again have the confidence of the whole German people as I have. There will probably never again be a man with more authority than I have. My existence is therefore a factor of great value.

Three days later (this is the account of a German diplomat):

> Suddenly he stopped and stood in the middle of the room staring. His voice was blurred and his behaviour that of a completely abnormal person. He spoke in staccato phrases: 'If there should be war, then I shall build U-boats, build U-boats, U-boats, U-boats.' His voice became more indistinct and finally one could not follow him at all. Then he pulled himself together, raised his voice as though addressing a large audience and shrieked: 'I shall build aeroplanes, build aeroplanes, aeroplanes,

aeroplanes, and I shall annihilate my enemies.' He seemed more
like a phantom from a story-book than a real person. I stared
at him in amazement and turned to see how Göring was
reacting, but he did not turn a hair.

Because Göring was used to it. This was the mad energy Hitler
sometimes harnessed in his demagoguery. After Stalingrad he
suffered an inflammation of the brain. His general symptoms,
now, included spectacular headaches, one trembling arm, one
dragging leg, untreatable insomnia, and acute and chronic depression (though he still managed frequent tantrums). His medica-
tion bespeaks him: the Hitlerian urine sample would duly reveal
that he was on hormone injections plus eight to sixteen doses,
daily, of a patented medicine called 'Dr Koester's Antigas Tablets'
(oh for an *l*), which turned out to consist largely of two poisons,
strychnine and atropine, thus greatly stoking the internal furnace.
In mid-April 1945 Goebbels sent for the horoscope of the Führer,
which prophesied victory. Hitler married for the first time on the
last full day of his life: 30 April . . . The other case, the Soviet
patient, as we shall go on to see, is much harder to read. This is
a case of inscrutable introversion, and of violent episodes. Here,
though, is a madman of much greater self-control – indeed, here
is a madman with *patience.**

*We cannot leave the ward without at least looking in on Vladimir Ilyich. He
is a scowl that occasionally allows itself a refreshing cackle. Lenin was courteous to
good Bolsheviks who agreed with him, and more than courteous to his wife, sister,
and 'mistress' (all of them good Bolsheviks who agreed with him). Other people,
though: they were not merely of no interest; they didn't even faintly register. Lenin
was a moral aphasic, a moral autist . . . When I read someone's prose I reckon to
get a sense of their moral life. Lenin's writing mind is cross-eyed in its intensity of
focus, painfully straitened and corseted, indefatigable in its facetiousness and iter-
ation, and constantly strafed by microscopic pedantries.

(viii.)

Stalin, unlike Hitler, did his worst. He did his worst, applying himself over a mortal span. In the year of his death he was developing what had every appearance of being another major terror, succumbing, at the age of seventy-three, to a recrudescent and semi-senile anti-Semitism. Hitler, by contrast, did not do his worst. Hitler's worst stands like a great thrown shadow, and implicitly affects our sense of his crimes. Had it come about, 'mature' Nazism would have meant, among other things, a riot of eugenics on a hemispherical scale (there were already plans, in the early 1940s, for further refinement of the Aryan stock). Josef Mengele's laboratory at Auschwitz would have grown to fill a continent. The Hitlerian psychosis was 'non-reactive', responding not to events but to its own rhythms. It was also fundamentally suicidal in tendency. Nazism was incapable of maturation. Twelve years was perhaps the natural lifespan for such preternatural virulence.

(ix.)

Bolshevism was exportable, and produced near-identical results elsewhere. Nazism could not be duplicated. Compared to it, the other fascist states were simply amateurish.

(x.)

At the end of his career Hitler faced defeat and suicide. 'When Stalin celebrated his seventieth birthday in 1949,' writes Martin Malia, staggeringly, '. . . he indeed appeared as the "father of the peoples" to about a third of humanity; and it seemed as if the worldwide triumph of Communism was possible, perhaps even imminent.'

(xi.)

Historians refer to it as the *Sonderweg* thesis: Germany's 'special path' to modernity – or, rather, Germany's special path to Hitler. But Russia has a special path too, and so does every other country, including the imaginary 'model' state from whose evolution Germany is thought to have diverged. The German combination of advanced development, high culture and bottomless barbarity is of course very striking. And yet we cannot wall off Nazism as inimitably German; and Bolshevism, clearly, cannot be quarantined as inimitably Russian. The truth is that both these stories are full of terrible news about what it is to be human. They arouse shame as well as outrage. And the shame is deeper in the case of Germany. Or so I feel. Listen to the body. When I read about the Holocaust I experience something that I do not experience when I read about the Twenty Million: a sense of physical infestation. This is species shame. And this is what the Holocaust asks of you.

(xii.)

But Stalin, in the execution of the broad brushstrokes of his hate, had weapons that Hitler did not have.

He had cold: the burning cold of the Arctic. 'At Oimyakon [in the Kolyma] a temperature has been recorded of – 97.8 F. In far lesser cold, steel splits, tyres explode and larch trees shower sparks at the touch of an axe. As the thermometer drops, your breath freezes into crystals, and tinkles to the ground with a noise they call "the whispering of the stars".'*

---

*From Colin Thubron's *In Siberia*. During blizzards whole camps were known to perish. Everyone died. Even the guards. Even the dogs.

He had darkness: the Bolshevik sequestration, the shockingly bitter and unappeasable self-exclusion from the planet, with its fear of comparison, its fear of ridicule, its fear of truth.*

He had space: the great imperium with its eleven time zones, the distances that gave their blessing to exile and isolation, steppe, desert, taiga, tundra.

And, most crucially, Stalin had time.

---

*The word for this is *agonism*: the permanent struggle of the self-appointed martyr. Militant Islam is obviously and proclaimedly agonistic.

PART II

IOSIF THE TERRIBLE:

SHORT COURSE

Census

There was a national census in 1937, the first since 1926, which had shown a population of 147 million. Extrapolating from the growth figures of the 1920s, Stalin said that he expected a new total of 170 million. The Census Board reported a figure of 163 million – a figure that reflected the consequences of Stalin's policies. So Stalin had the Census Board arrested and shot. The census result went undisclosed, but the board was publicly denounced as a nest of spies and wreckers, despite the fact that it had delivered its report to Stalin and not (say) to the London *Times*.

In 1939 there was another census. This time the Census Board contrived the figure of 167 million, which Stalin personally topped up to 170. Perhaps the Census Board added a rider to its report, saying that if Stalin found the figure too low, then it would have to be lowered still further: Stalin would have to subtract the membership of the Census Board.

The architects of the 1937 Census Board were shot for 'treasonably exerting themselves to diminish the population of the USSR'.

There it is – Stalinism: negative perfection.

*   *   *

Georgia

Accounts of the childhoods of the great historical monsters are always bathetic. Instead of saying something like 'X was raised by crocodiles in a septic tank in Kuala Lumpur,' they tell you about a mother, a father, a brother, a sister, a house, a home. It can be admitted that the family atmosphere at the Dzhugashvilis', in Gori, Georgia, left much to be desired. Iosif's mother and father hit each other and they both hit Iosif. But there is nothing in the early life that prefigures Stalin's inordinateness. It is the same with Hitler. He too was born on the periphery of the country he would rule (Upper Austria), and to peasant parents (though their situation would improve to the point where Hitler's status resembled Lenin's: a scion of imperial official-dom); both Adolf and Iosif served as choirboys; and both would grow to a height of five feet four. Hitler's father (somehow very appropriately) was more and more obsessed, as he grew older, by bee-keeping. Stalin's father was a semiliterate cobbler, and he drank.

Young Iosif Vissarionovich was the kind of kid who gives himself a nickname. The nickname was 'Koba'. Koba was the hero of a popular novel called, suggestively, *The Patricide*; but Koba was not the eponym. The main thing about Koba was that he was a Robin Hood figure, a taker from the rich and giver to the poor. Stalin had another nickname, 'Soso' (the Georgian diminutive of Iosif), which at this point might sum him up more accurately. Apart from his memory (obligatorily described as 'phenomenal'), he was an ordinary little boy. 'Stalin', of course, was another self-imposed nickname. Man of Steel. The Steel One.

He began learning Russian at the age of eight or nine (his parents were Georgian monoglots). In 1894, at the age of fifteen, he left the Gori Church School and won a kind of scholarship to the Tiflis Theological Seminary. He was expelled, or he dropped out, five years later. Thereafter he became a full-time revolutionary.

Two details from a boyhood. A schoolfriend later said that he had never seen Iosif cry. One thinks of the famous phrase that would gain fresh currency in the 1930s: Moscow does not believe in tears. On the other hand, Koba was a poet. These lines, for example, are thought to be from his pen:

> Know that he who fell like ash to the earth
> Who long ago became enslaved
> Will rise again, winged with bright hope,
> Above the great mountains.

Robert Conquest once suggested that 'a curious little volume might be made of the poems of Stalin, Castro, Mao and Ho Chi Minh, with illustrations by A. Hitler'. At the age of twenty, his artistic dreams frustrated, Hitler was a tramp: park benches, soup queues. Given just a little more talent, perhaps, he would have killed himself, not in the bunker, but in a cosy little studio in Klagenfurt.

We don't know how Stalin felt about his childhood. But we know how he felt about Georgia. Why take it out on your parents, when you can take it out on a province?

In 1921, with Stalin's full support, Lenin reannexed Georgia (which had been granted independence the year before) by invasion. Stalin went down south to attend a plenum of the new administration: his first visit for nine years. He addressed a group of railway workers and was heckled into silence with cries of 'renegade' and 'traitor'. At a later meeting he harangued the local Bolshevik leaders:

> You hens! You sons of asses! What is going on here? You must draw a white-hot iron over this Georgian land! . . . It seems to me you have already forgotten the principle of the dictatorship of the proletariat. You will have to break the wings of this Georgia! Let the blood of the petit bourgeois flow until they give up all their resistance! Impale them! Tear them apart!

Lenin was now favouring a softer line on the nationalities question, and especially on Georgia. Stalin was for maximum force.

In 1922 Stalin's violent highhandedness, his display of 'Great Russian chauvinism' (Lenin's phrase) on the matter of Georgia came close to ending his career: itself amazing testimony that the strength of his feelings now outweighed his self-interest. (Power, as we shall see, had an instantly deranging effect on Stalin; during the Civil War he was chronically insubordinate and trigger-happy; it took many years before he learned to control the glandular excitements that power roiled in him.) The Georgia question would have unseated Stalin – if Lenin's health had held. In May 1922 Lenin began to be buffeted by strokes, a month after his fifty-second birthday (he had also stopped three Russian bullets, we may recall, in 1918, and one of them was still lodged in his neck). I feel persuaded of Lenin's intention, not from all the references to Stalin's 'rudeness' (*grubost*: coarseness, grossness, crassness), but from this conversation between Lenin and his sister, Maria. Stalin had asked Maria to intercede for him; he played on her feelings, saying that he couldn't sleep because Lenin was treating him 'like a traitor'. Lenin's talk with his sister ended:

> ['Stalin says he loves you. And he sends warm greetings. Shall I give him your regards?']

'Give them.'

'But Volodya, he's very intelligent.'

'He's not in the least intelligent.'

This is said 'decisively' though 'without any irritation', suggesting that Lenin had long ceased to consider Stalin as a viable confederate. It is generally agreed that even a half-fit Lenin would have sidelined him, though Richard Pipes, in *Three 'Whys' of the Russian Revolution*, suggests that 'Stalin was far ahead in the competition for Lenin's post, possibly as early as 1920 but certainly by 1922.'

In 1935 Stalin went to see his mother, whom he had installed in the palace of the Tsar's Viceroy in the Caucasus (where she kept to a single room). It is thought that this much-publicized visit was part of a pro-family campaign to combat the falling birthrate. He asked her, inter alia, about the beatings she had given him in his childhood. She answered: 'That's why you turned out so well.'

In 1936, when old Ekaterina died, Stalin scandalized the remains of Georgian public opinion by failing to attend her funeral.

In 1937 the Great Terror reached Transcaucasia: 'Nowhere were victims subjected to more atrocious treatment,' writes Robert C. Tucker, 'than in Georgia.' Of the 644 delegates to the Georgian party congress, in May, 425 were either shot or dispatched to the gulag (the gulag was at its deadliest in 1937–38). Mamia Orakhelashvili, a founder of the republic, had his eyes put out and his eardrums perforated while his wife was forced to watch. The party chief Nestor Lakoba had already been poisoned and buried with honours in 1936; he was now exhumed as an enemy of the people, and his wife was tortured to death in the presence of their fourteen-year-old son (who was sent to the gulag with three young friends. 'When, later, they wrote to Beria requesting release to resume their studies,' writes Tucker, 'he ordered them returned to Tiflis and shot'). Budu Mdivani, the ex-premier, was arrested, tortured for three months, and shot. His wife, their four sons and their daughter were all shot.

When the interrogators started work on Mdivani he is said to have protested, 'You are telling me that Stalin has promised to spare the lives of Old Bolsheviks! I have known Stalin for thirty years. He won't rest until he has butchered all of us, beginning with the unweaned baby and ending with the blind great-grand-mother!' 'All of us' seems to refer to 'Old Bolsheviks'; but it could mean 'all Georgians' (or, conceivably, all Soviet citizens). The specific nature of Stalin's antipathy is in any case clear. It is usually attributed to his intense insecurity and his shame about his origins. Perhaps, too, he was trying to sever his last connections to anything human. In the 1930s, and beyond, Stalin killed everyone who had ever known Trotsky. But he was also killing everyone who had ever known Stalin – known him or seen him or breathed the same air.

Demian Bedny

Of all the writers with whom Stalin had dealings none was less distinguished than Demian Bedny. A hack and a McGonagall, Bedny was, ridiculously, the Soviet Union's proletarian 'poet laureate'. He had been active since the days of the Civil War, and his poems (or battle chants: 'Death to the vermin! Kill them all, to the last!') were posted on walls and scattered from aeroplanes). Trotsky praised his passion, 'his well-grounded hatred', and his ability to write, 'not only in those rare instances when Apollo calls', but 'day in and day out, as the events demand . . . and the Central Committee'. There were cries of 'Author! Author!' from Stalin, in 1926, when Bedny published an anti-Trotsky poem, 'Everything Comes to an End', which included the lines:

> Our party has served long enough
> as the target for spent politicians!
> It's time at last
> to put an end to this outrage!

As the show trial of the Old Bolsheviks Zinoviev and Kamenev approached its denouement, *Pravda* was full of mass resolutions and signed articles demanding the death penalty. Bedny's poem for 21 August 1936, was entitled 'No Mercy'.*

Demian Bedny, who was given a pension and a luxurious apartment in the Kremlin, had several run-ins with Stalin. Nadezhda Mandelstam tells the following tale of an early *froideur*. Apparently Bedny disliked lending books to Stalin because of the smears left in the margins by his 'greasy fingers'. He was incautious enough to confide this to his diary; a Kremlin secretary saw the entry and passed it on. It is obvious, incidentally, that Stalin never regarded his laureate as anything but a reasonably useful idiot. Stalin knew very well that poetry was more than a factory whistle . . .

In 1930 Bedny published 'Get Off the Oven-Shelf', a poem lamenting a decline in coal output in the Donbas (some of the

---

*At the same point in the Bukharin trial two years later the 'folk poet' D. Dzhambul contributed a similar piece called 'Annihilate'.

miners were newly recruited peasants), and 'Pererva', which addressed itself to a train crash (switchman negligence on the Moscow-Kursk line). Bedny's theme, here, was the torpor and wishfulness of the Russian temperament – what Lenin had called 'Oblomovism'. When this critique was itself criticized by the Central Committee, Bedny wrote to Stalin, putting his case for constructive satire on the national character in the tradition of Gogol and Shchedrin. Stalin's reply was, in Tucker's words, 'harshly negative'. He accused Bedny of perpetrating a 'slander' on the Russian proletariat.

Bedny had failed to see that Stalin was changing his stance towards Old Russia, and had now decided to exalt its folkloric traditions and historical heroes (he would rehabilitate not only Peter the Great but also Ivan the Terrible, in his own image). In Tucker's formulation, Stalin was becoming a 'right-radical Great Russian'. Bedny was thus most ill-advised when, in 1936, he wrote a comic opera called *Bogatyrs* (the great heroes), in which a sacred chapter in Russian history was raucously lampooned.

Robert Tucker:

> He portrayed these characters of Russian legend as drunkards and cowards . . . Prince Vladimir's adoption of Christianity in the tenth century, by leading the people of Kiev into the Dnieper River for a mass baptism in the dead of winter, was ridiculed as an episode in a drunken debauch.

Molotov attended the first night and walked out at the end of Act One ('An outrage!'). Bedny was evicted from the Writers' Union. And from his Kremlin apartment.

Our poet continued to write and publish – until 1938. At this point, his finger no nearer the pulse of events, he was moved to write an attack on Nazism, apparently unaware of the delicate manoeuvrings between Hitler and Stalin (who would soon be nominal allies). Called 'Inferno', Bedny's piece reimagined Germany in terms of the classical Hell (and in contrast, no doubt, to the Paradiso of the Soviet Union). At two o'clock in the morning Bedny was summoned to the offices of *Pravda*. The editor, Mekhlis, showed him his manuscript, which now bore Stalin's adjudication: 'Tell this newly appeared "Dante" that he can stop writing.'

'I have invented a new genre,' said Isaac Babel, the great short-story writer, in 1934: 'that of silence.' Babel ceased to be published in 1937; he was arrested in 1939, and shot in 1940.

Demian 'Bedny': Demian the Poor (his real name was Efim Pridvorov). He was a disgrace to poetry; and his physical appearance wore that disgrace. But we are relieved that he met no worse fate than penury – silence, in his case, being neither here nor there.

The Grey Blur, the Yellow Eyes

In November 1915 Lenin wrote to his colleague Vyacheslav Karpinsky asking for

> a big favour: find out (from Stepko [N. D. Kiknadze] or Mikha [M. G. Tskhakaya]) the name of 'Koba' (is it Iosif Dzh . . .? we've forgotten). It's very important!!!

This seems especially comic when we consider the historical revisions subsequently undertaken by Stalin. Films, paintings and textbooks routinely depicted scenes of Lenin and Stalin wisely planning the Revolution together (well before 1915), the 'great joy' and 'manly embraces' of their reunions, and so on. There is something boyishly transparent about the faked transcript of 1929, supposedly of Lenin's telegraphic communications in early 1918, when the new regime was struggling with the Treaty of Brest-Litovsk. Stalin's intention here is the retrospective validation, and magnification, of his own role (and, of course, the undermining of Trotsky's):

> 1. Lenin here. I've just received your special letter. Stalin isn't here and I haven't been able to show it to him yet . . . As soon as Stalin gets back I'll show him your letter . . . 2. I want to consult Stalin before replying to your question . . . 3. Stalin has just arrived and we are going to discuss the matter and give you our joint reply . . . Tell Trotsky we request a break in the talks and his return to [Petrograd]. Lenin.

'Our joint reply': a swift ascent, then, for 'Iosif Dzh . . .?' By 1915 Lenin had known Stalin for ten years. In 1912 he personally nominated him to the Central Committee. That same year Stalin twice crossed the Austrian border (illegally) to visit Lenin in Cracow. Lenin referred to him as 'my wonderful Georgian'. And yet he couldn't remember his *name*. 'It's very important!!!' observed Lenin. And so it is.

When the time came to falsify, or refalsify, the historical record, Stalin had much work to do. His prerevolutionary activities (agitprop and the organization of strikes) were mildly remarkable only for the frequency of his incarcerations. Between 1903 and 1917 he was arrested seven times and sentenced to imprisonment or, more usually, to internal exile (from which he escaped five times). Between 1908 and 1917 he spent only eighteen months at liberty. Even his part in the famous 'expropriations' appears to have been minor. The sensational heist in Tiflis (1907), with its guns, its bombs, its scores of injuries, its innocent dead (including the mutilated horses), was the work, not of 'Koba', but of 'Kamo' (the crazed Ter-Petrosian). Stalin's achievement, pre-1917, rests on the several articles he indubitably published in *Pravda*. Then came the October events in Petrograd.

The History of the All-Union Communist Party: Short Course was shepherded through the presses by Stalin in 1938 – during the first ebb of the Terror. Part primer, part ghosted autobiography, the *Short Course* would have eventual print runs in the tens of millions and become a cornerstone of the entire culture. Its popularity was perhaps not entirely manufactured and imposed. The *Short Course*, after all, was the best-known guide on how to avoid being arrested. By now, by 1938, almost everyone who remembered things differently was dead. This was one of the obscure desires of the Terror: to make a tabula rasa of the past . . . As the *Short Course* tells it, Stalin made the Revolution (and won the Civil War) more or less singlehanded – with the help and colleagueship of Lenin, and with the sinister hindrances of Trotsky. And the truth is ('a queer but undoubted fact', as Isaac Deutscher put it) that Stalin played no part in October at all.*

It seems to have been de rigueur for Stalin's contemporaries to describe him, at this stage (he would blossom fiercely during the Civil War), as 'a grey and colourless mediocrity', 'a grey blur' (with 'a glint of animosity' in 'his yellow eyes' – Trotsky), or 'just a small-town politician' (Lev Kamenev). Such assessments are

---

*He merits only two passing references in John Reed's *Ten Days That Shook the World*, and the book was later banned in the USSR for that reason. 'His name does not occur in any document relating to those historic days and nights' (Volkogonov).

usually quoted as examples of lack of prescience or as tributes to Stalin's powers of dissimulation. But it is clear that that's exactly what Stalin was, in 1917: a grey blur, with yellow eyes (several observers mention the 'tigerish eyes'). Still, even then Stalin had the ability to repel his peers. In March he suffered a preferment snub that Conquest finds 'quite astonishing when we consider that it was taken to outweigh his high official standing' (he was turned down for a minor promotion 'in view of certain personal characteristics'). We have here a figure both anonymous and liable to give offence. As soon as the guard dropped, in other words, something feral was revealed. The grey blur gave way to the yellow eyes.

When in 1912 Lenin nominated Stalin for the Central Committee he didn't put his name forward in the usual way but pushed him through by fiat, as if conceding that his protégé was not widely admired. Lenin indulged Stalin partly because of his background, the closest thing the Bolsheviks had to a proletarian (apart from Tomsky); and he felt that Stalin's working-class brutality was more ideologically 'honest' than the brainier brutality of himself and Trotsky and to lesser degrees all the other top men. In 1922, as we have seen, Lenin experienced a fundamental rejection of Stalin, a rejection of his low cultural level, his lumpen instability. He felt power ('immense power') concentrating itself in Stalin and, suddenly, it seems, he saw what that power had done and was doing to him. Stalin, in fact, was not corrupted so much as symbiotically reinvented by power.

When the new cabinet was announced, in 1917, Stalin was named fifteenth and last. (To reminisce about this placement was not encouraged, in 1937–38.) Stalin was Lenin's industrious, underbred mascot, his shaggy dog. Five years later, Lenin would

sense that the dog had begun to fizz with rabies. Two years
earlier, so far as Lenin was concerned, the dog didn't even have
a name.

We had better deal here with the baffling telephone conversation between Stalin and Lenin's wife, Krupskaya, on 22 December
1922, in which Stalin called her, among other things (such was
Party rumour), a 'syphilitic whore'.

The timing is important. At this stage Lenin-Stalin relations
were at their lowest point, after the Georgia altercation. On the
other hand, four days earlier the Central Committee had con-
ferred on Stalin responsibility for Lenin's medical care.* Thirteen
days *later* Lenin would compose his 'Testament' ('Stalin is too
rude', and so on). But Lenin wasn't told about the telephone call
until March, on the eve of his final stroke.

On 22 December 1922, Stalin learned that Krupskaya had
supposedly breached Lenin's medical regimen. In her own words
(a letter to Kamenev):

> Stalin subjected me to a storm of the coarsest abuse yesterday
> about a brief note Lenin dictated to me with the permission of
> the doctors. I didn't join the party yesterday. In the whole of
> the last thirty years I have never heard a coarse word from a
> comrade.

What can explain Stalin's reaction? The 'brief note' Lenin
dictated to Krupskaya was addressed to Trotsky, praising him for
his recent outmanoeuvring of Stalin (on the question of the

---

*With hindsight we may think that Stalin was hardly the automatic choice for
such a role. His real job was to cordon Lenin off from the new power vacuum,
which the Politburo was immediately and unsentimentally jockeying to fill.

foreign-trade monopoly). Evidence, to Stalin, of a Lenin-Trotsky bloc. But why would his aggression take the course it did? This was a clearly unforgivable intrusion, and prosecuted with such fury that Krupskaya (known to be an unmercurial woman, even as she nursed a dying husband) is said to have been reduced to hysterics (her nerves, she told Kamenev, were now 'at breaking point'). When Lenin heard about it, as he inevitably would, he moved at once, and again inevitably, to demote and discredit Stalin. Then, on 7 March, came Lenin's final stroke. He lived on, speechless, for another ten months; and Stalin survived.

If there is no rational explanation for Stalin's behaviour then an irrational one will have to serve. The prominent Chekist, Dzerzhinsky, on being mildly reproached for the savagery of his Georgian purge, agreed that the suppression had indeed got completely out of hand, adding, 'But we couldn't help ourselves.' We can well believe that the accession to and then the practice of power had that compulsive quality. One must feel one's way into it by imagining Bolshevik coercive force and the adjectives associated with it – naked, raw, brutal, merciless, absolute. On 25 May 1922, Stalin had experienced a runaway powersurge, on the occasion of Lenin's first stroke (with the massive booster of 13 December: strokes two and three). When it came to confronting Krupskaya, Stalin was all caught up in the thrills and heaves of the prospect of prepotence. He couldn't help himself.

Krupskaya was being perfectly serious when she said that had Lenin lived on, he would eventually have joined all the other Old Bolsheviks in Stalin's execution cellars. When he was told about the telephone call, Lenin wrote to Stalin: 'I have no intention of forgetting what has been done against me, and it goes without saying what was done against my wife I also consider to have been directed against myself.' Precisely. For the first and only time, and with unstoppable recklessness, Stalin had revealed a profound secret: his hatred of Lenin. To the extent that Stalin was a divided or a 'doubled' self, half of him hated Lenin as purely and passionately as the whole man hated Trotsky.

As instructed, Krupskaya delivered the 'Testament' to the Central Committee soon after Lenin's death. Stalin then announced his resignation.

But a year had passed, and political reconfigurations were already entrained, and Stalin's tactical offer was refused.

His ally throughout, his most loyal helper, was cerebral sclerosis. First, the disease weakened Lenin, then partly marginalized him, then silenced him, then, after a crucial delay, extinguished him – uncannily obedient, all the while, to Stalin's needs.

The Kremlin Complexion

'Lazar,' said Stalin, one day in the testing year of 1937, as he struck up a conversation with his industrious underling Lazar Moiseyevich Kaganovich. 'Did you know that your [brother] Mikhail is hobnobbing with the rightists? There is solid evidence against him.'

After a pause Kaganovich replied: 'Then he must be dealt with in accordance with the law.'

Kaganovich duly telephoned his brother Mikhail (a Bolshevik since 1905 and now Commissar for aircraft construction), who shot himself the same day in a colleague's toilet. Lazar Kaganovich died of natural causes in 1988.*

---

*During the mid-1980s David Remnick, with appropriately heartless persistence, badgered Kaganovich for an interview. He found what he expected to find:

Such abjection was a way of surviving Stalin: you gave him something of your blood, without wavering – though Poskrebyshev, Stalin's secretary, is said to have gone down on his knees in the hope that his wife might be spared the supreme penalty.

Nikita Khrushchev's daughter-in-law was jailed.

Vyacheslav Molotov's wife was sent to the gulag.

Mikhail Kalinin's wife was beaten unconscious by a female interrogator in the presence of head Chekist Lavrenti Beria, and then sent to the gulag.

Anastas Mikoyan's two sons were sent to the gulag.

Aleksandr Poskrebyshev's wife was sent to the gulag. Three years later she was shot.

These men formed Stalin's inner circle: they were the 'Kremlin complexion' crowd (chalky, with livid patches) who worked with him all day and drank with him all night. We must picture their faces round the dinner table, or flickering in the private projection room (musicals and Westerns in the earlier years; later, celebratory propaganda about collective farms and the like). We must picture their faces as they looked up from their desks the following day. These pale men had given Stalin something of their blood.

Rhythms of Thought

Stalin's two most memorable utterances are 'Death solves all problems. No man, no problem' and (he was advising his interrogators on how best to elicit a particular confession) 'Beat, beat and beat again.'

---

a twitching amnesiac on a state pension. This was the charge against Mikhail: he was Hitler's candidate for leading a fascist Russia. The Kaganoviches were Jewish.

Both come in slightly different versions. 'There is a man, there is a problem. No man, no problem.'* This is less epigrammatic, and more catechistic – more typical of Stalin's seminarian style (one thinks of his oration at Lenin's funeral and its liturgical back-and-forth).

The variant on number two is: 'Beat, beat, and, once again, beat.' Another clear improvement, if we want a sense of Stalin's rhythms of thought.

Succession

The years of Stalin's climb to ascendancy, 1922–29, are so undramatic – blocs, alignments, bureaucratic reshuffles, and a certain amount of doctrinal wheedling about Permanent Revolution (later to be condemned as 'Trotskyite contraband') and Socialism in One Country (Stalin's view that the USSR would have to survive without Communist revolutions in, for a start, Germany, France, England and the USA): these years are so undramatic that they are best sidestepped in favour of a brief glance at Trotsky and the question why, in the end, he gave Stalin so very little trouble. He gave Stalin trouble psychologically. But not politically.

It was by any standards a remarkably thin field that Lenin left behind him. No one can reckon on dying at the age of fifty-three; but the matter of the succession was one of the great integral carelessnesses of Leninism. The chain of command, according

---

*If Stalin had been a modern American he would not have used the word 'problem' but the less defeatist and judgmental 'issue'. Actually, when you consider what Stalin tended to do to his enemies' descendants, the substitution works well enough.

to *State and Revolution* (written in haste between the two revolutions of 1917), depended on '*unquestioning obedience* to the will
of a single person, the Soviet leader'. And when that Soviet leader
died – then what? Justified anxiety on this question shores up
the sense of gloom and failure in Lenin's later, post-stroke medi-
tations.

To begin with it looked as though the front-runner was the
Petrograd – now Leningrad – Party boss, Grigori Zinoviev. This
feels in itself remarkable, because nobody has ever had a good
word to say for him. Conquest is untypically categorical:
'[Zinoviev] seems to have impressed oppositionists and Stalinists,
Communists and non-Communists, as a vain, incompetent, inso-
lent, and cowardly nonentity.' Another party star was Lev
Kamenev, a more restrained and respectable personage but an
incorrigible trimmer and haverer. Zinoviev and Kamenev were
used to working in concert (they would also be suppressed in
concert); possibly their weaknesses might have balanced out in
some kind of ramshackle coalition. What else was there? Lenin,
showing his vanity and, in sickness, his muted will, recommended
broad-based consensus rule: rule by Politburo. But the system he
had half-accidentally constructed was shaped for rule by the
strongest personality. The inevitability of Stalin: Richard Pipes
thinks that Stalin was inevitable. Most historians, when dealing
with the Stalin ascendancy, reject 'inevitable' in favour of 'logical'.
. . . Kamenev, by the way, publicly and passionately called for
Stalin's overthrow on 21 December 1925 (Stalin's forty-sixth
birthday). At this stage he and Zinoviev had eleven years to live.*
Bukharin had thirteen.

---

*Do their deaths become them? Tucker quotes a witness to the following

Nikolai Bukharin, whom Lenin called 'the darling of the Party,' abased himself many times. 'I am so glad they have been shot like dogs,' he said, referring to Zinoviev and Kamenev, in 1936. At that time he was being vigorously menaced by Stalin. But he had abased himself earlier, under no such pressure, at Lenin's 'demonstration' trial of the Socialist-Revolutionists in 1922 (Pipes describes his role here as 'sordid'. He behaved like a one-man lynch mob). Bukharin was by all accounts almost drunkenly volatile, equally likely to burst into tears or laughter. When the Mandelstams sought his help, in the early 1930s, Nadezhda was astounded by the rage he flew into – on their behalf. But Bukharin had eloquence and insight; he had a much sharper sense of reality than any of his peers. Consequently he was the only eminence uncontaminated by the critical Bolshevik vice: murderous contempt for the peasants. ('Enrich yourselves,' he told them, thereby attracting a doctrinal rebuke.) And Collectivization, when it came, provoked this response from him, a response seldom found in these years, in these men: moral hesitation. Bukharin said privately that during the Civil War he had seen

> things that I would not want even my enemies to see. Yet 1919
> cannot even be compared to what happened between 1930 and

---

exchange, as the two men faced their executioners. Zinoviev: 'This is a fascist coup!' Kamenev: 'Stop it, Grisha. Be quiet. Let's die with dignity.' Zinoviev: 'No! . . . Before my death I must state plainly that what has happened in our country is a fascist coup.' (Tucker goes on to argue that 'fascist coup' was a reasonable analysis.) Volkogonov gives this, via one of the prison guards: 'Although they had both written to Stalin many times begging for mercy and were apparently expecting it (he had after all promised), they sensed this was the end. Kamenev walked along the corridor in silence, nervously pressing his palms. Zinoviev became hysterical and had to be carried.'

1932. In 1919 we were fighting for our lives. We executed people, but we also risked our lives in the process. In the later period, however, we were conducting a mass annihilation of completely defenceless men, together with their wives and children.

Conquest adds:

[Bukharin] was even more concerned with the effect on the Party. Many Communists had been severely shaken. Some had committed suicide; others had gone mad. In his view, the worst result of the terror and famine in the country was not so much the sufferings of the peasantry, horrible though these were. It was the 'deep changes in the psychological outlook of those Communists who participated in this campaign, and instead of going mad, became professional bureaucrats for whom terror was henceforth a normal method of administration, and obedience to any order from above a high virtue'. He spoke of a 'real dehumanization of the people working in the Soviet apparatus'.

It is here, and not in the aftermath of the Kirov murder (December 1934), that we see the quickening of the Great Terror. 'Koba, why do you need me to die?' began the forty-third unanswered letter that Bukharin wrote to Stalin, during the long course of his house arrest, trial, sentence. Why? *Zachto?* Bukharin said it himself, in 1936:

[Stalin] is unhappy at not being able to convince everyone, himself included, that he is greater than everyone; and this unhappiness of his may be his most human trait, perhaps the only human trait in him. But what is not human, but rather something devilish, is that because of this unhappiness he cannot help taking revenge on people, on all people but especially those who are in any way better or higher than he.

Anyone better or higher: a numerous company. In earlier and happier days the two men, Stalin and Bukharin, used to tussle playfully on the lawns of their *dachas*. Solzhenitsyn anecdotally reports that Bukharin would often put Stalin on his back. That would have been enough.*

Which leaves Trotsky. Lenin credited him with the highest 'ambition', but there was something fundamentally unserious about Trotsky's approach to the succession. In late 1922 he had to ask directions to Lenin's dacha in Gorky – where Stalin was a frequent and faithful visitor. Then there was the elementary ineptitude of his failure to return from holiday in order to attend Lenin's funeral. (It is not the case that Stalin duped him over the dates.) Trotsky's absence was widely remarked – as was Stalin's from another funeral, in 1936. The Russian philosopher Alexander S. Tsipko pinpoints two ingredients of Bolshevik elan: *disdain for the trivial* and *the desire to astonish the world*. Trotsky epitomized both. Stalin intended to astonish the world, as we shall soon see. But he had no disdain for the trivial. The Bolsheviks had created a world in which the activities of any group of two or more people had to be monitored by the state. Stalin accepted the implications of this. The totality of Trotsky's failure in the

---

*Bukharin died with defiant dignity. On balance he perhaps deserves the cadences of Arthur Koestler's fictional conclusion in *Darkness at Noon*:

> A shapeless figure bent over him, he smelt the fresh leather of the revolver belt; but what insignia did the figure wear on the sleeves and shoulder-straps of its uniform – and in whose name did it raise the dark pistol barrel?
> A second smashing blow hit him on the ear. Then all became quiet. There was the sea again with its sounds. A wave slowly lifted him up. It came from afar and travelled sedately on, a shrug of eternity.

Bukharin's wife spent six months in a small cell ankle-deep in water and went on to serve eighteen years. Their daughter survived. His first wife and all her close family were wiped out.

struggle for power is taken romantically by romantics. In fact his effort was lame, obtuse, even valetudinarian (an elderly tremolo comes off the page as we read about his various indispositions and recuperations). In the election to the Central Committee in 1921, Trotsky came in tenth – 'far below Stalin, and even after Molotov,' as Pipes points out. Anyway, there was no doubt who was temperamentally more suited to the job of nursing and patting and rubbing and generally tending to the gigantic paunch of the bureaucracy.

Theory

'Stop it, Koba, don't make a fool of yourself. Everyone knows that theory is not exactly your field.'

This interruption came from the lips of the old Communist sage David Ryazonov. It was a costly taunt.

Very soon after Lenin's death, in April 1924, Stalin gave a course of lectures, later printed in a short book called *The Foundations of Leninism*. It consisted almost entirely of quotations (without them, says Volkogonov, the book would contain little more than punctuation marks). The quotations were marshalled by a research assistant named F. A. Ksenofontov. He, too, would pay for his contribution.

In 1925 Stalin appointed Jan Sten, deputy head of the Marx-Engels Institute, as his private tutor. Sten's job was to tighten Stalin's grip on dialectical materialism. Twice a week, for three years, Sten came to the Kremlin apartment and coached his pupil on Hegel, Kant, Feuerbach, Fichte, Schelling, Plekhanov, Kautsky and Francis Bradley (*Appearance and Reality*). Stalin, ominously, found Sten's voice 'monotonous', but he managed to sit through the lessons, occasionally breaking in with such queries as 'Who uses all this rubbish in practice?' and 'What's all this got to do with the class struggle?' As Bukharin put it, Stalin was 'eaten up by the vain desire to become a well-known theoretician. He feels that it is the only thing he lacks.' Sten, with that monotonous voice of his, would not get off lightly.

The tutorials ended in 1928. By December 1930 Stalin felt himself equipped to lecture the lecturers. As the unchallenged dictator whose revolution from above (his 'Second October') was already launched in a wave of unprecedented hysteria and havoc, he found the time to address the Institute of Red Professors in the following terms:

> We have to turn upside down and turn over the whole pile of shit that has accumulated in questions of philosophy and natural science. Everything written by the Deborin group [Academician Abram Deborin was a temporarily influential thinker] has to be smashed. Sten and Karev can be chucked out. Sten boasts a lot, but he's just a pupil of Karev's. Sten is a desperate sluggard. All he can do is talk.

Sten and others were moreover accused of 'Menshivizing idealism' and of 'underestimating the materialistic dialectic'. It was impossible to ascertain what Stalin was prescribing – or proscribing. The final result of his intervention was that 'philosophy shrivelled up,' as Volkogonov puts it: 'no one had the courage to write anything more on the subject.'

Ksenofontov, Stalin's collaborator on *The Foundations of Leninism*, was told to abandon his work. He was later shot. Jan Sten was pronounced a 'lickspittle of Trotsky'. He was later shot. The fate of David Ryazonov ('Stop it, Koba') was slightly more unusual.

Ryazonov had a protégé, I. I. Rubin, who was among the defendants in the Menshevik trial of 1931. On his arrest Rubin was confined in what Solzhenitsyn calls the *box* ('constructed in such a way that [the prisoner] can only stand up and even then is squeezed against the door'). This went on for some time, but Rubin held out. The Chekists broke him by producing a stranger whom they threatened to shoot if Rubin's resistance continued. He witnessed two such murders before he signed. At his trial Rubin implicated Ryazonov as the possessor of documents adumbrating the full scope of the Menshevik conspiracy. 'You won't find them anywhere unless you've put them there yourself,' said Ryazonov, when summoned to the Politburo. He was sacked, expelled from the Party, and sentenced to internal exile. He was later shot.

It seems that the sole survivor of these theoretical exchanges was Abram Deborin, who died (in poverty) at the amazingly late date of 1963.

The Second October and the Breaking of the Peasantry

Collectivization (1929–33) was the opening and defining phase of Stalin's untrammelled power: it was the first thing he did the moment his hands were free. As a crime against humanity it eclipses the Great Terror, which it also potentiated, in two senses, rendering the purge both more certain and more severe. Collectivization makes you wonder what the fifty years of the gulag would have been like if telescoped in time (to half a decade) and distended in space (to fill the entire country). Only it was worse, demographically worse. During Collectivization Stalin is reckoned to have killed about 4 million children. For the man himself, though, and for the man's psychology, the most salient feature of Collectivization was the abysmal depth, and gigantic reach, of its failure. In his introductory administrative push, Stalin ruined the countryside for the rest of the century. It was here, too, that he lit out of all reality, and did so with full Bolshevik aggression. As the Party economist S. G. Strumilin put it: 'Our task is not to study economics but to change it. We are bound by no laws.' This was the first stage in Stalin's opaque – indeed barely graspable – attempt to confront the truth, to bring it into line, to humble it, to break it.

I was in my late twenties when I first realized – the moment came as I read a piece about Islam in the *TLS* – that theocracies are *meant to work*. Until then I thought that repression, censorship, terror and destitution were the price you had to pay for living by the Book. But no, that wasn't the idea at all: Koranic rule was meant to bring you swimming pools and hydrogen bombs. Collectivization, similarly, was *meant to work*. Stalin had earlier expressed doubts about the 'Left-deviation' (i.e., extremely doctrinaire) attitude to the peasantry: its policies, he said, would 'inevitably lead to . . . a great increase in the price of agricultural produce, a fall in real salaries and an artificially produced famine'. And his preparations for Collectivization, in the initial burst, were frivolously lax. Yet Stalin believed that Collectivization would *work*. Collectivization would astonish the world. This was a Stalinist rush of blood. And that is how Stalinism is perhaps best represented: as a series of rushes of blood.

In Bolshevik terms the peasantry was (as psychologists say when referring to a huge and unmentionable family dysfunction) 'the elephant in the living room'. The peasantry, in the Marxist universe, wasn't really meant to be there. In the Marxist universe

Russia was supposed to be more like Germany or France or England, with their well-developed urban proletariats. Yet the Russian peasants were intransigently actual: they comprised 85 per cent of the population. And, as landholders, they were technically bourgeois, technically capitalist.* Lenin had tried to socialize the countryside. Grain requisitioning was enforced by terror – and followed by famine. His agrarian policies also gave rise, in 1920–21, to a vast national uprising that proved a greater threat to the regime than all the armies of the Whites: part of a failed but genuine revolution that utterly dwarfed those of 1905 and February 1917. His response was the abashedly capitalistic New Economic Policy; and this was an enduring doctrinal embarrassment to the Bolsheviks. Originally an enthusiast, Lenin seemed to lose his appetite for Collectivization and what it would mean. The Right bloc in the Politburo concurred. The Left bloc was more restless for bold action but was reluctantly resigned to a socialization of the countryside that might take ten or twenty years. In 1928, with Trotsky finished, no one was talking with much ardour about forced Collectivization, let alone immediate forced Collectivization.† During the earlier years of the 1920s Stalin had presented himself as a godfearing centrist. Then, with the opposition defeated, he veered wildly Left. The argument with the professionals was easily settled. As 1929 wore on, writes

---

*The peasants, now tied to their collective farms, continued to be despised as essentially 'unsocialist' well into the 1960s.

†This is more or less the consensus view. Malia dissents from it; he sees Collectivization as structural to the Lenin-Stalin continuum, and he is eloquent. 'For a Bolshevik party the real choice in 1929 was not between Stalin's road and Bukharin's; it was between doing approximately what Stalin did and giving up the whole Leninist enterprise' (*The Soviet Tragedy*). The question remains: how approximately do we take the word 'approximately'?

Conquest, Soviet economists 'had the choice of supporting the politicians' new plans or going to prison'.

Stalin's aims were clear: crash Collectivization would, through all-out grain exports, finance wildfire industrialization, resulting in breakneck militarization to secure state and empire 'in a hostile world'. According to Robert Tucker, Stalin was beginning to picture himself as a kind of Marxist Tsar; he hoped to improve and replace Leninism (with Stalinism), and also to buttress the state 'from above', as had Peter the Great. What remains less clear is whether his strategy was thought through, or simply and intoxicatedly ad hoc. The Five Year Plan, after all, was not a plan but a wish list. It was certainly Stalin's intention, or his need, to regalvanize Bolshevism, to commit it, once again, to 'heroic' struggle. And yet, unlike Hitler, who announced his goals in 1933 and, with a peculiarly repulsive sense of entitlement, set about achieving them, Stalin is to be seen at this time as a figure constantly fantasticated not by success but by failure.

To get things going he needed an enemy and an emergency. The emergency was a 'grain crisis' after the disappointing but undisastrous harvest of 1927. The enemy was the village kulak. The kulaks (*kulak* means *fist*) were a pre-Revolutionary stratum of rich peasants: they were usurers and mortgagers and 'exploiters of labour'; and they all but disappeared during the rural terror of War Communism. Of course, under NEP, some peasants continued to be richer than others (by about half as much again, in extreme cases). It came down to one extra cow, one extra hired hand during the harvesting, one extra window on the face of the log cabin. On 21 December 1929, Stalin celebrated his fiftieth birthday, to hyperbolic acclaim; this date also marks the birth of the 'cult of personality', which would take such a toll on his mental health. Eight days later he announced his policy of 'liquidating the kulaks as a class'.

Solzhenitsyn is insistent ('This is very important, the most important thing') that Dekulakization was chiefly a means of terrorizing the *other* peasants into submission: 'Without frightening them to death there was no way of taking back the land which the Revolution had given them, and planting them on that same land as serfs.' (And Molotov spoke of dealing the kulaks 'such a blow' that 'the middle peasant will snap to attention before us'.) The Bolshevik 'class analysis' of the countryside seems, even by Party standards, desperately willed, vague, ignorant and contradictory;* but it did have the supposed virtue of siding with the least fit – the virtue of downward selection. There were meant to be three kinds of peasant (poor, middle, kulak), and three kinds of kulak (numerically bulked out by various 'subkulaks' or 'near-kulaks' or *podkulakniki*, meaning 'henchmen of kulak'). A plan approved in January 1930 stated that the first kind of kulak (the richest) was 'to be arrested and shot or imprisoned', writes Conquest, 'and their families exiled;

---

*A poem of 1936 about Collectivization pictured Stalin on an ebony steed:

> Past lakes, through hills and woods and fields
> Along the road he rides
> In his grey trenchcoat with his pipe.
> Straight on his horse he guides.
> He stops and speaks
> To peasantfolk
> Throughout the countryside
> And making necessary notes,
> Goes on about his ride.

Quoted by Tucker. Stalin was not on that horse. Volkogonov: 'Throughout his life he visited an agricultural region only once, and that was in 1928, when he went to Siberia to see to grain deliveries. He never set foot in a village again.'

and the second exiled merely; while (at this stage) the "non-hostile" third section might be admitted to the collective farm on probation.' The poorer peasants (who do not get a good press in the historiography: 'drunks', 'layabouts', 'windbags', 'unem-ployables', and so on) were encouraged, and paid, to denounce the richer peasants. Again, the extraordinary persistence of this theme: that a ruling order predicated on human perfectibility should reward, glorify, encourage and indeed necessitate all that is humanly base. In the context of the Bolsheviks' 'unprece-dented hypocrisy' (N. Mandelstam), we may consider, here, how the battle cry against 'exploitation of labour' accompanied the reenserfment, not just of the kulaks, but of the entire peasantry . . . The Bolsheviks found bourgeois morality, and bourgeois law, hypocritical. This belief somehow encouraged a fabulous expansion in hypocritical possibility. The Bolsheviks took hypocrisy to places it had never been before; their hypocrisy was highly innovative, highly refined, and almost wittily symmetrical. It was negative perfection.

Working in consort with tens of thousands of Party activists, the punitive organs fanned out from the cities, with rifles, and bundles of orders and instructions. Not all Soviet villages contained kulaks, but all Soviet villages had to be terrorized, so kulaks had to be found in all Soviet villages. Stalin was, of course, using a quota system (as he would in the Great Terror). He seemed to have in mind just under 10 per cent: about 12 million people. The agitators and Chekists had had three years of strident indoc-trination (and active service: grain requisitioning, the exaction of levies), with all the usual machismo emphases on hardness and mercilessness; and they were themselves half-terrorized (from both sides); and Stalin's quotas were always *minimums*

which it was an honour to exceed. This is from Vasily Grossman's
Forever Flowing:

> The fathers were already imprisoned, and then, at the begin-
> ning of 1930, they began to round up the families too . . . They
> would threaten people with guns, as if they were under a spell,
> calling small children 'kulak bastards', screaming 'Blood-
> suckers!' And those 'bloodsuckers' were so terrified that they
> hardly had any blood of their own left in their veins. They were
> as white as clean paper.

Stalin had for a while been putting it about that the poor and
middle peasants were flocking to the collective farms 'spontaneously' – a discordant adverb, because spontaneity was not a
quality he usually praised. Collectivization, to the peasants, meant
the surrender of their goods, animals and even their physical
beings to the state. The choice they faced was to collectivize or
be themselves dekulakized. Stalin's objective was Lenin's objective of 1921: state monopoly of food.

Thus anarchy, plunder, mania and sadism were visited on the
countryside. Peasant resistance took two main forms, one
predictable, the other unforeseen. First, outright insurrection. The
Cheka reported 402 riots and revolts in January 1930, 1,048 in
February, and 6,528 in March.* These were often quelled by the
armed forces: cavalry, armoured cars and even fighter aircraft.
The peasants' other main strategy, though, which showed a
dreadful decorum, could not be answered or reversed. This is the
account of an activist quoted by Tucker:

> I called a village meeting, and I told the people that they had
> to join the collective, that these were Moscow's orders, and if

*'In all of 1930 nearly 2.5 million peasants took part in approximately 14,000
revolts, riots, and mass demonstrations against the regime' (Nicolas Werth).

they didn't they would be exiled . . . They all signed the paper that same night, every one of them. Don't ask me how I felt and how they felt. And the same night they started to do what the other villages of the USSR were doing when forced into collectives – to kill their livestock.

'Everyone had a greasy mouth,' as another activist disgustedly noted: 'everyone blinked like an owl, as if drunk from eating.' This was the peasantry's last supper. And it accounted for roughly half of the national herd.

Launched over the latter part of 1929, Collectivization was already a clear catastrophe by late February 1930. There were differences, but Stalin had reached Lenin's impasse of 1921. In the earlier case, Lenin accepted defeat, withdrawal and compromise. In other words, he accepted reality. Stalin did not. The peasantry no longer faced a frigid intellectual. It faced a passionate low-brow whose personality was warping and crackling in the heat of power. He would not accept reality. He would break it.

Stalin's first move was a feint towards accommodation. On 2 March 1930, all Soviet newspapers ran the famous article 'Dizzy with Success' (which Stalin had not shown to the Politburo). Causing consternation at every Party level, the piece jovially blamed the recent abuses and excesses on a triumphalist *apparat*. In April, showing a primitive, semi-subliminal self-awareness, Stalin elaborated as follows:

> [The unfortunate consequences] arose because of our rapid success in the collective farm movement. Success sometimes turns people's heads. It not infrequently gives rise to extreme vanity and conceit. That may very easily happen to represen-tatives of a party like ours, whose strength and prestige are almost immeasurable. Here, instances of Communist vain-glory, which Lenin combatted so vehemently, are quite possible.

The new line brought temporary concessions. Collectivization was slowed and even partly reversed. But Dekulakization accelerated. The gulag could not expand fast enough to contain the deportees. In his long novel *Life and Fate* Grossman describes the feelings of a Soviet citizen threatened by arrest (here he coincidentally echoes Stalin: 'How much does the Soviet Union weigh?'):

> He could feel quite tangibly the difference in weight between the fragile human body and the colossus of the State. He could feel the State's bright eyes gazing into his face; any moment now the State would crash down on him; there would be a crack, a squeal – and he would be gone.

The peasantry would now experience what Grossman repeatedly calls 'the rage of the State'. When Pasternak travelled to the countryside in the early 1930s to 'gather material about the new life of the village', he fell ill and wrote not a word for an entire year. 'There was such inhuman, unimaginable misery, such a terrible disaster, that it began to seem almost abstract . . .' What he saw 'would not fit within the bounds of consciousness'. No, not *his* consciousness. What he saw was the reification of another's consciousness, another's mind, another's rage.

In the autumn of 1930 the cycle of violence became a spiral: kaleidoscopic and vertiginous. Here is part of a requisitioner's report:

> . . . 12 per cent of all the farmers have been tried already, and that doesn't include the deported kulaks, peasants who were fined, etc . . . The prisons are full to bursting point. Balachevo prison contains more than five times as many people as it was originally designed to hold, and there are 610 people crammed into the tiny district prison in Elan. Over the last

month, Balachevo prison has sent 78 prisoners back to Elan, and 48 of them were less than ten years old . . . [V]iolence seems to be the only way of thinking now, and we always 'attack' everything. We 'start the onslaught' on the harvest, on the loans, etc. Everything is an assault; we 'attack' the night from nine or ten in the evening till dawn. Everyone gets attacked: the shock troops call in everyone who has not met his obligations and 'convince' him, using all the means you can imagine. They assault everyone on their list, and so it goes on, night after night.

Listing five types of torture used to force peasants to reveal grain reserves, the writer Mikhail Sholokhov added, in a letter to Stalin: 'I could give a multitude of similar examples. These are not "abuses" of the system; this is the present system for collecting grain.' On 7 August 1932, Stalin promulgated one of the most savage laws in all history. The peasants called it the 'five-stalk law' or simply the 'ear law'. '[A]ny theft or damage of socialist property' became punishable by ten years or, as the saying went, by nine grams (of lead). A whole family could be shattered for a pilfered handful. Sentences given between August 1932 and December 1933 ran to 125,000, with 5,400 executions.

Where can Stalin's rage go next, how can it expand and intensify? A woman widowed that fortnight by starvation is given ten years in the gulag for stealing a few potatoes. It starts to be the practice that orphaned children are shot en masse. The Cheka executes vets and meteorologists. Suddenly 20,000 Communist activists and managers are arrested (for 'criminal complacency' in the struggle), to terrorize the terrorizers, to pile terror upon terror, and then more terror, and then more, until Stalin, the escalationist, turns to nonconventional or nuclear terror: famine.

As grain yields fell, requisitioning quotas grew, with only one possible outcome. Stalin just went at the peasants until there was nobody there to sow the next harvest.

Women

He was twice a widower.

Of his first wife, Yekaterina (Kato) Svanidze (m. *c.* 1905: two years after his first arrest), Conquest writes in *Stalin: Breaker of Nations*:

> We know little about their brief life together, though acquaintances say that while she prayed for his redemption from his dangerous career she was, in the Georgian tradition, obedient to his wishes; on his side, the official Social Democratic notion of the equality of the sexes played no part. Nonetheless, though occasionally brutal, he is reported to have been very fond of her.

Kato died of typhus in 1907. In his *Stalin*, Dmitri Volkogonov describes (but does not reproduce) photographs of her funeral showing Koba 'short and thin, his shock of hair uncombed, standing at the graveside with a look of genuine grief on his face'. After the ceremony Stalin said to an old friend: 'This creature softened my stony heart. She is dead and with her have died my last warm feelings for all human beings.' Some historians take Stalin's little speech on such good trust that they eschew quotation marks and simply paraphrase it in the third person. It was not that simple, or not that natural. If, in a work of fiction, I were to put those words into the mouth of a character, it would be on the following understanding: *Here is a man who has always been puzzled by – and perhaps even ashamed of – his lack of human feeling. The death of the young wife relieves him of that puzzlement and shame (it is not his fault; the world did it). He can henceforth ally himself with feelinglessness.* Kato left behind her a six-month-old son, Yakov. As Koba threw himself into the cycle of arrest, exile and escape (one year of freedom in the next decade), Yakov remained in Georgia with his maternal aunt and uncle. Certainly, Stalin never showed anything but contempt for him, and played a strange part in his terrible death.

Stalin made the acquaintance of his second wife, Nadezhda (Nadya) Alliluyeva, when she was an infant of two or three. The Alliluyevs were cultured Old Bolsheviks who regularly put Stalin up during his visits to prewar St Petersburg. It is said that he once saved Nadya and her sister Anna from some risk of drowning; and there's no question that she idealized him over the years – the gruff agitnik, with his moustache, his tousled quiff, his multiple arrests. After the Revolution, at the age of sixteen, she became Stalin's secretary, and then, a year later, his wife. Vasily was born in 1921, Svetlana in 1926. Nadya shot herself in the head after a party in the Kremlin to celebrate the fifteenth anniversary of the Revolution. November 1932: in a sense, as we shall see, she was just another victim of Collectivization. While he contemplated her in the open coffin Stalin was seen to make a gesture of dismissal and heard to mutter, 'She left me as an enemy.'

During his longest exile, it is said, Stalin sired a child in Siberia. And there were rumours that in his later years he would sometimes sleep with his housekeeper, Valentina Istomina. And that is about all. Considering what he could have got up to, and considering what Beria (for instance) actually did get up to, Stalin's sexual life was remarkably prim. One can hardly avoid a comparison with Hitler (whose only 'great love', Geli Raubal, shot herself in September 1931, and whose companion, Eva Braun, attempted suicide in the autumn of 1932, and again in 1935, and again in 1945, successfully, with her husband at her side). Both Stalin and Hitler felt threatened by intelligent women. Stalin: 'a woman with ideas . . . a herring with ideas: skin and bones'. Hitler: 'A highly intelligent man should take a primitive and stupid woman.' Both responded to (frequent) complaints of neglect with a curse or a taunt; and both enjoyed inflicting humiliation. Hitler's sexuality, or asexuality, was by far the more extreme: he was a monorchic neuter, an impotent, a terrible virgin. In him the will to power entirely subsumed the erotic energies. More generally Nazism, and also Bolshevism, exude the confusions of crypto-homosexuality, homosexuality enciphered and unac- knowledged – the cult of hardness, with all the female qualities programmatically suppressed. Heterosexuality has clarity, and homosexuality has clarity; but much violence waits in the area in between. Nazism, of course, killed many thousands of homo- sexuals. Bolshevism, with its contradictory traditions of permis- siveness and sans-culotte puritanism, alighted only rarely on a sexual enemy – 'German bedstraw', for example (women suspected of fraternizing with the occupation forces during the war).

There are variations in the accounts of Nadya's last night. During the Kremlin banquet (hosted by the cretinous Kliment Voroshilov) Stalin 'insulted' Nadya; there seems to have been an exchange along the lines of 'Hey, you, have a drink!' (Nadya was allergic to alcohol), followed by 'Don't you *hey* me!' He also threw a doused cigarette at her (or, in a variant, a lit cigarette which went down her dress). Nadya walked out; she was followed by her friend Polina Molotov, who joined her in a calming stroll round the Kremlin courtyard. Back in the Stalin apartment, Nadya sought her bedroom (it was separate bedrooms by now), and shot herself with a German revolver. She had written a note . . . In a long-suppressed section of his memoirs Khrushchev reports that Nadya telephoned the dacha and was told by an oafish duty-officer that Stalin was 'with a woman'. This feels discountable. It is the only rumour of an infidelity in Stalin's fourteen-year marriage; and it goes against our sense of the parochial diffidence of his sexuality (there are glints of disgust, too: that 'herring'). Nor is there much cogency in another rumour, that Stalin assisted in or expedited Nadya's suicide. There was, after all, the suicide note.

Svetlana Stalin, then seven, would go on to reveal that the note was 'partly personal, partly political'. It was November 1932: one wonders if Stalin was still divisible in these terms. He was already nearly all political, and after the events of this night he would finally dispense with the personal . . . The precipitant of Nadya's suicide was almost certainly political, too. She had recently enrolled as a chemistry student at the Industrial Academy in Moscow. A good Communist, she would ride there in the tram. It tests the empathetic powers to imagine even a tenth of the gangrenous nausea experienced by Nadezhda Alliluyeva (a serious, cultured, strong, pretty, motherly woman of thirty-one), seated at her desk, while classmates told her about the real situation in the Ukraine (where they had spent the summer, as activists). Nadya challenged her husband, and again we must imagine the tenor of this exchange. Stalin, typically, seems to have brazened his way out (as he did with Lenin over the Krupskaya business, in a letter which arrived just after Lenin's final incapacitation). He told Nadya that such talk was 'Trotskyite gossip'.

But she came back at him, later, having heard more from her classmates, including an account of two brothers who were arrested for trading in human flesh. This time Stalin's response was to rebuke Nadya for political indiscipline, to arrest the students at the Industrial Academy, and to order a purge of all colleges that had contributed manpower to Collectivization. Talking about famine would soon become a capital crime in the USSR. Nadya's execution was self-execution, but it anticipated that law.

At this time, Svetlana writes, her mother succumbed to 'devastating disillusionment'. Nadya came to see that 'my father was not the New Man she had thought when she was young'. But Stalin was a New Man, right enough: he had dreadfully burgeoned. Unprecedented power was his, and he had launched it on an experiment. The experiment had failed (and become, simply, a war of extermination waged against the guinea pigs). In the countryside, now, instead of growing fat on the loyally thrumming grain factories of which a German philosopher had fleetingly dreamed, the peasants were eating each other, and eating themselves.

Nadya Alliluyeva didn't know the half of it. She was ignorant of the fact that 5 million would die in the Ukraine alone. She was ignorant of the fact that they would die of her husband's *set purpose.*

If you want to know how a man felt about his wives then you look at how he treated his children. We shall do so. You would also look at how he treated his wives' families. And Stalin's feelings, as always, are written in crimson. This is Alan Bullock's summary:

> On the side of his first wife, Ekaterina Svanidze, her brother Alexander, once one of Stalin's closest friends, was shot as a

spy; at the same time his wife was arrested and died in camp, while their son was exiled to Siberia as 'a son of an enemy of the people'. Ekaterina's sister, Maria, was also arrested and died in prison. On the side of his second wife, Nadezhda Alliluyeva, her sister Anna was arrested in 1948 and sentenced to ten years for espionage; Anna's husband, Stanislav Redens, had already been arrested in 1938 as 'an enemy of the people' and was later shot. Ksenia, the widow of Nadezhda's brother Pavel, and Yevgenia, the wife of Nadezhda's uncle, were both arrested after the war and not released until after Stalin's death.

Afterword. When Milovan Djilas personally protested that the Red Army was raping Yugoslav women, Stalin said of his universal soldier: 'How can such a man react normally? And what is so awful in his having fun with a woman, after such horrors?' The women of Yugoslavia, it seems, were treated less harshly than certain of their sisters. Solzhenitsyn, an artillery officer in East Prussia at the time of his arrest (1945), later wrote: 'All of us knew very well that if the girls were German they could be raped and then shot. This was almost a combat distinction.' To what extent, in Stalin's view, was this also a matter of 'having fun with a woman'?

Men and Mountains

All the Party bosses had institutions named after them. As well as the Stalin Chemical Works, there was the Voroshilov Weaving Mill, the Zinoviev Paper Mills, the Bukharin Glass Factory, and so on. Old towns were also renamed: there were suddenly places called Ordzhonikidze, Kalinin, Kirov. In his *Stalin* Conquest comments:

> Meanwhile over the years, the country had to endure not only Stalingrad and Stalino (eventually six Stalinos in all), but also Stalinabad, Stalinsk, Stalinogorsk, Stalinskoye, Stalinski, Staliniri (the capital of South Ossetia), Mount Stalin (the highest peak in the USSR – later to be joined by the highest peaks in Czechoslovakia and Bulgaria), Stalin Bay, the Stalin Range, and various villages simply 'name of Stalin' . . .

In 1938, a year that saw 4.5 million supererogatory arrests and perhaps 500,000 executions, the Cheka chief, citing 'workers' suggestions', put before the Politburo the notion that Moscow should be renamed Stalinodar. Showing, now, a more traditional Bolshevik self-effacement, Stalin vetoed the change. He always said that the cult of personality, while useful politically, was distasteful to him. 'In general,' writes Conquest, 'his sporadic and ineffectual criticisms of the cult may be seen as a ploy to add modesty to the rest of the panoply of his virtues.'

When Janusz Bardach, prodded by obscenities and rifle butts, staggered out of the slave ship (his destination was the isolator at Kolyma), he saw, emblazoned on the cliff face, the words

GLORY TO STALIN, THE GREATEST GENIUS OF
    MANKIND.
GLORY TO STALIN, THE GREATEST MILITARY LEADER.
GLORY TO STALIN, THE GREATEST LEADER OF THE
    INTERNATIONAL PROLETARIAT.
GLORY TO STALIN, THE BEST FRIEND OF WORKERS
    AND PEASANTS.

And much more.

The 'cult of personality', of course, became the official euphemism for the Twenty Million. We may feel that the phrase is both derisory and appropriate. According to Marx, *personality* played no part in history: the course of that locomotive was determined by the railtracks of political economy, and not by the quirks of the stoker. Well, the Bolsheviks submitted this theory, among many others, to graphic refutation. Stalin did have a personality, and so did Lenin.* Personality made a difference. In Stalin's case, the difference was the Andes of dead bodies, one of whose peaks (call *that* mountain after him) disgorged its contents before the eyes of Varlam Shalamov.

1933: The Terror-Famine

We speak of famine 'raging', 'stalking the land', holding people 'in its grip'. Describing the immobility and silence within the villages, Vasily Grossman writes: 'Only famine was on the move. Only famine did not sleep.' Metaphorically we invest famine with volition and intent, but famine is just an absence – an absence of food, then an absence of life. It has a smell, noted for its extreme longevity: that of purulence. And Grossman writes that, despite the stillness, 'everything felt fierce and wild . . . And the earth crackled' . . . In considering the Terror-Famine of 1933, it is now asked of the reader forcefully to repersonify famine and call him Stalin. It is Stalin who is holding people in his grip, Stalin who is stalking the land, Stalin who is raging.

*And so did Khrushchev, whose 'secret speech' of 1956 was entitled 'On the Cult of Personality and Its Consequences' (and dealt only with the purge of the Party, and not of the nation). One of Stalin's more energetic administrators (in 1937 he was sent to the Ukraine to kill 30,000 people), Khrushchev showed, nonetheless, that it was possible to recross Solzhenitsyn's 'threshold' and pick up the remains of his humanity.

The use of famine as a weapon of the state against the popu-
lace is generally considered to be a Stalinist innovation (later
taken up by Mao and other Communist leaders), but Lenin's famine of 1921–22 had its terroristic aspects. Both famines had the
same cause: punitive food-requisitioning. Whereas Stalin nur-
tured and consolidated the mass starvation, Lenin, by contrast,
reluctantly and tardily permitted the American intervention,
which saved over 10 million lives. Yet in the Ukraine, at least,
Lenin's famine overlapped with terror. As the historian H. H.
Fisher put it in 1927: 'The Government of Moscow not only failed
to inform the American Relief Administration of the situation
in the Ukraine, as it had done in the case of much more remote
regions, but deliberately placed obstacles in the way . . .' Conquest
adds: 'Indeed, between 1 August 1921 and 1 August 1922, 10.6
million hundredweight of grain was actually taken from the
Ukraine for distribution elsewhere.' All his adult life Lenin had
been an admirer of famine as a 'radicalizer' (and secularizer) of
the peasantry. And what else but terror-famine could he have
had in mind when, in 1922, he warned Kamenev: 'It is a great
mistake to think that the NEP put an end to terror; we shall
again have recourse to terror and to economic terror.' So, once
again, Stalin in 1933 was merely showing himself to be 'Lenin's
most able pupil'. His only qualitative novelty, apart from the
Party purge, was the show trial. And we may recall Solzhenitsyn's
comment of the 'demonstration' trial of the SRs in 1922: Lenin
was 'so nearly there'.

Both Lenin and Stalin considered the Ukraine the most re-
fractory of all the republics. During the chaos of 1918–20, when
the administration in Kiev changed hands thirteen times, the

Bolsheviks invaded, or reinvaded, in annual campaigns. And throughout the Stalin push of 1929–33, and beyond, every imaginable Ukrainian institution was repeatedly purged. The thoroughness of Stalin's attempt at de-Ukrainianization can be gauged from an account given in Shostakovich's *Testimony*. It concerns the fate of the *kobzars* – peasant poets (many of them blind) who went from village to village with their verses and songs. They were not, one would have thought, an immediate threat to Soviet power, though they could be listed in separate categories of undesirables ('outdated elements,' for example, or simply 'others' – a much-used classification). But they nonetheless reminded the Ukrainian peasants that they had once had a country. The *kobzars*, several hundred of them, were invited to their first All-Ukrainian Congress. 'Hurting a blind man,' lamented Shostakovich, '—what could be lower?' Some were imprisoned, but 'almost all' were shot, because (as Conquest notes) a blind man would not be worth feeding in the gulag.

Stalin, then, had two reasons for assaulting the Ukrainian peasants: they were peasants, and they were Ukrainian. Thus the USSR continued to export grain, and continued to store it. The food requisitioning continued until March 1933 – the epicentre of the famine. By now the collection brigades only bothered with households that weren't obviously starving. The Ukraine had other similarities to the 'vast Belsen' of Conquest's description: armed guards, and watchtowers, manned day and night, to detect and deter thefts of the crop. Despite blockading, and barricading, hundreds of thousands of peasants made their way to the cities, where they crawled around at knee height among the crowds, who themselves formed swaying, howling lines in front of the 'commercial' bread shops* (the cities, too, were ravaged, Stavropol losing 20,000, Krasnodar 40,000, Kharkov 120,000). In December 1932, to combat 'kulak infiltration of the towns', the regime tightened restrictions on internal travel:

> The Central Committee and the government are in possession of definite proof that this massive exodus of the peasants has been organized by the enemies of the Soviet regime, by counterrevolutionaries, and by Polish agents as a propaganda coup against the process of collectivization in particular and the Soviet government in general.

Within the villages, within the families, Grossman writes, 'Mothers looked at their children and screamed in fear. They screamed as if a snake had crept into their house. And this snake was famine, starvation, death.' This snake was Stalin. At first the children cried all day for food; then, in addition, they cried for food all night. Some parents fled their children. Others took them to the towns and left them there. The Italian consul in Kharkov gave this report:

> So for a week now, the town has been patrolled by *dvorniki*, attendants in white uniforms, who collect the children and take them to the nearest police station . . . Around midnight they are all transported in trucks to the freight station at Severodonetsk. That's where all the children who are found in stations or on trains, the peasant families, the old people . . . are gathered together . . . A medical team does a sort of selection process . . . Anyone who is not yet swollen up and still has a chance of survival is directed to the Kholodnaya Gora buildings, where a constant population of 8,000 lies dying on straw

---

*These were black-market outlets *run by the government*. Their prices were high.

beds in the big hangars. Most of them are children. People who are already beginning to swell up are moved out in goods trains and abandoned about forty miles out of town . . .

Some parents killed their children. And other parents ate their children. *Zachto?* 'Why, what for, to what end?' as Grossman asks. His narrator goes on:

> It was then that I saw for myself that every starving person is like a cannibal. He is consuming his own flesh, leaving only his bones intact. He devours his fat to the last droplet. And then his mind goes dim, because he has consumed his own mind. In the end the starving man has devoured himself completely.

Twenty pages earlier Grossman similarly defines the fate, not of the victim, but of the executioner:

> [O]nly one form of retribution is visited upon an executioner – the fact that he looks upon his victim as something other than a human being and thereby ceases to be a human being himself, and thereby executes himself as a human being. He is his own executioner.

This, perhaps, is the meaning of the Terror-Famine of 1933: the self-cannibalized were destroyed by the self-executed. And this is the surreal gangrene of Stalinism.

About 5 million died in the Ukraine, and about 2 million died in the Kuban, Don and Volga regions and in Kazakhstan. These were formerly the richest agricultural lands in the USSR.

Poison Pen

In the 1930s, Nadezhda Mandelstam tells us, the verb *to write* assumed a new meaning. When you said *he writes* or *does she write?* or (referring to a whole classroom of students) *they write,* you meant that he or she or they *wrote reports to the organs.* (Similarly, the Cheka's rigged cases were called 'novels'.) To 'write' meant to inform, to denounce. Solzhenitsyn calls it 'murder by slander'.

Denunciation in Russia has a long history, going back at least as far as the sixteenth century and the testingly protracted reign of Ivan the Terrible (1533–84). 'Spy or die' was, more or less, the oath you swore. This practice, increasingly institutionalized under the old regime, was a tsarist barbarity that Lenin might have been expected to question. And he did waver, to the extent that he unsuccessfully proposed (in December 1918) that false denouncers should be shot. More moderate voices prevailed, and the punishment arrived at was one or two years depending on the gravity of the case. Solzhenitsyn is scandalized by this laxity. In the gulag a *five*-year term, compared to the far more usual *tenner* or *quarter* (twenty-five years), was colloquially known as 'nothing'.

It was during the Collectivization period that denunciation made its great leap forward. In the villages, as we have seen, the poorer peasants were incited to denounce the richer. 'It was so easy to do a man in,' explains Grossman: 'you wrote a denuniciation; you did not even have to sign it.' By the mid-1930s, when terror turned towards the towns and cities, denunciation was being praised in the press as 'the sacred duty of every Bolshevik, party and nonparty'. Quickly and predictably, denunciation now went through the roof. The process was quintessentially Stalinist in that a) it cultivated all that is most reptilian in human nature, and b) it selected downwards (those that were last would now be first).

And it was also, again, surreal. You might denounce someone for fear of their denouncing you; you could be denounced for not doing enough denouncing; the only disincentive to denunciation was the possibility of being denounced for not denouncing sooner; and so on. There were cases of denunciation for *state bounty*. From *The Great Terror*:

> In one Byelorussian village depicted in a recent Soviet article, fifteen rubles a head was paid, and a group of regular denouncers used to carouse on the proceeds, even singing a song they had composed to celebrate their deeds.

A single Communist denounced 230 people; another denounced over a hundred in four months. 'Stalin required,' as Conquest says, 'not only submission, but also complicity.' After his release from the gulag, just as he was finding himself as a writer, Solzhenitsyn came under extremely menacing pressure to become a *writer* in Nadezhda Mandelstam's sense. It has been estimated that in an average office every fifth employee reported to the Cheka. As Dmitri Volkogonov writes: 'Who could have imagined how many "spies and wreckers and terrorists" would be discovered. It was almost as if they were not living among us, but we among them!'

Tribute must now be paid to the most prodigious denouncer of all, the great Nikolaenko, scourge of Kiev. This unbelievable termagant was singled out for special praise by Stalin himself: 'a simple person from down below', she was nonetheless a 'heroine'. In Kiev, pavements emptied when Nikolaenko stepped out; her presence in a room spread mortal fear. Eventually Pavel Postyshev (First Secretary in the Ukraine, candidate member of the Politburo) expelled Nikolaenko from the Party. Stalin reinstated her 'with honour'. In a speech of 1937 he said, marvellously (for this episode is another example of the epiphanic, multifaceted negative perfection of Stalinism):

> [In Kiev, Nikolaenko] was shunned like a bothersome fly. At last, in order to get rid of her, they expelled her from the Party. Neither the Kiev organization nor the Central Committee of the Communist Party of the Ukraine helped her to obtain justice. It was only the intervention of the Central Committee of the Party which helped to disentangle that twisted knot. And what was revealed by an examination of the case? It was revealed that Nikolaenko was right, while the Kiev organization was wrong.

Assuming that this translation is a sensitive one (and I think it is): 'justice' is rich, and so is 'obtain' justice; 'bothersome fly' and 'that twisted knot' are rich; the rhetorical question near the end is rich; that closing 'while' is rich.

A vindicated Nikolaenko went back to her denunciations, and Kiev was in any case most viciously purged. Postyshev, chastened, demoted, transferred, now developed a reputation for exceptional ferocity in his function of purging his new fief, Kuibyshev. Later, as the Terror turned, he was attacked by Moscow for (of all things) exceptional ferocity: 'by cries of "vigilance" hiding his brutality in connection with the Party'. He was arrested in February 1938, and later shot.

Meanwhile, a twice-vindicated Nikolaenko was still hard at work – on her denunciations. There is much talk of the 'little Stalins' all over the USSR, but Nikolaenko was a true Stalinette: accession to power dismantled her sense of reality. When the new, post-purge bosses, headed by Khrushchev, had established themselves in Kiev, Nikolaenko denounced Khrushchev's deputy,

Korotchenko. Khrushchev defended his man, a posture Stalin adjudged to be 'incorrect': 'Ten per cent truth – that's already truth, and requires decisive measures on our part, and we will pay for it if we don't so act.' But then Nikolaenko denounced *Khrushchev*, a first-echelon toady and placeman, for 'bourgeois nationalism', and Stalin finally conceded that she was nuts. She helped destroy about 8,000 people.

Anyone who has ever received a poison-pen letter will have been struck by a sense of the author's desperate impotence. In the USSR, under Stalin, the poison worked: it had power. That was how it was: the *writer* and the poison pen.

I have not read any account of the fate of Nikolaenko. Either she was reexpelled, or her subsequent denunciations were for the most part tactfully ignored. She might of course have been shot – though Stalin showed a slight but detectable squeamishness about killing Old Bolshevik women.

As for the impressionable Postyshev, condemned by Moscow for his lack of moderation and restraint . . . This is *The Great Terror*:

> Postyshev's oldest son, Valentin, was shot, and his other children were sent to labour camps. His wife, Tamara, was viciously tortured night after night in the Lefortovo, often being returned to her cell bleeding all over her back and unable to walk. She is reported shot.

Heavy Industry

Soviet industry moved forward, and staggered about the place, like a titanic infant, with every manner of thunderous accident (collisions, explosions), with peasant boys twirling off frozen scaffolding, with many deaths, sudden or premature, in the usual atmosphere of myth and coercion, of error and terror – but it did move forward. John Scott, an American volunteer at the Morlock newtown of Magnitogorsk (250,000 workers), wagered that 'Russia's battle of ferrous metallurgy alone involved more casualties than the battle of the Marne.' And there were also fabulous inefficiencies: the regular unavailability, in the whole of Moscow, of a single 'light bulb or a bar of soap' (Tibor Szamuely), for instance, or the inability of the White Sea-Baltic Canal, constructed by the 'fart power' (Solzhenitsyn) of hundreds of thousands of slaves, to carry heavy shipping. Inefficiencies, when undeniable, had to be blamed on someone; and so Stalin (following Lenin) institutionalized the crime of *wrecking* – 'notwithstanding', as Solzhenitsyn says, 'the nonexistence of this concept in the entire history of mankind'.* Whereas the real wrecker, the 'super-wrecker' (Tucker), was of course Stalin.

One of the partial and deforming 'triumphs' of industrialization was ideological. Until now the Bolsheviks, contra Marx, formed a 'superstructure' without a proper proletarian 'base'. During the decade of the Big Break, about 30 million peasants were forced to find work in the cities. Martin Malia is characteristically panoptic:

> [Stalin] launched from above a second revolution that rebuilt Mother Russia as a Soviet pseudo-America and converted her superfluity of peasants into real proletarians. Thus the Party's supreme achievement was to transmogrify its status as 'super-structure' into the demiurge for creating the industrial and worker 'base' that was supposed to have created *it*.

*John Scott did see one case during his several years at Magnitogorsk: some outgoing kulaks spiked a turbine.

Soviet Communism can look back on two achievements. Industrialization made up for what Malia calls Russia's 'deficit of modernity' – though it deepened the systemic abnormality that led to the state's collapse. That was one achievement. The other was the defeat of Hitler. Both owed everything to the Russian people: their tears, their sweat, their blood.

Kazakhstan

Until 1930 the economy and culture of Kazakhstan, in Soviet Central Asia, was based on nomadism and transhumance (the seasonal movement of livestock). The plan was to Dekulakize these wanderers, and then Collectivize them. Once denomadized, the Kazakhstanis would devote themselves to agriculture. But the land was not suitable for agriculture. What it was suitable for was nomadism and transhumance. The plan didn't work out.

Over the next two years Kazakhstan lost 80 per cent of its livestock. And 40 per cent of its population: famine and disease.

The plan didn't work out.

Congress of Victors – 1

'The year 1937 really began on the 1st of December 1934.' This is the famous opening sentence of Eugenia Ginzburg's *Into the Whirlwind*. The year 1937 refers to the onset of the Great Terror; and 1 December 1934, refers to the murder of Sergei Kirov. The Terror did 'begin' in 1934 – but earlier in the year. I think we can pinpoint it.

On 26 January the Seventeenth Party Congress opened in the conference hall of the Great Kremlin Palace. The Congress styled itself the Congress of Victors. In *Stalin in Power* Robert Tucker redubs it the Congress of Victims, and on understandable grounds: of its 1,996 delegates, 1,108 would perish in the Terror. One can think of other names for this Congress. Congress of Vultures, one might say, after briefly consulting the reality of the countryside – or Congress of Vampires. And Congress of Vaudevillians, too: in January/February 1934 the Party began to absent itself from actuality. It entered the psychotheatre in Stalin's head.

As the Congress of Victors opened, the USSR was just steadying itself after veering back from total ruin. Collectivization had resulted in a series of world-historical catastrophes. Something like 10 million peasant dead (this was Stalin's own figure, in conversation with Churchill) might be acceptable to a good Bolshevik, the political objective having been achieved (unmediated control of peasant produce). But a moment of tranquil thought would have told anyone that Stalin's Big Break had turned out to be a primitive fiasco. The USSR had lost more than half of its livestock. About a quarter of the peasantry had fled the countryside for the cities, where the housing crisis was already legendary. In 1932 Moscow itself tottered with hunger – and Moscow, as Reader Bullard noted, was 'much better off for food than the provinces, even a short distance away'. (The long entry on 'shortages' in Bullard's index itemizes, among other things, books, candles, cement, clothing, coal, door handles and locks, electricity, fertilizers, fuel, glass, household utensils, lightbulbs, matches, metal, onion-seed, paper, petrol, rubber, salt, soap, and string. When you sent a parcel, you asked the recipient to return the wrapping.) Six-fold inflation coincided with sharp cuts in wages and the extortion of regular 'state loans'. It was a Russia of ration cards and labour books – and of increasing 'passportization', a most un-Leninist, not to say frankly tsarist, imposition. Such was the background, then, as the Old Bolsheviks (most of the comrades were of the October generation) gathered in Moscow for the Congress of Victors. These ageing idealists would also have been aware that the showpiece advances of industrialization had been achieved through a vast and burgeoning network of slave labour.*

It would not be true to say that Stalin got through the cataclysms of 1929–33 without hearing some sceptical murmurs from his colleagues. Zinoviev, Kamenev and Bukharin were by now abject and impotent figures (who would humble themselves further in the course of the Congress). But the Bolshevik fetish of unity, or of helpless and desperate cohesion, was not quite universal. Dissidence emerged most strongly in the person of M. N. Ryutin, who serves, in the present context, as something of a hero – minor, tarnished, yet unbroken. In 1930 he circulated an anti-Stalin treatise later known as the Ryutin Platform, was denounced, arrested, imprisoned, released and reinstated 'with a warning'. In 1932 he circulated the much shorter and more trenchant 'Appeal to Party Members'. He was again denounced, arrested, imprisoned. And here we see a crucial escalation in the level of the Stalin malevolence: its glandular sensuality, and its passionate attention to detail . . . The Politburo was now faced with Stalin's demand that Ryutin be executed for treason. With Kirov leading, the Politburo refused to cross that line: it refused to kill an old comrade (or, more precisely, it refused to seal an old comrade's fate before trial). Even Molotov was against it. Stalin could only

---

*Agriculture, it would eventually emerge, did not subsidize industry: industry subsidized agriculture. And Dekulakization was a net loser, too. Total dispossession of the supposed peasant plutocrats failed to cover the cost of their deportation.

carry Kaganovich. In the meantime he had Ryutin transferred from a political prison to a tougher one in Verhne-Uralsk. We can imagine his continuing interest in Ryutin's welfare. And this went on for *five years*: Stalin, we may be sure, threw absolutely everything he had at him, and Ryutin never confessed. (He was shot in 1937, as were his two sons; his wife was killed in a camp near Karaganda.) Dissidence, in the end, was effortlessly crushed; it simply informed Stalin, with incensing clarity, that there were things he couldn't yet do, and that his version of reality had not yet prevailed.

So, just after 'the culmination of the most precipitous peace-time decline in living standards known in recorded history',* Stalin took the podium at the Congress to a standing ovation – of which, said *Pravda*, 'it seemed there would be no end'.

But then something went wrong with the authorized reality, and eight days later the Terror was entrained.

Prolonged and Stormy Applause

No doubt Stalin ended the applause himself, on that occasion – with a diffident elevation of the palms, perhaps. But ending the applause for Stalin was a mortally serious business. Who could end the applause for Stalin when Stalin wasn't there?

At a Party conference in Moscow Province, during the Terror years, a new secretary took the place of an old secretary (who had been arrested). The proceedings wound up with a tribute to Stalin. Everyone got to their feet and started applauding; and no

---

*From Alec Nove's evenhanded *An Economic History of the USSR: 1917–1991*. The cover of my paperback bears the striking advisory, 'New and Final Edition.'

one dared stop. In Solzhenitsyn's version of this famous story, after five minutes 'the older people were panting with exhaustion'. After ten minutes:

> With make-believe enthusiasm on their faces, looking at each other with faint hope, the district leaders were just going to go on and on applauding till they fell where they stood, till they were carried out of the hall on stretchers!

The first man to stop clapping (a local factory director) was arrested the next day and given ten years on another charge.

There existed at the time a gramophone record of one of Stalin's longer speeches. It ran to eight sides, or rather seven, because the eighth consisted entirely of applause.

Now close this book for a moment and imagine sitting there and listening to that eighth side, at night, in the Moscow of 1937. It must have sounded like the approach of fear, like the music of psychosis, like the rage of the state.

Congress of Victors – 2

As the Congress of Victors proceeded, the Stalin confabulation seemed remarkably robust. Six months after the culmination of the worst famine in Russian history, the country's rulers proceeded in a spirit of raucous triumphalism. The smile of Stalin's moustache presided over the self-abasements of his most distinguished adversaries. Bukharin:

> In his brilliant application of Marx-Lenin dialectics, Stalin was entirely correct when he smashed a whole series of theoretical premises of the right deviation which had been formulated above all by myself.

Zinoviev:

> We now know that in the struggle which Comrade Stalin
> conducted on an exclusively high level of principle, on an exclu-
> sively high theoretical level, we know that in that struggle there
> was not the least hint of anything personal.

And Kamenev, incredibly, described Ryutin and his bloc as 'rabid
kulak scum' who deserved 'more tangible' disciplining than mere
theoretical refutation. Kirov was positively boyish:

> Our successes are really tremendous. Damn it all, to put it
> humanly, you just want to live and live – really, just look what's
> going on. It's a fact!

It was not a fact. It was data from Stalin's parallel universe. When
unpleasant truths did succeed in fighting their way to the surface,
the Bolshevik template supplied the expected scapegoats: those
stunning losses of livestock, for example, were attributed to the
characteristic barbarism of the kulaks.

The fact was that facts were losing their value. Stalin had
broken the opposition. He was also far advanced towards his
much stranger objective of breaking the truth. Or it may have
been the other way about: actuality, under Stalin, was such that
dread and disgust forbade you to accept it – or even to contemplate it. As the onetime Marxist Leszek Kolakowski persuasively
writes:

> Half-starved people, lacking the bare necessities of life,
> attended meetings at which they repeated the government's
> lies about how well off they were, and in a bizarre way they
> half-believed what they were saying . . . Truth, they knew, was
> a Party matter, and therefore lies became true even if they
> contradicted the plain facts of experience. The condition of

their living in two separate worlds at once was one of the most
remarkable achievements of the Soviet system.

The astounding servility of the Victors of 1934, who were as yet
unterrorized, is usually explained as follows: if Stalin could not
now be removed (they reasoned), he could at least be softened
and mollified, flattered, humoured. What this amounted to was
collusion in psychosis. They acted out Stalin's psychosis, and in
so doing, predictably and disastrously, they fed and fattened it.

But now reality intervened.

On the last day of the Congress the delegates were as usual
given their say on the composition of the new Central Committee.
While neither universal nor equal, the vote was at least direct and
secret. Just over 1,200 delegates were handed a list of nominees
and then crossed out the names of the men they were voting
against. Volkogonov describes the result as 'unbelievable!' Most
of the vote-counters were, of course, later shot, but one survivor
claimed that Stalin had received 120-odd negative votes (to Kirov's
three). Other sources, including Khrushchev, give a figure of 300.
Stalin fudged the figures and went on, in any case, to pack the
Central Committee with Stalinists . . .

Those 300 votes would mean the death of a generation. As
Tucker points out, Stalin had always suspected that he was
surrounded by dissemblers and double-dealers: now he had
proof. How many of the Congress eulogists had struck his name
from the ballot? Tucker adds that he had further evidence of
treachery. He knew of another person who had dissembled, who
had feigned moderation and indifference to advancement, who
had schemed and dreamed and finally prevailed. That person
was himself.

Meanwhile, in the world outside the Stalin psychosis . . . A population that is utterly crushed, in all senses, has only one means of protest: in a kind of genetic hunger strike, it starts to cease to reproduce itself. Since 1917 the Bolsheviks had systematically undermined the family. Divorce was encouraged (to achieve it you were simply obliged to notify your spouse by postcard); incest, bigamy, adultery and abortion were decriminalized; families were scattered by labour-direction and deportation; and children who denounced their parents became national figures, hymned in verse and song. This is Moshe Lewin:

> The courts dealt with an incredible mass of cases testifying to the human destruction caused by [the] congestion of dwellings. The falling standards of living, the lines outside stores, and the proliferation of speculators suggest the depth of the tensions and hardship. Soon the cumulative results of such conditions were to cause widespread manifestations of neurosis and anomie, culminating in an alarming fall in the birth-rate. By 1936, in fact, the big cities experienced a net loss of population, with more children dying than being born, which explains the alarm in governing circles and the famous laws against abortion proclaimed in that year.

Even Stalin bestirred himself. He was photographed with his smiling children, and duly trundled down to Tiflis to pay that single visit to his mother.

Kolyma Tales

Varlam Shalamov was arrested and sent to camp in 1929. He was twenty-one, and a law student; and unlike many other millions so designated, he really *was* a Trotskyite. That 'T' in his crime-description folder ('Anti-Soviet Trotskyite Activities') would have dramatically worsened his first two terms. He was tried and sentenced a third time in 1943 – for having praised Ivan Bunin – and reclassified as a mere Anti-Soviet Agitator. He got out of Kolyma in 1951 and, after two years of internal exile, he got out of Magadan. Then he wrote *Kolyma Tales*.

Nature simplifies itself as it heads towards the poles (and we head north now because so many scores of thousands were doing so, as Stalin's rule developed, and as the camps crazily multiplied). Nature simplifies itself, and so does human discourse:

> My language was the crude language of the mines and it was as impoverished as the emotions that lived near the bones. Get up, go to work, rest, citizen chief, may I speak, shovel, trench, yes sir, drill, pick, it's cold outside, rain, cold soup, hot soup, bread, ration, leave me the butt – these few dozen words were all I had needed for years.

Life was reduced. *Kolyma Tales* is a great groan from someone chronically reduced. Solzhenitsyn captured the agony of the gulag in the epic frame, in 1,800 unflagging, unwavering pages. Shalamov does it in the short story – for him, the only possible form. His suffering in the gulag was more extreme, more complete and more inward than that of Solzhenitsyn, who candidly observes:

> Shalamov's experience in the camps was longer and more bitter than my own, and I respectfully confess that to him and not me was it given to touch those depths of bestiality and despair towards which life in the camp dragged us all.

Shalamov told Nadezhda Mandelstam that he could have spent a lifetime 'quite happily' in the camp described in *One Day in the Life of Ivan Denisovich*. Whereas Kolyma, in the late 1930s (after Stalin's speech demanding worse conditions), amounted to negative perfection. Osip Mandelstam was on his way to Kolyma, in

1938, when he died of hunger and dementia in the transit prison at Vtoraya Rechka.

Kolyma Tales . . . Two prisoners take a long trek, at night, to exhume a corpse: they will exchange its underwear for tobacco. One prisoner hangs himself in a tree fork 'without even using a rope'. Another finds that his fingers have been permanently moulded by the tools he wields (he 'never expected to be able to straighten out his hands again'). Another's rubber galoshes 'were so full of pus and blood that his feet sloshed at every step – as if through a puddle'. Men weep frequently, over a lost pair of socks, for instance, or from the cold (but not from hunger, which produces an agonized but tearless wrath). They all dream the same dream 'of loaves of rye bread that flew past us like meteors or angels'. And they are forgetting everything. A professor of philosophy forgets his wife's name. A doctor begins to doubt that he ever was a doctor: 'Real were the minute, the hour, the day . . . He never guessed further, nor did he have the strength to guess. Nor did anyone else.' 'I had forgotten everything,' says one narrator: 'I didn't even remember what it was like to remember.' All emotions evaporate: all emotions except bitterness.

In Volume Two of *The Gulag Archipelago* Solzhenitsyn sharply disagrees with what he takes to be Shalamov's conclusion, that '[i]n the camp situation human beings never remain human beings – the camps were created to this end'. Arguing for a more generous estimate of spiritual resilience, Solzhenitsyn adduces Shalamov's own person. Shalamov, after all, never betrayed anyone, never denounced, never informed, never sought the lowest level. 'Why is that, Varlam Tikhonovich?' asks Solzhenitsyn (and note the coaxing patronymic). 'Does it mean that you found a footing on some stone – and did not slide down any further? . . .

Do you not refute your own concept with your character and verses?' A footnote then adds, 'Alas, he decided not to refute it', and goes on to tell of Shalamov's 'renunciation' of his own work in the *Literaturnaya Gazeta* of February 1972. Here, for no clear reason, Shalamov denounced his American publishers and declared himself a loyal Soviet citizen. 'The problematics of the *Kolyma Stories*,' he wrote, 'have long since been crossed out by life.' Solzhenitsyn adds: 'This renunciation was printed in a black mourning frame, and thus all of us understood that Shalamov had died. (Footnote of 1972.)' In fact, Shalamov died in 1982. And even so, even metaphorically, Solzhenitsyn got the date wrong.

Shalamov 'died' in 1937, if not earlier. Despite its originality, its weight of voice, and its boundless talent, *Kolyma Tales* is an utterly exhausted book. Exhaustion is what it describes and exhaustion is what it enacts. Shalamov can soar, he can ride his epiphanies, but his sentences plod, limp and stagger like a work gang returning from a twelve-hour shift. He repeats himself, contradicts himself, entangles himself, as if in a dreadful dream of retardation and thwarted escape. In a poem that made Solzhenitsyn 'tremble as though I had met a long-lost brother', Shalamov spoke of his vow '[t]o sing and to weep to the very end'. And this he did, with honour. But he had encountered negative perfection, as Solzhenitsyn had not; and it broke him.

On the other hand, the book lives, and to that extent Solzhenitsyn's point remains pertinent. In 'The Red Cross' Shalamov writes:

> In camp a human being learns sloth, deception and viciousness. In 'mourning his fate', he blames the entire world . . . He has forgotten empathy for another's sorrow; he simply does not understand it and does not desire to understand it.

Shalamov did not forget empathy. In the four-page story 'An Individual Assignment' the young prisoner Dugaev is working sixteen hours a day and fulfilling only a quarter of his norm. He is surprised, one night, when his workmate Baranov rolls him a cigarette.

> Greedily Dugaev inhaled the sweet smoke of home-grown tobacco, and his head began to spin.
>   'I'm getting weaker,' he said.
>   Baranov said nothing.

Dugaev has difficulty sleeping, and is losing the inclination to eat; his work deteriorates further. The story ends:

> The next day he was again working in the work gang with Baranov, and the following night soldiers took him behind the horse barns along a path that led into the woods. They came to a tall fence topped with barbed wire. The fence nearly blocked off a small ravine, and in the night the prisoners could hear tractors backfiring in the distance. When he realized what was about to happen, Dugaev regretted that he had worked for nothing. There had been no reason for him to exhaust himself on this, his last day.

The cigarette Baranov gave him: that was Dugaev's final smoke.

At the moment of arrest, wrote the poet, 'you tire as in a lifetime.' In Shalamov's Kolyma, every moment was that kind of moment.

The Kirov Murder

On 2 December 1934, *Pravda* solemnly informed its readers that on 1 December at 16:30, in the city of Leningrad in the building of the Leningrad Soviet (formerly Smolny), at the hands of a murderer, a concealed enemy of the working class, died Secretary of the Central and Leningrad committees of the All-Union Communist Party (Bolshevik) and member of the Presidium of the Central Executive Committee of the USSR, Comrade Sergei Mironovich Kirov. The gunman was under arrest.

As *Pravda* hit the stands, a special train containing Stalin and a numerous entourage was arriving from Moscow.

At this point Borisov, Kirov's personal bodyguard, had only hours to live.

The gunman, a 'misfit' called Leonid Nikolayev, lasted till just after Christmas. Together with many other alleged conspirators, he was shot (at night, in the cellars of Liteyni Prison). About a million would follow in the Terror.

On the opening page of *Stalin and the Kirov Murder* Conquest writes:

> Single events – even accidental ones – have often turned the path of history. The assassination of the Archduke Franz Ferdinand, just over twenty years previously, brought on a perhaps otherwise avoidable Great War. At any rate, that is the only individual crime (or dual crime, since the Archduke's morganatic* wife was also killed) with which the Kirov murder can be compared.

Enormous and sanguinary convulsions were helped into being by Nikolayev's bullet. Soviet society, which had steadied into a kind of breadline normality after the epic flounderings of 1929–33, was set to experience a new crescendo of the state's rage. For all its drama and complexity, however, the Kirov murder was

---

*This word repays a visit to the dictionary: '(Of marriage) between man of high rank and woman of lower rank, who remains in her former station, their issue having no claim to succeed to possessions of father.' So: a kind of pre-nup.

essentially a monstrous diversion: a red herring the size of a killer whale. It was something of an irrelevance even for Kirov. The Terror was coming anyway, and he would have been among its chief victims.

Nearly all historians are 99 per cent sure that Stalin oversaw the Kirov murder through the Moscow Cheka (and one well-placed commentator, Volkogonov, calls it 'certain'). I am now told that post-glasnost research has rendered this view more doubtful.* All *cui bono?* considerations point to Stalin: he had at least a dozen reasons for wanting Kirov dead (or 300 reasons: those votes at the Congress of Victors). No other event would have served Stalin so well as a springboard for mass repression. And the subsequent fates of nearly every key player in the murder (no man, no problem) speaks of Stalinist assiduity. True, the crime and the cover-up were haphazardly managed; it is particularly hard to understand the Cheka's selection of Niko-layev, a figure of almost epileptic instability. But he finished the job: Kirov was dead. Anyway, Stalin's guilt in the matter, when set beside his greater guilt, is another near-irrelevance. Perhaps we should throw our hands in the air and attribute Nikolayev to mere Stalinian voodoo, like his magically timed, stroke-inducing affronts to Lenin in 1922–23. The point is that the momentum for terror had already gathered. Kirov's murder gave rise to a prodigiously exaggerated version of the Rohm purge (30 June 1934); but its real equivalent was the Reichstag Fire of

---

*J. Arch Getty and R. T. Manning (eds.): *Stalinist Terror: New Perspectives.* Getty calls the standard interpretation 'folkloric'. Revision begets revision. (A still more recent book swings the argument back the other way.) If Getty goes on revising at his current rate, he will eventually be telling us that only two people died in the Great Terror, and that one very rich peasant was slightly hurt during Collectivization.

the previous year. Nikolayev simply saved Stalin the trouble of torching the Kremlin.

The top Leningrad Chekists were in attendance when the night train from Moscow pulled into the station. Stalin approached their chief, Medved, and, instead of patting him on the back, slapped him across the face. A student of Machiavelli, Stalin knew that the Prince must be an actor. At Kirov's state funeral there was a more sinister piece of showmanship: Stalin kissed Kirov's corpse.

Borisov, the personal bodyguard, was not with Kirov when Nikolayev struck (it is thought that some Moscow Chekists detained or distracted him at the door). Late in the morning of 2 December, he was sent by lorry to the Smolny, there to be interrogated by Stalin. On Voinov Street there was a minor accident. The driver and the three Cheka guards were unhurt. Borisov was dead. They had used iron bars on him in the back of the truck.

Downward selection had long been about its work, and the cadres were ready; the punitive organs were ready. As Sergo Ordzhonikidze, who would kill himself three years later, remarked to none other than Sergei Kirov in January 1934: 'Our members who saw the situation in 1932–33 and who stood up to it are now tempered like steel. I think that with people like that, we can build a state such as history has never seen.'

Children

Svetlana was the Cordelia of the Stalin children, in that love flowed, or seeped, between the tyrant and the daughter. This, unbelievably, is from Stalin's pen:

> My little housekeeper, Setanka, greetings!
>   I have received all your letters. Thank you for the letters!
> I haven't replied because I'm very busy. How are you passing
> the time, how's your English, are you well? I'm well and
> cheerful, as always. It's lonely without you, but what can I do
> except wait. I kiss my little housekeeper.

One assumes that the above predates Nadezhda's suicide in 1932
(when Svetlana was six). At that point, Svetlana would write,
something 'snapped inside my father'; 'inwardly things had
changed catastrophically'. Outwardly, too: Stalin, at the time, was
personally supervising one of the greatest man-made disasters in
history; and Nadezhda's death, as we have seen, was a political as
well as a personal indictment. Thereafter, in any case, family life
and family feeling quickly evaporated.

Stalin's relationship with Svetlana effectively ended in 1943.
The daughter's activities, like the sons', were monitored by the
organs, and wiretaps revealed that Svetlana was having an affair
with a Jewish scenarist called Alexei Kapler, whom Stalin promptly
dispatched to Vorkuta (espionage: five years). 'But I love him!'
protested Svetlana.

> 'Love!' screamed my father, with a hatred of the very word I
> can scarcely convey. And for the first time in his life he slapped
> me across the face, twice. 'Just look, nurse, how low she's sunk!'
> He could no longer restrain himself. 'Such a war going on, and
> she's busy the whole time fucking!'

There followed a long estrangement, punctuated by occasional
cruelties, occasional thaws. When they spent some time together
in the early 1950s, Svetlana reports that '[w]e had nothing to say
to one another.' This is Khrushchev:

> He loved her, but he used to express these feelings of love in
> a beastly way. His was the tenderness of a cat for a mouse. He
> broke the heart first of a child, then of a young girl, then of a
> woman and mother.

Stalin linked Svetlana to Nadezhda and to his own most spectacular failure. Still, there had been paternal love – reflexive and
perfunctory, perhaps, but love. The boys had to get along without
it. And while Svetlana, with her marriages, her wanderings, went
on to have a pained but articulate life, Yakov and Vasily were
doomed.

Vasily (1921–62), Svetlana's full brother, has a present-day
analogue in the person of Uday Hussein.* The children of these
autocrats, unlike the autocrats, grew up in a scripted reality, and
faced a different kind of assault on their mental health. Nor
were Vasily Stalin's prospects improved when, after his mother's
suicide, Stalin absented himself too, entrusting Vasily's nurtu-
rance to Vlasik, the head of his security guards. Also Stalin is
said to have regularly beaten Vasily, a little implausibly, given
his otherwise religiously observed indifference to him (there is
no doubt that he beat Yakov, with method and invention). The
main difficulty facing the child of an autocrat, I imagine, is
that reality won't tell you what you're worth. Later you will
notice that everyone is terrified of you (except of course your
father). Vasily decided to become a fighter pilot. In his *Stalin*,
Colonel General Dmitri Volkogonov takes a scandalized look
at the personal dossier of Lieutenant General Vasily Stalin. A

---

*A reputedly prolific rapist and murderer, Uday, we are relieved to learn, is
now in a wheelchair following an assassination attempt. Like Uday, Vasily was the
kind of young man who thinks it's funny to fire live rounds at restaurant chande-
liers.

record of dazzling promotions ('deputy and later commander of the Air Force') is interleaved with numerous confidential reports about Vasily's incompetence (and brutishness). 'Showered with honours and the blessings of well-wishers seeking their own ends,' Volkogonov goes on, 'Vasily had, almost unnoticed, become a fully-fledged alcoholic.'

Three weeks after Stalin's death Vasily suffered a demotion: he was, in fact, dismissed from the service (and forbidden to wear military uniform). He was thirty-two, and died nine years later. Khrushchev found him uncontrollable. There were periods of prison and exile. He said that he was thinking of becoming the manager of a swimming pool. At the age of forty he was an invalid. There were four wives. There were seven children; three of them – to stress, in parting, an apparently sympathetic anomaly – were adopted.

Yakov (1907–43), the half-brother, Yekaterina's boy, suffered the most dramatically and movingly. Stalin really hated him. It took me several days of subliminal work to accept this. The standard interpretation may seem ridiculous, but it is probably the right interpretation. We have seen something of Stalin's violent insecurity about his provenance. This insecurity was now turned on Yakov. Stalin hated Yakov because Yakov was Georgian. Yakov was Georgian because his mother was Georgian; Yakov was Georgian because Stalin was Georgian; yet Stalin hated Yakov because Yakov was *Georgian*. The racial and regional tensions within the USSR constitute an enormous subject, but Stalin's case was, as usual, outlandish. We have to imagine a primitive provincial who (by 1930 or so) had started to think of himself as a self-made Peter the Great: an Ivan the Terrible who had got where he was *on merit*. Thus Stalin was Russia personified; and Yakov was

Georgian. Yakov is said also to have been of a mild and gentle disposition, to his father's additional disgust.

Raised by his maternal grandparents, Yakov joined the Stalin household in the mid-1920s. He spoke little Russian, and did so with a thick accent (like Stalin). Nadezhda seems to have liked him and fully accepted him. But Stalin's persecution was so systematic that towards the end of the decade Yakov attempted suicide. He succeeded only in wounding himself; and when Stalin heard about the attempt he said, 'Ha! He couldn't even shoot straight' (Volkogonov has him actually confronting his son with the greeting, 'Ha! You missed!'). Soon afterwards Yakov moved to Leningrad to live with Nadezhda's family, the Alliluyevs.

Like Vasily, Yakov joined the armed forces, as a lieutenant (rather than a field marshal), reflecting his more peripheral status. He was the better soldier, and fought energetically until his unit was captured by the Reichswehr. This placed Stalin in a doubly embarrassing position. A law of August 1941 had declared that all captured officers were 'malicious traitors' whose families were 'subject to arrest'. Thus Yakov came under the first category – and Stalin came under the second. As a kind of compromise, Stalin arrested Yakov's wife. When the Nazis tried to negotiate an exchange, Stalin refused ('I have no son called Yakov'). He feared all the same that the supposedly feeble Yakov might be pressured into some propagandist exhibition of disloyalty. He need not have so feared. Yakov passed through three concentration camps – Hammelburg, Lübeck, Sachsenhausen – and resisted all intimidation. It was precisely to avoid succumbing (Volkogonov believes) that Yakov made his decisive move. In a German camp, as in a Russian, the surest route to suicide was a run at the barbed wire. Yakov ran. The guard did not miss.

We have seen what Stalin did to the families of Yekaterina and Nadezhda. Yakov's wife was Jewish, and Stalin had opposed the marriage for that reason. Nonetheless she was released after only two years in prison: a rare manifestation of slaked appetite.

Reason and the Great Terror – 1

The question of Stalin's sanity is one we will keep having to come back to. Compromised by power (and by increasing isolation from unwelcome truths), his sense of reality was by now unquestionably very weak; but it would be wrong to think of him in a continuous state of cognitive disarray. This underestimates his vanity and his pedantry. He habitually assessed himself in the context of legitimization: world-historical legitimization. And at times his internal world was luridly cogent.

First he looked to Lenin. It hadn't been difficult to find a Leninist warrant for Collectivization: state monopoly of food had always been considered a worthy socialist goal. Finding a Leninist warrant for the massacre of Leninists was more uphill. Pondering the implications of the Kirov murder, Stalin would have recalled August 1918. The attempted assassination of Lenin (and, on the same day, the successful assassination of Uritsky, head of the Petrograd Cheka) had launched the Red Terror, which, however, was directed outwards. Stalin wanted it directed inwards, too. Lenin *had* purged the Party, and approved of purges (quoting Lassalle to Marx: 'a party grows stronger by purging itself'), but his was a paper purge, a 'quiet' terror, dealing only in expulsions, like the one Stalin was prosecuting in the period 1933–35. Robert C. Tucker elaborates:

> After 1917, when membership in what was now a ruling party
> grew attractive to careerists and the like, Lenin looked to the
> purge as a means of weeding out such people . . . and on one
> occasion he even called for a 'purge of terrorist character' –
> specifically, summary trial and shooting – for 'former officials,
> landlords, bourgeois and other scum who have attached them-
> selves to the Communists . . .'

For Stalin these were tantalizing words.

He spoke often and interestedly about purging from as early
as 1920. 'The purge theme in [Lenin's] *What Is To Be Done?*',
writes Tucker, 'struck a responsive chord in the young man.' He
praised purging again in 1927: 'What did Lenin seek then [in
his Party reshuffle of 1907–08]? One thing only: to rid the Party
as quickly as possible of the unstable and snivelling elements,
so they wouldn't get in the way. That, comrades, is how our
party grew.' Tucker continues, in a rather uncharacteristic
passage:

> After saying this, Stalin went on: 'Our party is a living organ-
> ism. Like every organism, it undergoes a process of metabo-
> lism: the old and outworn moves out; the new and growing
> lives and develops.' In brief, party people opposed to him were
> shit.

The drive to purge was career-long. Purging was hard, and hardness was a Bolshevik virtue. Stalin was never really sure that he
was the cleverest or the bravest or the most visionary or even the
most powerful. But he knew that he was the hardest.

In his quest for precedent, Stalin went further back (skipping
Marx and Engels, who were contemptuous of terror as *malum
per se*). When he mused about his historical destiny, Stalin's
thoughts turned to the great Russian tyrants, in particular Ivan

the Terrible (the first to style himself Tsar) and Peter the Great (the first to style himself Emperor). By his various interventions in historiography and the arts, Stalin personally rehabilitated the image of Peter I, transforming him from 'the premature industrial capitalist and syphilitic sadist'* of the orthodox view to an altruistic modernizer and statebuilder. In Paris in 1937 Alexei Tolstoy (the supreme hack and opportunist) drunkenly admitted to direct influence on his own fiction and drama:

> [While I was working on Peter] the 'father of the peoples' revised the history of Russia. Peter the Great became, without my knowing it, the 'proletarian tsar' and the prototype of our Iosif! I rewrote it all over again in accordance with the party's discoveries . . . I don't give a damn! These gymnastics even amuse me. You really do have to be an acrobat.

Thus the Petrine epoch (1682–1725) provided the model: bureaucratization, the deepening of enserfment, the large-scale use of slave labour, the entrenchment of the punitive organs – and, later, imperial expansion.

Peter I was Stalin's lodestar during the Collectivization period. Later in the 1930s, as the Terror approached, Stalin looked to Ivan IV, Ivan Vasilievich Grozny – Ivan the Dread. A recreational hands-on torturer, a frothing debauchee (seven wives, and boasts of 'a thousand virgins'), and a paranoid psychotic (he murdered his own son, as incidentally would Peter), old Ivan seems an unlikely candidate for Communist rehabilitation. But he was a purger. And so, in the Stalin-sponsored history textbook of 1937, Soviet schoolchildren were now leadenly advised that

*This valuable formulation is, again, Robert Tucker's. He has made the Tsar Stalin theme very much his own, and in this section I am gratefully indebted to his *Stalin in Power*.

Lenin disguised (July, 1917).

Krupskaya.

Koba between arrests.

Trotsky.

Besprizornye: a group of the homeless millions.

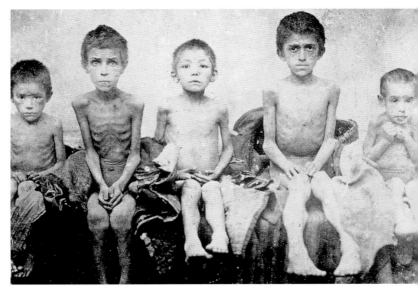

Lenin's famine.

The Cheka assembles evidence for a literary investigation.

Gorky with Cheka chief Yagoda (right).

Solzhenitsyn.

Evgenii Kibrik's "Lenin Arrives at the Smolny during the Night of October 24". Stalin was elsewhere at the time.

Two losing finalists of a competition sponsored by the Hungarian Workers' Party. The winner, a sixty-foot bronze, was destroyed in the Hungarian uprising of 1956.

Lenin in 1923.

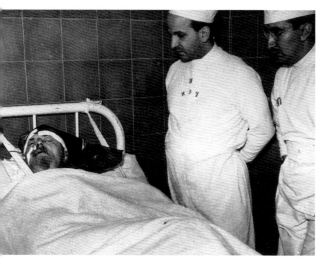

Trotsky lies dying
in a hospital in
Mexico City,
August 21, 1940.

The White Sea-Baltic Canal.

Troops fighting in the Red October Factory in Stalingrad.

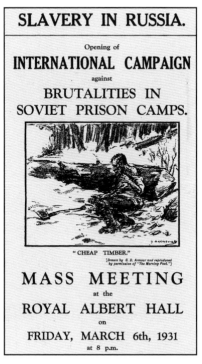

SLAVERY IN RUSSIA.

Opening of

INTERNATIONAL CAMPAIGN

against

BRUTALITIES IN
SOVIET PRISON CAMPS.

"CHEAP TIMBER."
[Drawn by G. D. Armour and reproduced by permission of "The Morning Post."]

MASS MEETING

at the

ROYAL ALBERT HALL

on

FRIDAY, MARCH 6th, 1931

at 8 p.m.

Boris Efimov's caricature of Trotsky and others wallowing in a trough entitled "Vaterland" (1938).

Anthropophagi, 1920.

[u]nder the reign of Ivan IV, Russia's possessions were enlarged manifold. His kingdom became one of the biggest states in the world . . . Ivan discovered that he was being betrayed by the big patrimonial boyars. These traitors went into the service of the Poles and Lithuanians. Tsar Ivan hated the boyars, who lived in their patrimonies like little tsars and tried to limit his autocratic power. He began to banish and execute the rich and strong boyars.

As early as 1934, at the Congress of Victors, Stalin repeatedly used the obsolete word *vel'mozhi* (which, like *boyar*, means *grandee*) to describe the laxer Party chieftains. And in a 1937 conversation with Sergei Eisenstein, even more ominously, Stalin echoed the Ivanian principle of destroying every traitor 'together with his clan' (*rod*: family and retinue). In his correspondence with the organs during the Terror, Stalin used the alias 'Ivan Vasilievich' . . .

Iosif the Dread already had something else in common with Peter the Great and Ivan the Terrible: failure. The 'enlightened' brutality of Peter's revolution from above, it is generally felt, did more to divide and deform the country than it did to elide it with Europe. Ivan's failure, by contrast, was near-infinite. The state simply disintegrated around him. His reign was followed by the Time of Troubles, a period of chaos and civil war – and a huge secondary purge of the population, cutting the census by about a third. In his attempt to account for Ivan's failure, Stalin said (to the filmmaker Eisenstein) that Ivan was fatally hampered by religion. After murdering a boyar clan, Stalin incredulously related, Ivan would repent for a whole year instead of just getting on with the work. (This is a good example, not only of Stalin's ghoulish practicality, but also of his congenital deafness to the spirituality of other people; he did not recognize the souls of other people.)* Also, Stalin said, there were 'five' clans that Ivan had failed to liquidate. Ivan's failure was a failure of rigour.

In 1934, 1935, 1936, for Stalin, *failure* was the elephant in the Kremlin office, study and living room, in the light and space of the various dachas, in the billiard saloon of the Crimean villa. During these interim years Stalin was digesting failure, massive and irreversible failure. He had had political success, true. (It seems to be an oddity of the Communist system that failure, if sufficiently massive, and irreversible, tends to consolidate power.) But his Second October had failed.

Stalin couldn't fully bring himself to know what everyone knew. The most precipitous economic decline in recorded history does not exactly go unnoticed. And there was the matter of the millions of dead, common knowledge throughout the Party, and of some concern, no doubt, even to an assembly as somnambulistic as the Congress of Victors.

The Great Terror was an emanation from Stalin's body. Its source lay in the effort of the mind to overcome the evidence of the gut.

Show Trial

Stalin told Eisenstein (whose two-part *Ivan the Terrible* appeared in the 1940s) that Ivan had unwisely spared 'five' boyar clans. He didn't get this from the history books: no such number has ever been specified. It appears that Stalin was thinking of the popular

---

*'The Pope? How many divisions does *he* have?' is Stalin's most famous expression of this indifference.

nineteenth-century play, *Tsar Fedor Iovannovich*, in which a character says that Ivan was survived by 'five boyars'.

Nearly every night there were screenings in the private projection rooms in the Kremlin or the various dachas. Khrushchev says that Stalin was particularly keen on Westerns: 'He used to curse them and give them proper ideological evaluation, but then immediately order new ones.' Milovan Djilas was also invited to the Kremlin movie theatre; he noted that 'throughout the performance Stalin made comments – reactions to what was going on, in the manner of uneducated men who mistake artistic reality for actuality.' One is reminded, here, of the magnificent paragraph in *The Truce*, when Primo Levi joins the largely Russian audience at a picture show in a Ukrainian transit camp:*

> It seemed as though the people in the film were not shadows to them, but flesh-and-blood friends or enemies, near at hand. The sailor was acclaimed at every exploit, greeted by noisy cheers and sten-guns brandished perilously over their heads. The policemen and jailers were insulted with bloodthirsty cries, greeted with shouts of 'leave him alone', 'go away', 'I'll get you', 'kill them all'. After the first escape, when the exhausted and wounded fugitive was once more captured, and even worse, sneered at and derided by the sardonic asymmetrical mask of John Carradine, pandemonium broke out. The audience stood up shouting, in generous defence of the innocent man; a wave of avengers moved threateningly towards the screen ... Stones, lumps of earth, splinters from the demolished doors [earlier there was a showtime stampede], even a regulation boot flew against the screen, hurled

*The film was *The Hurricane* (1937). 'Through miles of raging ocean he defied man's law!' ('The simple life on a South Pacific island is disrupted, not only by a vindictive governor but by a typhoon. Tolerable island melodrama' – Halliwell.)

with furious precision at the odious face of the great enemy, which shone forth oversize in the foreground.

Such a – what to call it? – lumpen, credulous primitivism, or imaginative semiliteracy, might help explain an aspect of the later Show Trials of the period 1936–38, in which renowned Old Bolsheviks, including Bukharin, Kamenev, Zinoviev (and, in absentia, Trotsky), 'confessed' to a series of phantasmagoric crimes: namely, Stalin's confidence (not at all widely shared by his circle) that world opinion would, as he said, 'swallow it'. Some Western observers, it is true, took these unnatural melodramas at face value; others (like the American Eugene Lyons) were left 'limp with the impact of horrors half-glimpsed'. The horrors were half-glimpsed, and Soviet citizens, it seems, half-believed the extorted confessions of the accused. This remark of Solzhenitsyn's feels doubly significant: 'I was keenly interested in politics from the age of ten;* even as a callow adolescent I did not believe [Judge Andrei] Vyshinsky and was staggered by the fraudulence of the famous trials . . .' Even a youth could instantly penetrate the imposture. Still, one can imagine a less exceptional child gradually losing this innocent certainty and succumbing to the moral rot, and the floating reality, of mature Stalinism.

In later years, as we have already mentioned, Stalin's cinematic tastes narrowed. Out went the cowboy films, the comedies and musicals. Stalin preferred to watch propaganda: pseudo-newsreels about life on the collective farms. The boards groan

---

*I.e., from 1928, the year of the inaugural 'Shakhty' case (fifty-three technicians and engineers were accused of industrial sabotage). The Show Trials were Stalin's contribution; they remain distinct from Lenin's 'demonstration' trials of the early 1920s, which were fixed but not scripted. Both types of trial used torture.

with fruit and vegetables, with suckling pig, with enormous geese. After their banquet the reapers return singing to the fields . . . What kind of pleasure did these portrayals give him? Did he 'believe' them – did he think they were 'real'?

Reason and the Great Terror – 2

'In my opinion,' said Khrushchev, 'it was during the war that Stalin started to be not quite right in the head.' Well, he should know, but Khrushchev's view is a curious one, suggesting as it does that the Stalin of 1929–33 and 1936–38 enjoyed cloudless mental health. Not *quite* right? Stalin did many profoundly crazy things during the war, particularly in the period 1941–43. But common intuition turns Khrushchev's judgment on its head. The Nazi invasion irrefutably informed Stalin that his alternate world was nonexistent, and this is why, as we'll see, it stupefied and unmanned him. The Nazi invasion was an avalanche of reality. It made a colossal demand: Stalin had to reach down, reach back, and find and resurrect what was left of his sanity.

As early as September 1941, three months after the invasion, when Stalin was shown the trial protocols and 'draft sentence' of his floundering commander-in-chief on the western front, he said, 'I approve the sentence [execution], but tell Ulrikh to get rid of all that rubbish about "conspiratorial activity".' And as late as 1946 (just before the psychosis resumed), Stalin summoned the rather-too-popular Marshal Zhukov to the Kremlin and side-lined him, saying, 'Beria has just written me a report of your suspicious contacts with the Americans and the British. He thinks you'll become a spy for them. I don't believe that nonsense.' So, dismayingly but with factual candour, Stalin calls the 'reason'

for the Great Terror exactly what it was: rubbish and nonsense
. . . Analogously, he never asked his citizens to fight the Great
Patriotic War in order to defend Marxism-Leninism, the
Revolution, or the dictatorship of the proletariat. He asked them
to fight it in the name of *Rus'*, of the Orthodox Church, of span-
gled tsarist generals . . .

There have been several attempts – none of them, perhaps,
very ardent – to adumbrate a 'rational' Terror. Stalin did it to
preempt a fifth column in the event of war. Stalin did it to Russify
(or at least de-Semitize) the Party machine. Stalin did it to fore-
stall any opposition to his intended rapprochement with Hitler.
Stalin did it to obliterate all memory of his indifferent performance in the Revolution and the Civil War. Stalin did it to prevent
the dissemination of the fact that he had once been an agent of
the *Okhrana* (the Tsar's secret police). The absurdity of this last
suggestion (offered by certain Old Bolsheviks, on no evidence)
prompts me to make one of my own: Stalin did it to create a
favourable reception for his *History of the Communist Party of
the Soviet Union: Short Course* (1938) – the ultimate how-to book
on avoiding arrest.

It is mildly and briefly tempting to argue that, during the
1930s, Stalin purged every section of society that was capable of
dethroning him. The peasantry could bring him down (as it
had very nearly brought Lenin down in 1921), so he purged it;
the Party could bring him down, so he purged it; the Cheka
could bring him down, so he purged it; the military could bring
him down, so he purged it. But the Comintern couldn't bring him
down, and he purged the Comintern – along with every other
Soviet institution. Here is an often-quoted joke: the Chekists
rap on the door at four in the morning, to be told, 'You've got

the wrong apartment. The Communists live upstairs.' Yet the number of Party members swept away in the Terror has been described as proportionately 'tiny' and even 'negligible'. The purge was truly exponential in character. Arrests were carried out on the basis of a quota per area; the arrestees were then pressured to implicate others; these others were then pressured to implicate yet others . . .

For the USSR the Terror constituted a vast and multiform deficit. Most obviously, and most irrationally, Stalin decapitated the armed forces, whose *weakness* could (and almost did) bring him down. According to the Soviet press (in 1987), the military purge accounted for:

3 of the 5 marshals
13 of the 15 army commanders
8 of the 9 fleet admirals and admirals Grade I
50 of the 57 corps commanders
154 of the 186 divisional commanders
16 of the 16 army political commissars
25 of the 28 corps commissars
58 of the 64 divisional commissars
11 of the 11 vice commissars of defence
98 of the 108 members of the Supreme Military Soviet

Lower down, 43,000 officers were 'repressed' between 1937 and 1941. One soldier likened the purge to 'a Tartar massacre', but even this understates the case. As Roy Medvedev put it: 'Never has the officer corps of any army suffered such losses in any war as the Soviet Army suffered in this time of peace.'

These 'losses' were not only emblazoned across the pages of *Pravda*: as Alan Bullock notes, the government 'took the trouble to have the proceedings translated and published abroad'. How were they interpreted in London, Paris and Washington, and in Berlin, as war neared? Monitors of the purge would have to assume either a) that all Soviet society was writhing with incensed disaffection or b) that Stalin was a maniac. Berlin (for instance) would have known that commanders Yakir and Feldman, both of them Jews (and both of them executed), were *not* working for the Nazis. So interpretation b) would have been likely to predominate. After the army purge of 1937–38, it is certain, Hitler felt easier about Soviet military strength, and his assessment was confirmed by the Red Army's prolonged humiliation at the hands of tiny Finland in the land-grabbing Winter War of 1939–40, the Slavic multitudes being horribly mauled by the blue-eyed snipers in their camouflaged ski suits. Hitler decided he could take Russia in a single campaign.

Beria to Stalin on 21 June 1941: 'My people and I, Iosif Vissarionovich Stalin, remember your wise prediction: Hitler will not attack in 1941!' Hitler attacked the very next day; and Stalin, in Khrushchev's words, became overnight 'a bag of bones in a grey tunic'. This was the strategic fruit of the Great Terror.

Why, then? *Zachto?* The briskest and most matter-of-fact kind of answer would go something like: to obliterate all possible opposition to the development of totalitarian rule (and, by selecting downwards, to install fresh cadres of callow obedience and brutality). Yet this doesn't account for the range, depth and duration of the Terror; nor, in particular, does it explain Stalin's need for *confessions*. The untrammelled use of the death penalty was something Stalin needed, physically, viscerally. He also needed confessions – and innumerable man-hours were devoted to extracting them even in cases that were never intended to be made public. It had to do with the size – the totality, the negative perfection – of the surrender Stalin demanded of his victims. In an especially fascinating chapter of *The Great Terror* ('The Problem of Confession') Conquest writes:

> The principle had become established that a confession was the best result obtainable. Those who could obtain it were to be considered successful operatives, and a poor [Chekist] had a short life expectancy. Beyond all this, one forms the impression of a determination to break the idea of the truth, to impose on everyone the acceptance of official falsehood. In fact, over and above the rational motives for the extraction of confession, one seems to sense an almost metaphysical preference for it.

Thus the Terror enforced Stalin's version of reality (past and present). It endeavoured to concretize his alternate world.

Again it is perhaps helpful to see Stalin, not as a fixed or static entity, but one constantly warped and distended by office. The Terror brought Stalin more power; but it was in itself an unprecedented *exertion* of power, too: a double escalation. If, as the commonplace has it, power is a drug, then in some cases the drug will stop working unless the dosage is increased – exponentially in this instance. For Stalin, power was a thing of the senses and the membranes. And he invariably sought the upper limit. Collectivization ended when the peasants were all collectivized (and the kulaks all dekulakized). The Terror-Famine ended when there was no one left to sow the next harvest. Gulag went on expanding until it seemed about to burst. The Terror continued until even the temporary prisons, the schools and the churches, were all full, and the courts were sitting twenty-four hours a day.

By then, 5 per cent of the population had been arrested as some sort of enemy of the people. It is often said that not a family in the country remained unaffected by the Terror. If so, then the members of those families were also subject to sentence: as members of the family of an enemy of the people. By 1939, it is fair to say, all the people were enemies of the people.

The question 'why?' – in any kind of narrative – is never quite satisfied by the answer 'individual psychosis'; such an answer feels like a hole or a loose end. Hence the revisionist talk of 1936–38 as being a 'consensus operation' (J. Arch Getty), or as a time of 'terror, progress, and social mobility' (Sheila Fitzpatrick). These writers are in quest of something that isn't there: common sense. Another way round the lone-madman theory is to view the purges as a 'logical' outcome of Bolshevik ideology and praxis. Having gone ahead with the dogmatic policy of Collectivization, and having reached the unexpected result of economic and moral penury, what can a good Bolshevik do but become even more radical? One can say that Stalin's psyche was perhaps uniquely amenable to such a course.* Apropos, here, is Santayana's definition of the fanatic: he redoubles his efforts while forgetting his aims. He doesn't want to think or to know. He just wants to *believe*.

Nor should we neglect the obvious point – that Stalin did it because Stalin liked it. He couldn't help himself. The Terror was, in part, an episode of sensual indulgence. It was a bacchanal

---

*Only Stalin, perhaps, was capable of presiding over the systemic deformity he had created. His doubled mind was well suited to the methodology of 'the two truths', as the *apparat* privately called it. Malia evokes the ubiquitous unreality as follows: 'In short, there is no such thing as socialism, and the Soviet Union built it.'

whose stimulant was power; and the cycle became ever more vicious. Typically, Stalin emerged from his lost weekend much strengthened and refreshed; typically, too, the titanic hangover was reserved for his doppelganger, his alter ego, his fairground mirror – the USSR.

I will close this section with a little kaleidoscope of unreason: 'They don't put old women like me on tractors,' a peasant complained to her cellmates, thinking she had been denounced as a *traktoristka* (tractor-driver) rather than a *trotskista* (Trotsky-ite); when the time came to acknowledge 'excesses' in the un-masking of Trotskyites, Stalin officially noted that these excesses were the work of Trotskyites as yet unmasked; all the directors of the major foundries in the Ukraine were arrested, and a few months later their replacements were arrested too (it was only the third or fourth batch that managed to keep their seats); one Byelorussian commissar was arrested (and shot) for refusing to use torture, and other chiefs were killed simply for not killing enough; early in his reign Chekist Yezhov decreed that prison windows should be boarded up and prison-yard gardens asphalted over; any *genuine* spy was treated as an exotic and a celebrity by fellow prisoners; footballers, gymnasts, philatelists and Esperantoists were arrested for their connections abroad; a science student was arrested for having a pen pal in Manchester, even though his letters consisted almost entirely of Soviet prop-aganda; after a night-long interrogation, a ten-year-old boy admitted his involvement with a fascist organization from the age of seven (what happened to him? Before exacting the supreme penalty, did they wait for his twelfth birthday?); a twelve-year-old boy was raped by his interrogator, protested to the duty officer, and was duly shot . . . It was later – in the 1940s – that a man was sentenced to fifteen years for, among other things, 'unfavourably contrasting the proletarian poet Mayakovsky with a certain bourgeois poet', the bourgeois poet being Pushkin, whose centenary, as it happened, passed with some fanfare in that year of 1937.

And so we must imagine the railway station at Kiev and the arrival of the special train from Moscow containing a large Cheka force led by Khrushchev, Molotov and Yezhov. The Chekists have a quota: the enemies of the people they will be expected to unmask must comprise a minimum of 30,000 souls.* That will mean 30,000 confessions. Given a (low) 'conveyor' average of forty grillings per prisoner, that will mean over a million interrogations. The Chekists will need their special rubber aprons, their special rubber hats, their special rubber gloves.

Interventions

Philosophy and political economy were not the only specialisms in which Stalin (that fabulously overweening ignoramus) put himself about. Hitler confined his cultural interventions to the fields where he felt, wrongly, that he had a competence: art and architecture. But Stalin's superbity was omnivorous. His intention, or need, was to inundate an entire society with his own quiddity. And among Stalin's characteristics we must now include an infinite immunity to embarrassment. In September 1938, as if signalling an end to the fulminant phase of the Terror, the *Short Course* appeared and entrenched itself as Stalin's official biography. By that time most of the Old Bolsheviks, who knew it to

---

*For comparison: there were 14,000 executions, nationwide, in the last half-century of Tsarist rule.

be false, were dead – but not all of them were. Over five hundred
Old Bolsheviks put their signatures to a thank-you note to Stalin
in the pages of *Pravda* in 1947 ('with words of love and gratitude'). And there remains the impenetrable anomaly of the inner
circle: Voroshilov, Molotov, Kaganovich, and so on. *They* knew,
for example, that it was Trotsky, not Stalin, who had dominated
October and the Civil War; and they knew that Trotsky was not
'a fascist spy'. How could Stalin tolerate the existence, let alone
the constant proximity, of this little reservoir of silent truth? Was
it not a daily, and a nightly, reproach and reminder?* As earlier
noted, Stalin had inflicted a blood wound on most of the men
in his sanctum. This was intimate humiliation; and the collusion
in Stalin's aggrandizement took the humiliation further. Still, the
survival of the cronies (increasingly precarious for all of them
after the war) remains a serious lacuna in Stalin's personality
mechanism. One thing it suggests is that he never 'came to believe'
in his own novel.

You are inclined to imagine Stalin muttering a few words to
Molotov (say) about the political utility of his personal deifica-
tion, but it must have been far more aggressive than that. After
all, one of the purposes of the Terror, as Tucker asserts, was to
impose on the Party a dramatic revision of Marx. It was a tenet
of Marxism, as we have seen, that 'personality' remained an
'insignificant trifle' (in Lenin's phrase) when set against the
master forces of history. Well, Stalin himself was a bellowed
rebuttal of that notion. *His* Marxism would have room for
'heroes' – great men who, as he saw it, could detect pattern in

---

*Stalin worked with these men and spent most evenings in their company.
Dinner would usually end around 4 A.M. Day became night for all the *apparatchiki*,
to the further detriment of their Kremlin complexions.

the *tormenta* of events and thus urge history forward. Such a one was Iosif Vissarionovich, 'the universal genius', as he now came to be called. He owned the physical spaces of Russia. But he wanted the mental spaces too. He wanted to fan out into every mind.

We cannot hope, as Stalin hoped, to be all-inclusive. Here are just a few examples.

Astronomy. Research on sunspots was felt to have taken an un-Marxist turn. In the years of the Terror more than two dozen leading astronomers disappeared.

History. This was naturally a dangerous trade in a period when the past was undergoing revision from above. But Party history and Russian history were far from being the only sensitive areas: parenthetical observations on Joan of Arc, the Midas legend, and Christian demonology, for example, could be taken as criminal deviations from the Moscow line. Stalin's gavel was of course a heavy instrument. In 1937 the main school of Party historians was arrested en masse and accused of 'terrorism'. '[I]t is extraordinary,' writes Conquest, 'how many of the leading terrorist bands were headed by historians.' Of the 183 members of the Institute of Red Professors just under half were suppressed.

Linguistics. In the early 1930s Stalin championed the teachings of N. Marr, who held a) that language was a class phenomenon (a superstructure over the relations of production), and b) that all words derived from the sounds 'rosh', 'sal', 'ber' and 'yon'. Linguisticians who held otherwise were jailed or shot. In 1950, when Stalin was seventy (and up to his armpits in the Korean crisis), he nonetheless found the time to write or at least supervise an enraged 10,000-word denunciation of the Marrists. This is Conquest, in a quietly typical strophe: '"These academicians", [Stalin] was horrified to have to report, "had arrogated to themselves too much power."' The Marrists were now removed in their turn.

Biology. 'Stalin made his most notorious intervention into scientific life,' Tucker succinctly notes,

> by supporting an upstart plant breeder, Trofim Lysenko, in a series of sensational projects to make agriculture flourish, which came to nothing, and a crusade to destroy the science of genetics, which succeeded.

The USSR was full of little Stalins, but Trofim Lysenko was a middleweight Stalin (like Naftaly Frenkel): he was a vicious charlatan who fought the truth with the weapon of violence. Of peasant stock, and semi-educated, Lysenko followed Lamarck on the inheritance of acquired characteristics, in defiance of elementary Darwinism. Twice in 1935 Lysenko had the opportunity to address an audience that included Stalin. On both occasions he attributed his most recent failures to sabotage by hostile colleagues. Stalin, who naturally responded to this theme (wrongheaded debacles blamed on enemies), greeted the first speech with a cry of 'Bravo, Comrade Lysenko, bravo!,' and greeted the second with the bestowal of an Order of Lenin (the first of eight). Serious biologists were now subject to arrest, and Lysenko 'was on his way to the total pogrom of genetics that he would carry through in 1948 with Stalin's blessing'. He remained influential well into the 1960s.*

Religion. It may seem inapt to consider this matter under the heading of 'interventions': Stalin's activities here were hardly a matter of theological nicety. From the outset the Bolshevik line had been 'militant atheism'. Apart from the imposition of pauperism and oppression, 'no action of Lenin's government', Richard Pipes believes,

> brought greater suffering to the population at large, the so-called 'masses', than the profanation of its religious beliefs, the closing of the houses of worship, and the mistreatment of the clergy.

In common with any other gathering of two or more people, organized worship was 'viewed as prima facie evidence of counter-revolutionary intent'. The brutal mauling of the church, and particularly the Russian Orthodox Church (backwards, corrupt, and fatally compromised by its links with the Tsarist gendarmerie), was perhaps politically intelligible: hence the lootings and lynchings, the priest-hunts, the rigged trials,[†] the executions. But

---

*To the mortification of Sergei Nikitich Khrushchev, who was a rocket scientist and kept telling his father that Lysenkoism was without rational foundation. See the memoir *Khrushchev on Khrushchev*, a partial, limited, and strangely honourable book.

[†]In these trials of 1922 dozens of prelates were charged with obstructing the confiscation of church valuables. Lenin was again using the 1921 famine as a political convenience: he claimed that these valuables would be used to defray humanitarian aid. They would not be so used. Solzhenitsyn gives us a moment of transcendental hypocrisy during the trial of Patriarch Tikhon. '[S]o it was sacrilege according to the laws of the church,' said the Presiding Judge, 'but what was it from the point of view of *mercy*?'

it was the regime's extraordinary intention to stamp out private, even individual, worship too (aiming to replace 'faith in God with faith in science and the machine'). In one of their eerily post-modernist convulsions, the Bolsheviks deployed the weapon of orchestrated mockery: blasphemous and semi-pornographic street carnivals, with cavorting Komsomols garbed as priests, popes, rabbis. The press claimed that these parades were greeted with spontaneous delight, but the people, as a witness feelingly wrote, looked on with

> dumb horror. There were no protests in the silent streets – the years of terror had done their work – but nearly everyone tried to turn off the road when it met this shocking procession. I, personally, as a witness of the Moscow carnival, may certify that there was not a drop of popular pleasure in it. The parade moved along empty streets and its attempts at creating laughter were met with dull silence . . .

Yes, and what kind of laughter would *that* have been? During this period, church weddings were declared void (and funeral rites forbidden). Laughter and Leninism: the unholiest marriage of all.

Quiescent in the later years of NEP, the assault on religion was resumed in 1929. While he collectivized and dekulakized, Stalin also desacralized. Priests were associated with kulaks, and classified with them, and shared their fate. One admires the scandalized tone of this Chekist's accusation: 'the local priest . . . came out openly against the closing of the church'. Normally the bells were taken first (their tolling, it was perfunctorily explained, disturbed the rest of hardworking atheists) and later melted down for industrial use; icons were smashed or burned; the profane harlequinades were revived, with, assuredly, even less success than in the cities. By the end of 1930, 80 per cent of the village churches had been closed, or converted to such uses as storage points for kulaks awaiting deportation. Meanwhile, 'proper steps' had been taken 'to prevent prayer meetings at home'.

It seems safe to say that by June 1941 religion had disappeared from Stalin's alternate world. But then reality reintruded, in the form of a rampant *Wehrmacht*: the greatest war machine ever assembled, and heading straight for him. He knew that his citizens would not lay down their lives for socialism. What would they lay down their lives for? Consulting this sudden reality, Stalin saw that religion was still there – that religion, funnily enough, belonged to the real.

Voices from the Yezhovshchina*

(i.)

This is the voice of Stepan Podlubny (b. 1914), a factory-school apprentice:

> 6 December 1937. No one will ever know how I made it through the year of 1937 . . . I'll cross it out like an unnecessary page, I'll cross it out and banish it from my mind though the black spot the massive ugly black spot like a thick blood

*Genrikh Yagoda (shot in 1938) was replaced as head of the Cheka by Nikolai Yezhov (shot in 1940), who was in turn replaced by Lavrenti Beria (shot in 1953). Yezhov's period in office (1936–38), and the Great Terror itself, are sometimes called the *Yezhovshchina*: the time of Yezhov's rule . . . The quotes in the present section are all from *Intimacy and Terror: Soviet Diaries of the 1930s*, edited by Véronique Garros, Natalia Korenevskaya and Thomas Lahusen. The book is by turns boring, startling, sickening and inspiring. Some know it and some don't – but all the voices are crippled.

stain on my clothes, will be with me most likely for the rest
of my life.

It will remain because my life during these 341 days of
1937 has been as ugly and disgusting as the clotted blood that
oozes out in a thick red mass from under the corpse of a man
dead from the plague.

The source of Stepan's distress is revealed in an earlier entry: he
has been an informer since 1932. (Solzhenitsyn writes: 'I hesitate
to sully the shining bronze countenance of the Sentinel of the
Revolution, yet I must: they also arrested persons who refused
to become informers.') The Podlubnys had been dispossessed as
kulaks in 1929. Stepan's mother concealed her origins and was
sentenced to eight years for this crime. The extracts end as
follows:

They consider her a danger to society. You'd think they'd caught
a bandit, but even bandits get lighter sentences than that. Well,
so what, you can't break down a stone wall with just your head.
Can this be the end of justice on earth. No there will be justice.
Many people have perished in the name of justice, and as long
as society exists, people will be struggling for justice. Justice
will come. The truth will come.

Many years later Stepan Podlubny donated his diary to the Central
Popular Archives as 'an act of repentance'.

(ii.)

This is the voice of Leonid Potyomkin (b. 1914), an engineer who
would later be Vice Minister of Geology (1965–75):

Welcome to the year 1935 in the country of Socialism! . . . After
class I go to a lecture: 'The Low-life Scum of the Zinoviev
Group and the City Administrative Committee Decision about

the Party Meeting at the Mining Institute'. The speaker is a charming young woman, a student in our institute's graduating class. She is a good speaker and her Party spirit is enchanting to watch and to listen to . . .

[10 July 1935]. The perfect speech of the commissar of the regiment serves as an example of cogency in its presentation of clear thoughts penetrating the entire depths of the essence of phenomena. In terms of its enthusiasm, the clarity of its sound structure and the delightful culture of its language. With a deep awareness of the meaning of the words I uplift my voice with astounding force and join the chorus as we march to my favourite song, the march from the film *Happy Fellows*.

Leonid had been to see *Happy Fellows* (which was incidentally the toast of Stalin's screening-room) back in January, when he doggedly noted that its 'cheerfulness and musicality make for a pleasant spectacle, arousing cheerfulness in the spectator'.

(iii.)

This is the voice of Vladimir Stavsky (b. 1900), General Secretary of the Union of Soviet Writers and Chief Editor of *Novy mir*.*

What happiness!

To celebrate the New Year with the people nearest and dearest to my heart! My dear, darling Lyulya! We've been through so much suffering, so much sorrow! But now the path to happiness is before us! The path of heroism and triumph! . . . You are so dear to me! A fellow human being in the best

---

*Stavsky was known as the 'executioner of Soviet Literature'. For example, it was he who denounced Osip Mandelstam. He also had a history of alcoholism (the editors of *Intimacy and Terror* remark on his 'tormented handwriting', which was 'deciphered only with great difficulty'). We catch him here at a vulnerable moment (midnight on New Year's Eve, 1938/39); and it is of course painfully clear on internal evidence alone that Stavsky is stinking drunk.

sense of the word. The snow is pouring down from the spruces and pines, I know. The night is darkest blue, and there's not a star in the sky. But in our hearts, yours and mine, we have stars, and sky, and happiness! . . .

My darling! The whole richness of life appears before my eyes, all of life beats in my heart, my beloved!

And I want to live, together with the epoch, together with Stalin, together with you, my beloved, my darling!

And we will triumph!

And we will be happy!

I love you! My darling!

(iv.)

This is the voice of Lyubov Vasilievna Shaporina (b. 1879), the founder of the Leningrad Puppet Theatre and the wife of the composer Yury Shaporin:

[10 October 1937]. The nausea rises to my throat when I hear how calmly people say it: He was shot, someone else was shot, shot, shot. The words . . . resonate through the air. People pronounce the words completely calmly, as though they were saying, 'He went to the theatre' . . .

[22 October 1937]. On the morning of the 22nd I woke up about three and couldn't get back asleep until after five . . . Suddenly I heard a burst of gunfire. And then another, ten minutes later. The shooting continued in bursts . . . until just after five . . . That is what they call an election campaign. And our consciousness is so deadened that sensations just slide across its hard, glossy surface, leaving no impression. To spend all night hearing living people, undoubtedly innocent people, being shot to death and not lose your mind. And afterwards, just to fall asleep, to go on sleeping as though nothing had happened. How terrible . . .

[2 November 1937] . . . The poor girls, what they've had to

go through: in the morning their mother is taken away, and then they're picked up and taken to a place that is no better than prison . . .

I don't understand anything, it all seems like a dream to me. In the morning they were still a family, and now there's nothing, everything has shattered.

[6 February 1938]. Yesterday morning they arrested Veta Dmitrieva. They came at 7 in the morning, locked them in their room and conducted a search . . . Veta said goodbye to Tanechka (age 4), she said, 'When I come back, you'll be all grown up.'

[11 March 1938] . . . People in Moscow are in such a panic, it's made me sick, literally . . . Irina's aunt, a lawyer, said that every night two or three defense lawyers from her office are arrested. Morloki was arrested on 21 December, and on 15 January Leva, our simple-minded theatre fan and prop man, was exiled to Chita. At that rate they might as well arrest the table or sofa . . .

[24 January 1939] . . . The city is freezing for lack of coal and firewood. Our theatre is using the building of the Tram Worker's Park. You'd think that, even if they won't give you any books, you'd at least be able to get some coal. There's not any, not a speck, they don't even give it out through official channels, and there won't be any before summer. There's no firewood. No electrical supplies, no stockings, no cloth, no paper. If you want to buy some manufactured product you have to spend all day in line, and stay overnight too . . .

[19 February 1939] . . . I. I. Rybakov died – in prison. Mandelstam died in exile. People everywhere are ill or dying. I have the impression that the whole country is so completely exhausted that it can't fight off disease, it's a fatal condition. It's better to die than to live in continual terror, in abject poverty, starving.

The 'election' referred to on 22 October 1937 ('Irina came home from school and said, "They told us there are mass arrests going on right now. We need to rid ourselves of undesirable elements before the election!"'), was a charade designed to celebrate the new Stalin Constitution. On 12 December Lyubov Vasilievna Shaporina went along to cast her vote:

> Quelle blague! I went into the booth, where supposedly I was going to read the ballot and choose my candidate for the Supreme Soviet – 'choose' means you have a choice. There was just one name, already marked. I burst out laughing uncontrollably, right there in the booth, just like a child. It took me a long time to compose myself. I leave the booth, and here comes Yury, stony-faced. I lifted my collar and ducked down into it so that only my eyes were visible; it was just hilarious.
>
> Outside I ran into Petrov-Vodkin and Dimitriev. V.V. was going on and on about some irrelevant topic and laughing wildly. Shame on them for putting grown people in such a ridiculous, stupid position. Who do we think we're fooling? We were all in stitches.

There has never been a regime quite like it, not anywhere in the history of the universe. To have its subjects simultaneously quaking with terror, with hypothermia, with hunger – and with laughter.

Ech . . .

The day before Lyubov Vasilievna Shaporina basked in 'the sun of the great Stalin Constitution', Stalin himself addressed the voters and candidates who had gathered in the vast auditorium of the Bolshoi Theatre:

> Never before in the world have there been such genuinely free and genuinely democratic elections, never! History knows no

other example [applause] . . . our elections are the only genuinely free and genuinely democratic elections in the whole world [loud applause] . . .

Stalin's appearance was an unexpected treat, that night at the Bolshoi. 'The audience rose as one as he took the rostrum,' writes Volkogonov, and the 'storm of applause lasted for several minutes.' Stalin began his oration in jovial style:

> Comrades, I must admit I had no intention of speaking. But our respected Nikita Sergeyevich [Khrushchev] dragged me here, I might say, by force . . .
>
> Of course, I could have said something light about anything and everything [laughter] . . . I understand there are masters of that sort of thing not just in the capitalist countries, but here, too, in our Soviet country [laughter, applause] . . . But still, as I'm out here now, I really should say something [loud applause]. I have been put forward as a candidate for Deputy . . . Well, it's not done for us Bolsheviks to decline responsibility. I accept it willingly [stormy, prolonged applause]. For myself, comrades, I want to assure you that you can count on Comrade Stalin [a stormy, prolonged ovation].

This was some scene. Ground zero of the Great Terror – and here was the Party, joined in a panic attack of collusion in yet another enormous lie. They clapped, they laughed. Did *he* laugh? Do we hear it – the 'soft, dull, sly laugh', the 'grim, dark laughter, which comes up from the depths'?

While I was getting through the shelf of books I have read about him, there were four occasions when Stalin made *me* laugh. Laugh undisgustedly and with warmth, as if he were a comic creation going enjoyably through his hoops. These are all things Stalin *said*. Nothing Stalin *did* makes you laugh.

One. On hearing that his grain-collection campaign of 1927 had fallen far short of its norm, Stalin identified the situation as 'a kulak strike!' – reaching, with charming reliability, not for one but for two categories of execration.*

Two. There is something inimitably *Stalin* in the remark he was 'in the habit of repeating' after the war, according to Svetlana. He was in the habit of repeating: 'Ech, together with the Germans we would have been invincible.' It is not so much the shocking cynicism (and ideological debauchery) of the sentiment; rather, one thrills to the boundless *realpolitik* packed into that humble, provincial, mountain-dwelling three-letter expletive, *Ech* . . .

Three. This concerns the terrible case of Pavel Morozov. Pavel ('Pavlik') was a fourteen-year-old peasant boy who, in the early 1930s, denounced his father (for kulak leanings). The father was shot. And Pavlik was soon after murdered by a band of villagers said to include his grandfather and his cousin. Stalin briefly interrupted his preparations for exalting Pavlik as a hero and martyr of socialism (statues, songs, stories, inscription in the Pioneer 'Book of Heroism', the Moscow Palace of Culture renamed in his honour), to remark, privately: 'What a little swine, denouncing his own father.'†

Four. On 29 June 1941, a week into the Nazi invasion, Stalin attended a meeting with the military and learned the true dimensions of the discomfiture – and the true dimensions of his own

---

*I would later read that Stalin was simply echoing Lenin, who, faced with a similar disappointment, referred rather less pithily to 'a kulak grain strike'.

†Conquest makes the parenthetical point that Stalin, it would seem, harboured no decisive resentment towards *his* father. Iosif Vissarionovich was perhaps mildly susceptible to the verities he set out, in the interests of political security, to eradicate.

miscalculation, paralysis, willed myopia, and lack of nerve. 'Lenin left us a great inheritance and we, his heirs,' said Stalin 'loudly', and searching for the appropriate modulation at this world-historical node, 'have fucked it all up.'*

In the nightmare of the dark /
All the dogs of Europe bark

We should consider him, for the time being, not as a political or ideological entity but as a physical system, a will, a constitution, a quivering organism.

Stalin's summary of the situation on 29 June seemed fairly accurate – and would have seemed entirely so if he had recast the sentence in the first-person singular. Soviet unpreparedness for the Nazi invasion is of course legendary. And Stalin's refusal to believe in its imminence was no mere perversity or dereliction: it was the result of herculean self-hypnosis. He staked his being on it; and he lost. When the news came through ('they are bombing our cities'), Stalin's psyche simply fell away. It prostrated him; he became a bag of bones in a grey tunic; he was nothing but a power vacuum.

Despite the global astonishment it caused, the Nazi-Soviet Pact of 1939 was a construable move on Stalin's part, even an obvious one, given the dilatory hauteur of the Allies' approaches

---

*I follow Volkogonov's phrasing. The less elaborate 'Lenin founded this state, and we've fucked it up' is given by most historians (and I have come across 'All that Lenin created we have lost', presumably in some transitional version of events). But Colonel General Volkogonov has a natural authority on the war years. Hereabouts his pages are anecdotally rich with three generations of top-brass table talk.

to Moscow. It was the later, supplementary agreement, the Borders
and Friendship Treaty, that Volkogonov regards as 'Stalin's greatest
mistake'. In the USSR Nazism had always been

> properly defined as a terroristic, militaristic, dictatorial regime
> and the most dangerous phalanx of world imperialism. To
> Soviet minds, it was the embodiment of the class enemy in
> concentrated form . . . It is now difficult to establish precisely
> who suggested introducing the word 'friendship' into the title
> of the treaty. If it was the Soviet side, it testifies to political
> mindlessness.

The way Stalin saw it, the imperialist powers would embroil
themselves in a marathon bloodbath in Europe, after which a
strengthened Red Army would do some empire-building of its
own among the ruins. This dream was rather seriously undermined when Hitler took France in six weeks – leaving Stalin
pacing the floor and giving vent to many a 'choice' obscenity (the
adjective is Khrushchev's). By June 1941 Hitler's war record went
as follows: Poland in twenty-seven days, Denmark in twenty-four
hours, Norway in twenty-three days, Holland in five, Belgium in
eighteen, France in thirty-nine, Yugoslavia in twelve, and Greece
in twenty-one. Hitler had never been diffident about his plans
for the USSR. In *Mein Kampf* (1925) he had proposed to cut a
path eastward with fire and sword, and to enslave the Slavic
undermen. After he came to power *Mein Kampf* was aggressively
reissued 'with no deletions'. Even Stalin fully accepted that it was
only a question of when. In the broadest sense Soviet preparations for war were gargantuan, but they were off-centre, and
fatally medium-term.

Stalin received not fewer than eighty-four written warnings
of the coming attack, from sources as various as Richard Sorge

(his masterspy then stationed in the German Embassy in Tokyo) and Winston Churchill (who had decryptions from Bletchley Park). Any reasonably observant passenger on the Moscow-Berlin railway line would have prophesied war; for weeks, men and munitions had been thundering east, to form the largest concentration of poised violence *ever*. In the early months of 1941 there were 324 violations of Soviet airspace by German reconnaissance planes (which, if forced to land, were repaired and when necessary refuelled by Soviet engineers). The German ambassador in Moscow dismantled all precedent by giving the exact day; a German deserter earned summary execution (as a provocateur) by giving the exact hour. Russian commanders who put their troops on alert were sharply menaced from above (even by such comparative realists as Zhukov). On 14 June an official statement dismissed rumours of war as 'clumsy fabrications'. At this time all German vessels left all Russian ports. On 21 June Lavrenti Beria demanded the recall of the Soviet minister in Berlin for 'bombarding' him with disinformation, promising, moreover, 'to grind him to dust' in the gulag.

Just after midnight on 22 June the goods train laden with Soviet-donated matériel, bound for Berlin, crossed the border.* Soviet frontier guards could hear the engines of the tanks as they manoeuvred into position . . . At three o'clock in the morning, just outside Moscow, Stalin sought his couch in the Kuntsevo dacha. The evening meal had perhaps been lighter and briefer than usual: many of the top commissars were already heading

---

*In accordance with the Pact's reciprocal trade deals. German consignments were generally skimpy and tardy. Russian consignments were always fiercely punctual (and often topped up by direct order from Stalin). This particular goods train was of course the last.

south for their summer holidays. 'Stalin had hardly laid his head on the pillow,' writes Volkogonov, when Zhukov called the dacha and told the duty officer: 'Wake him up immediately. The Germans are bombing our cities.' When Stalin came to the phone Zhukov told of the air attacks on Kiev, Minsk, Sevastopol, Vilna . . . 'Did you understand what I said, Comrade Stalin?' He could hear the sound of Stalin's breathing. Again he asked: 'Comrade Stalin, do you understand?' Only when the German embassy confirmed that the two nations were now at war ('What have we done to deserve this?' cried Molotov) did Stalin give the order to begin fighting back.

Before we consider the psychological peculiarities of the case, it is necessary to register the gravity of Stalin's misreading, and the price of his tenacity in error. In the first weeks of the war the Soviet Union lost 30 per cent of its ammunition and 50 per cent of its reserves of food and fuel. In the first three months the air force lost 96.4 per cent of its planes (this staggering figure is Volkogonov's). By the end of 1941 Leningrad was besieged and German troops were approaching the southern suburbs of Moscow. By the end of 1942, 3.9 million Russian soldiers had been taken prisoner – 65 per cent of the Red Army. Only a few days after the launch of Operation Barbarossa (original, and more brutal, codename: Operation Fritz), informed opinion in London and Washington – and Moscow – held that the war was already lost.

How is it to be explained, Stalin's posture as hostilities approached? It would be pat, but also accurate, to say that from 1933 to 1941 the only human being on earth that Stalin trusted was Adolf Hitler. (One assumes, too, that the latter gave his personal assurance that any trouble on the border would be the work of mutinous generals; this would strike a chord with the susceptible Stalin, who was still purging his army.) Different historians give different emphases. For example, Stalin believed that Russian mobilization would repeat the blunder of 1914, leading to a German ultimatum, and war (Conquest); Stalin was enervated, mentally wiped out, by the speed of the German success in France (Tucker); Stalin's rapprochement with militant fascism induced a generalized confusion in his political reflexes (Volkogonov). In his lopsided but very busy book, *Blood, Tears and Folly: An Objective Look at World War II*, Len Deighton makes the point that Stalin was the victim of his own paranoia – or reverse-paranoia. He felt that the imperialists were trying to lure him into a quagmire: this, after all, was what he had wanted to do to the imperialists. All writers agree that Stalin underestimated Hitler's fanaticism. Germany, Stalin thought, would never risk a war on two fronts. But there was no second front, until 1944.

In *Russia's War* (and how much of it *was* Russia's war) Richard Overy says that in 1941 Stalin was engaged in 'a personal battle with reality'. This is surely right, and we can take the point further. For years that battle had seemed to be going very well, what with the innumerable little victories of 1937–38. Stalin, remember, was a figure unstoppably giganticized by power. He had become a Saturn. And he *very much wanted* Hitler to refrain from attacking him in 1941. And what he very much wanted had a habit, by now, of coming to pass. Stalin felt that reality was obedient to his will; like King Lear, he thought the thunder would peace at his bidding. Hitler was fantastic, inordinate, unbelievable. But he was dourly real.

After the Great War, Churchill said that he had beaten all the lions and tigers – and did not now intend to be beaten by 'the baboons'. He meant the Bolsheviks. It is of course always a moral error to compare your adversaries to beasts, and such 'animal-ization' is a considerable twentieth-century theme (Lenin was already talking about the 'insects' and 'vermin' arrayed against him, in 1917). Still, Stalin's behaviour in early 1941 bears marked similarities to a certain manoeuvre in baboon praxis. If a weak baboon is threatened by a strong baboon he will sometimes symbolically offer up his rear end, as if for passive intercourse. The weak baboon is actually showing some psychological nous. Stalin tried it, and merely got what he seemed to be asking for. Maybe, too, he was half baboon, half ostrich, under the impression that if he couldn't see reality, then reality couldn't see him.

Zoya Kosmodemyanskaya

One of the most extraordinary photographs in *The Russian Century: A History of the Last Hundred Years** is that of the corpse of Zoya Kosmodemyanskaya.

Zoya Kosmodemyanskaya was a young partisan captured by the Germans in the battle for Moscow. When the Russians counter-attacked they found her body on a village gibbet. In January 1942 her story was told in *Pravda*. There followed a poem, a play, and a cult. In the play Zoya Kosmodemyanskaya sees Stalin in a vision just before her death, and he solaces her with the information that Moscow has been saved (neglecting, inter alia, to explain why her father and grandfather were both shot in the Terror). In any event, one glance at the corpse of Zoya Kosmo-demyanskaya and you would understand the nature of the enemy

---

*This is more than a picture book. Brian Moynahan's text is a fresh and vigorous distillation.

you faced. The Nazi policy of what might be called innovatory
barbarism earned them the furious enmity of a wavering population which, even as things stood, produced nearly a million
turncoats. Stalin knew that the Russian people wouldn't fight for
him. But they would fight for Zoya Kosmodemyanskaya. *She*
would make them 'bellow like bulls when they attack'.

There are two photographs of this young woman in *The
Russian Century*. One shows her being marched off to captivity
with a placard round her neck, no doubt disclosing her crime
(arson); it is an exceptionally beautiful face, both dark and pale,
and of softly Jewish cast. The faces of her captors are businesslike,
matter-of-fact, even quietly regretful . . . In the second photograph she wears the noose of a taut rope, though the body has
been cut down. Her black hair is fanned out on the snow. Her
'perfect' right breast is visible – but you can't quite say that,
because a breast owes part of its perfection to the other breast,
and the other breast has here been hacked off. Her head is bent
at an impossible angle. And her face is unforgettably that of a
martyr. The eyes are closed, the mouth is full but tightly clenched.
Her face expresses preternatural self-sufficiency, and an entirely
effortless superiority to her murderers and mutilators. It is the
face of another world, another cosmos. She was eighteen.

As the Russians retreated in the first few weeks of the war they
left behind them, in Poland, the Baltic states, and the Ukraine,
Cheka-manned prisons full of the 'usual suspicious elements' –
meaning, very broadly, anyone with an education. The prisoners
were almost invariably killed, even the ordinary criminals and
those merely awaiting trial. One can see the logic of dynamiting
a cellful of suspects (women suspects: this happened in the
Ukraine). But the more typical preference was to administer a

slow death. There are many accounts of prison floors strewn with genitals, breasts, tongues, eyes and ears. *Arma virumque cano*, and Hitler-Stalin tells us this, among other things: given total power over another, the human being will find that his thoughts turn to torture.

Accounting, as a Catholic, for his belief in evil as a living force, the novelist Anthony Burgess once said, 'There is no A. J. P. Taylor-ish explanation for what happened in Eastern Europe during the war.' Nor is there. Of the many characteristics shared by the two ideologies, however, one in particular proved wholly corrosive: the notion that mercilessness is a virtue. In the millenarian confrontation of the antichrists, the twin sons of perdition, cruelty became competitive, both between and within the opposed forces. Hereabouts a line is crossed, and one thinks of the fuddled brute in the court report who has stabbed his victim ninety-three times (or some such outlandish figure). The first thrust will be justified by the one that comes after. Every further thrust will be justified by the one that came before.

Hitler spelled it out. In March 1941, nearly three months before the campaign began, he told his senior officers that the war against Russia would be different from the war against France. The war against Russia would be one of annihilation: *Vernichtungskrieg*. And under the cover of that, under its fog and night, its foul breath, would come the *Vernichtungslagers*, the to-nothing camps of Auschwitz-Birkenau, Maidanek, Treblinka, Belzec, Chelmno, Sobibor.

The Taste Inside Stalin's Mouth

On the day that Barbarossa broke, Stalin was so uncertain of his stomach that only a single glass of tea passed his lips. That glass of tea did not wash away the 'taste of wormwood' which (as he told his secretary, Poskrebyshev) had lodged itself in his mouth on 22 June 1941. When he questioned his great war-winning general, Zhukov, about the chances of holding Moscow, Stalin said, 'I ask you this with pain in my heart . . .' A pain in the heart, a flutter in the gut, and a new taste in the mouth. Wormwood: a sour perennial herb of the genus *Artemisia*. Wormwood: bitterness or grief, or a cause of these.

When his generals told him the truth about the western front, Stalin collapsed as a regnant presence. Some accounts have him holed up for a week or more at Kuntsevo in a state of semi-hibernation. In Volkogonov's version we are offered an abruptly reclusive figure who would, nonetheless, occasionally lurch into the Defence Council with a volley of obscene abuse and then lurch out again. On 1 July a delegation arrived at the dacha. 'Why have you come?' asked Stalin with the 'strangest' look on his face. He clearly expected dethronement or arrest; and he would have gone quietly. To his obvious surprise, Molotov and Kaganovich and the rest of them patiently suggested that the country should resist the Germans and that Stalin should lead this effort. His reply is usually given as 'Fine' – though Conquest's 'All right' sounds more appropriately robotic (it consorts with the taste of wormwood in his mouth). The battle for Moscow hadn't begun. The battle with reality would last until Stalingrad in the winter of 1942–43.

At first he tried to prosecute the war through terror: the familiar psycho-chaos of fear and fantasy. He used the methods, and the personnel, of the Civil War.* Trotsky's innovation, the

---

*Old comrades from the days of Tsaritsyn (later Stalingrad; later still,

'blocking unit' (which ensured certain death with shame to those evading possible death with honour), was widely revived. Captured officers would be aware that their families now faced arrest.* Stalin kept ordering his blinded, shattered, trapped or fleeing forces to undertake obliterating counterattacks; failure invited summary trial and execution. At a time when the camps were being combed for competent military men, Stalin took the trouble to shoot 300 officers who were already in prison. As Kiev was falling he disdained all counsel and refused on principle to let the army retreat: 650,000 soldiers were taken prisoner, therefore becoming, by Order 270 (August 1941), 'traitors to the motherland'. In other countries returning POWs were greeted by brass bands and bunting; in the USSR, soldiers who had fought their way out of encirclement were greeted with the *super* or the gulag. In 1941 and 1942 'no fewer than 157,593 men – a full sixteen divisions' (Volkogonov) were executed for cowardice.

All his life Stalin was a consistently terrible little man. He never had anything resembling a finest hour – but the battle for Moscow shows him at his meagre apogee. In a crisis so severe that the government apparatus was being carted off to the Urals (the 'Highway of Enthusiasts', which led eastward, was thick with fleeing bureaucrats watched by jeering crowds) and there were plans to mine every significant piece of real estate in the capital

---

Volgograd): the feral factotum Mekhlis, the ex-tailor Shchadenko, the Quasimodo-like Kulik, and the tirelessly incompetent Voroshilov. In Teheran in 1943, when Churchill, in an atmosphere of historic emotion, presented Stalin ('by order of the King') with the Sword of Stalingrad, Voroshilov succeeded in dropping it as he solemnly bore it from the room.

*Men of other ranks would be aware that their families would be 'denied state assistance': i.e., ration cards, medical treatment, and the right to vote (this last a 'platonic' deprivation, according to Moshe Lewin).

(including the Metro), Stalin chose not to retreat. His train was waiting, but he stayed. In addition he astonished the Politburo with the proposal that the October Parade should take place as usual, which it did, in a snowstorm; the Germans were kilometres from the suburbs; and stretchers were ready to remove the dead and injured from Red Square if the Luftwaffe attacked. Stalin stood, as they say. He knew about failure; the author of Collectivization certainly knew something about failure. But this? All historians regard Stalin's failure of 1941 as perhaps the most abject in world history. But he stood, he stood there, and he took it, like the sleet in his face.

Bolshevik Bravery

It is suggestive that Stalin, adding to his copious demerits, should question the courage of the Russian soldier, who would soon be astonishing the world with his (and her) heroic madness. Perhaps we should take a look at the physical bravery of the main politicals.

Trotsky was brave, but I have never read anyone who claimed that Lenin, when danger neared, was other than a double-quick decamper (and Zinoviev was known as 'panic personified'). Trotsky was physically brave. A sense of invulnerability was an ingredient of his charisma. It was still with him on 20 August 1940, in Mexico. When the assassin Ramón Mercader drove the icepick into Trotsky's head there came a cry – a cry that is variously described but seemed to convey outrage, infinite and incredulous outrage. And Trotsky resisted, and fought with his assailant.* When Mercader struck, Trotsky had been at his desk, working on a biography of the man who had him murdered.

Stalin. In a playful demonstration of strength Tukhachevsky once swept him off his little feet and held him head-high; Stalin's face, it is said, was a picture of rage and terror. It was terror only during the flight to Teheran in 1943. When the plane bobbed through the air pockets, Stalin's knuckles whitened on the armrests as he grimaced with undisguisable fear. The plane had an escort of twenty-seven fighters. Stalin had never flown before. And he never flew again.

For the third and final Big Three summit, in 1945, Stalin travelled to Potsdam, by rail, under the protection of fifteen hundred regular soldiers and 17,000 Cheka troops. The nightly removal to Kuntsevo was always a major military operation. If Stalin took his daughter for a stroll in the grounds of the Kremlin, there would be a tank looking over his shoulder or idling just ahead.

In Teheran, Churchill toasted him as 'Stalin the Mighty'. And that was the trouble. As a fighting man, or as a political bully of fighting men, in the Civil War, Stalin showed plenty of 'contempt for life', without perhaps ever attaining the truly radical refinement of that ethos: contempt for death. His performance was

---

*Trotsky hung on until the following day. As he lay dying in the hospital he had a strange visitor: the twenty-five-year-old Saul Bellow (who remembers the stain of blood and iodine on Trotsky's short grey beard). The living Trotsky is evoked in Bellow's novel *The Adventures of Augie March* (1953); in a book full of extraordinary passages, this is a superextraordinary passage, and powerfully romantic, embodying all the intensity of hope that our artists and thinkers directed towards 1917 . . . When Ramón Mercader was released from prison and journeyed to Moscow in the 1960s, he formally inherited the award that had been been granted (by Stalin) to his mother. It was, of all things, the Order of Lenin.

strikingly mercurial; but I have never seen any suggestion that he
was shy of danger.

The trouble was power, and the inflationary effects of power.
That was the trouble on the plane to Teheran: all this weight, all
this value, all this *me*, subject to the uncontrollable physics of
weather and aviation.

Retributively, fear of death became his internal great terror.
When Lenin died the embalmers of his corpse were nominated
as the Immortalization Commission. Stalin wanted immortalization while he was still alive, and one of his later 'interventions'
took the form of an increasingly lively interest in gerontology;
like Mao, he exhausted various quackeries with the usual results.*

Hatred of death, in Stalin's case, duly arrived at its negative
apotheosis. Towards the end he started killing doctors.

It loves blood / The Russian earth

So wrote Anna Akhmatova, who, after the war, would be earning
her living by cleaning floors. And it did love blood, the Russian
earth.

The battle for Moscow was Germany's first defeat in the
Second World War; it roughly coincided with Pearl Harbor (7
December) and with Hitler's declaration of war against the USA
(11 December) – surely, for Hitler, the moment of irreversible
hubris. These events produced an enormous and complementary
expansion in the psyche of his adversary: 1942 saw a series of

---

*For a time Stalin's chief longevity coach was Dr Alexander Bogomolets, who
claimed that he (Stalin) might live to be 150 (he would now be 122). Dr Bogomolets
died of natural causes at the age of sixty-five.

superambitious disasters for the Red Army. Dmitri Volkogonov describes Stalin's military thinking as 'primitive' (or indifferent to losses); he learned 'by blood-spattered trial and error' – but he did learn. He desisted, on the whole, from killing his generals, and started attending to them; Zhukov would soon be talking to Stalin 'brusquely', as if to an inferior. In October 1942 Stalin recalled the political commissars (Volkogonov's 'military illiterates') from their 'dual commands' at the front. He created new decorations and restored Tsarist ranking systems; the shoulder-boards which in the Civil War had been nailed into the bare flesh of White officers now appeared on the uniforms of the Reds.

Stalin's mental journey, by 1943, proceeded in the opposite direction to that of Hitler. One moved towards reality; the other moved away from it. They crossed paths at Stalingrad. And as the war turned on the hinge of that battle (and on the new psychological opposition), Stalin might have concerned himself with a 'counterfactual': if, instead of decapitating his army, he had intelligently prepared it for war, Russia might have defeated Germany in a matter of weeks. Such a course of action, while no doubt entailing grave consequences of its own, would have saved about 40 million lives, including the vast majority of the victims of the Holocaust.

I have been saying that the invasion pressed Stalin into a semblance of mental health. Certainly, in August 1945, remission ended, and the patient's sanity once again fell apart. And even during the war he found time for a domestic atrocity that typically (i.e., insanely) combined the gratuitous and the literalistic. As early as the summer of 1941, Stalin evicted the Volga Germans from the lands they had occupied for two centuries and deported them to Central Asia and Siberia. In 1943–44 other minor nationalities followed: the Kalmyks, the Chechens, the Ingushi, the Karachai, the Balkars, and the Crimean Tartars; then the Crimea and the Caucasus were partly cleansed of Greeks, Bulgars, Armenians, Meskhetian Turks, Kurds, and Khemshins. In Stalin's view these were all suspect populations likely to turn to the Nazis; he told Khrushchev that he wanted to do the same to the Ukrainians but – despite his efforts in the 1930s – there were still too many of them (*c.* 40 million).* The achieved deportations involved about 1.2 million people, most of them women, children and the elderly; the men were all in the army (where the Chechens and the Ingushi alone produced thirty-six Heroes of the Soviet Union). In its reports on these operations the Cheka keeps praising its own 'efficiency'; and the deportations were not conducted with quite the raucous brutality of Dekulakization. All the families were dispossessed (Solzhenitsyn says that they were usually given an hour to pack); they were dispatched by rail, river and road;† their fatality rate, over the next three or four years, was about 20–25 per cent. For the deportees now joined the kulaks in that enormous category, the 'specially displaced': they were internal refugees, itinerant slave labour, asked to adapt to new lands, new languages, new climates . . .

---

*When Khrushchev passed on Stalin's remark in his Secret Speech of 1956, the assembled delegates of the Twentieth Party Congress reacted with wild laughter. It takes a beat or two before one can see why *Bolsheviks* should find this funny. Were they amused by the elephantiasis and demented circumspection of Stalin's paranoia? Partly, perhaps. More likely, though, the laughter was an expression of moral aftershock, and an expression of sheer relief that such enormities were now in the past. They laughed because they *could* laugh. But the sound of that laughter, one imagines, remained disturbingly confused.

†By 1944 the trucks used for the deportations included many Studebakers, donated (not for this purpose) by the Americans as part of the Lend-Lease aid programme.

These actions naturally constituted a significant military deficit for the USSR. The extraordinarily thorough and labour-intensive excision of the Volga Germans came at a time when the western front had disintegrated: Beria's initial circular went out on the day that the Germans reached the Neva (and the siege of Leningrad began to solidify). True, Stalin was still in the process of reining himself in; yet in 1943–44 – the golden age of his mental equilibrium – he still felt the need for the broadest possible canvas of power and pain. Traitor nations, traitor *ethnicities*: such suspicions would resurface after the war, forming the greatest and blackest irony of the entire period.

Meanwhile, across the border, Hitler's psychological trouble was revealing itself as clinical – as organic. In early 1941 he was already sufficiently 'confident' to undertake the invasion of Russia a) without a war economy, and b) *without antifreeze.* That is to say, he gambled on victory in a single campaign: a physical impossibility. We have seen how Chancellory-watchers all over the world were deceived by Hitler's spell of success; he himself would have been the more deceived, to put it mildly. Recent work by Ian Kershaw and others has suggested that the 'authoritarian chaos' of Hitler's polity was fundamentally irrational and self-destructive, and his plans for the east delusional.*
After Stalingrad, in any event, Hitler would scream at the bringers of bad news with foam visible in the corners of his mouth. 'If ever a building can be considered the symbol of a situation,' wrote Albert Speer, 'this was it': the walls of his bunker in East Prussia were sixteen feet thick; they 'locked him up inside his delusions'. After the briefcase-bomb attempt on his life (July

*Hitler planned to turn Russia into a 'slave empire'. This does sound delusional. But then it occurs to you that a slave empire is what they had there already.

1944), Hitler came to believe that Stalin's purge of the Red Army
had been an act of Benthamite justice and precision. He started
doing what Stalin had stopped doing: he reimposed Party discipline, installing political officers at all military HQs. Having
earlier lost his voice, Hitler, after the bomb attack, lost his
hearing. His isolation was complete.

It loves blood, the Russian earth. The great battles represented
inconceivable concentrations of hatred. Stalingrad, where the
front was reduced to a street, a house, a room, a ceiling, a wall,
a window; where swarms of rats 'flowed like a warm river over
the living and the dead'; where, indeed, the Germans were
confronted by *Rattenwaffe*, ratwar,* in which the Slavic undermen (Hitler's 'swamp animals') took the fight to them in the
runnels and the sewers ('deep war', in Ilya Ehrenburg's phrase),
and prevailed. Or the meshuggah megabattle of Kursk (July
1943), where, during a violent thunderstorm, fascism and Communism clashed with 'indescribable fury and horror', as Alan
Bullock writes: huge densities of 'armour crashed into each other
to form a roaring, whirling tangle of over a thousand tanks
locked together in combat for over eighteen hours' – in an area
of barely three square miles. Or the Siege of Leningrad, begun
during the battle for Moscow and not lifted for 900 days, with
a million dying in the first winter, the 'road of life' over frozen
Lake Ladoga (the first trucks disappeared under the ice; many
horses died en route and were delivered as meat), the relief vehi-
cles making the return journey with refugees, the director of the
Hermitage weeping on the railway platform as the first treasures

---

*Antony Beevor: *Stalingrad*.

rolled east, and Shostakovich, to the sound of guns, writing the symphony that expressed the murderous violence pressing in on the beleaguered city . . .

After the Winter War against Finland (1940–41), most observers, as we know, dismissed the Red Army as a toothless dinosaur. But at least one German officer saw it differently:

> . . . unprejudiced observers also noticed some very positive characteristics of the Soviet soldier: his incredibly tough conduct in defence, his imperviousness to fear and despair, and his almost unlimited capacity to suffer.

It was these qualities, particularly the last, that turned the war – together with the great expansion of previously trapped energy, and trapped meaning, in the Russian breast. The effort was nationwide, typically huge-scale, passionate, and bootstrap: typically 'sacrificial'. About 6 million workers were transported east, with their families – and also their factories, which were often reassembled and up and running in a matter of days. Such feats were underscored by a churning netherworld of forced-labour camps where conditions were sometimes worse than in the gulag. The zeks themselves now experienced fresh privations: the food quota was cut, and the living space halved – and not because the archipelago was getting any smaller. Of the 5.7 million POWs taken by the Germans, 4 million died in captivity (the USSR was not a signatory of the Geneva Convention; the Russian soldier suffered hardest, always and everywhere). Stalin wanted the remaining 1.7 million. And he got them. About 15–20 per cent were cleared by the Cheka. The rest faced execution or the camps.

Stalin's city, Stalingrad, was once Tsaritsyn: the scene of some of his more controversial activities during the Civil War. The pivotal victory there must have been savagely gratifying.* When he kissed the Sword of Stalingrad at Teheran (November 1943), when he heard Churchill salute 'Stalin the Mighty': what extravagant vindication. And the second Big Three meeting, at Yalta fourteen months later, with the ageing Prime Minister and the dying President paying Stalin's convenience the courtesy of travelling all the way to the Crimea, was another occasion for gorgeous complacency. Then the final summit in July, at Potsdam, among the shards and splinters of the Reich. Roosevelt was dead, and Churchill (halfway through the conference) lost office and was replaced by Clement Attlee.† Hitler was dead, too, and the detailed dismantling of Hitlerism would begin at Nuremberg. Stalin could take a look around and see exactly where he stood. Presiding over an empire greater than any Tsar's, he was now, without question, the preeminent personage on earth.

The Saddest Story

Within the USSR, throughout the quarter-century of his rule, Stalin was an extremely popular leader. It is something of a humiliation to commit that sentence to paper, but there is no avoiding it. Hitler was also a popular leader; but he had some economic successes, unlike Stalin, and he targeted relatively

*And Stalin's wartime pleasures *were* savage. In early 1944, while clearing the southern front, General Ivan Konev ambushed 30,000 German troops retreating in open terrain. After thorough work by the Russian tanks and artillery, a Cossack cavalry unit effected the kind of slaughter (as one witness said) 'that nothing could stop until it was over'. Subsequently there was no Churchillian talk, from the Kremlin, about the inevitable moral rot of warfare. 'Stalin was reported to be delighted with the massacre' (Overy), and Konev was made a marshal.

†Stalin was much perplexed, here, by the mysteries of democracy.

small minorities (the Jews comprised about 1 per cent of the population). Stalin's targets were majority targets, like the peasantry (85 per cent of the population). And although Hitler's invigilation of the citizenry was intimidating and persistent, he did not go out of his way, as Stalin did, to create a circumambience of nausea and fear. In a land where 'people leaving for work said farewell to their families every day, because they could not be certain they would return at night' (Solzhenitsyn), Stalin was always extremely popular.

Of course, Stalin's popularity was wholly – Hitler's merely largely – a matter of manipulation. For the citizen the process began in nursery school, and was reinforced by every means and from every direction and at all times. As in Germany, this was the birth of mass-media propaganda; people were unaware, then, that propaganda was propaganda – and propaganda worked. To love Stalin, suggests Volkogonov (who loved Stalin), was a form of 'social defence': it conditioned you to avoid trouble. *Sakharov* loved Stalin, and, like Volkogonov, was distraught at his death. 'It was years,' he later wrote, 'before I understood the degree to which deceit, exploitation and outright fraud were inherent in the whole Stalinist system. That shows the hypnotic power of mass ideology.' Moreover, Stalin made a ridiculous amount of headway in putting it about that the Cheka worked independently of the Kremlin. There's the famous anecdote – the two men meeting in the streets of Moscow, during the height of the Terror: 'If only someone would tell Stalin!' and so on. And this was not a joke, and these were no ordinary Ivans. The two men were Ilya Ehrenburg and Boris Pasternak.

The love for Stalin: it is very nearly the saddest story of all. You can see Dmitri Volkogonov slowly shaking his head as he writes, 'No other man in the world has ever accomplished so fantastic a success as he: to exterminate millions of his own countrymen and receive in exchange the whole country's blind adulation.' What has Stalin gone and done here? What is the nature of this particular crime – what is its content? It feels like some form of rape: a travesty of love, prosecuted by force. He took you early, too, in your school uniform. So, another enormous and contaminating lie, implanted in the childish heart.

Love signalled the totality of his victory. *1984* ends as follows:

> He gazed up at the enormous face. Forty years it had taken him to learn what kind of smile was hidden beneath the dark moustache . . . But it was all right, everything was all right, the struggle was finished. He had won the victory over himself. He loved Big Brother.

Into the Sere

No one is ever going to tell us about the physiology of autocratic rule, about the addiction to power and how this affects the system. But it seems fair to assume, in Stalin's case, that he bore the marks of an addiction so lavishly slaked. Presiding over what can confidently be called the least relaxing regime in human history cannot itself have been relaxing. (The hourly fear of assassination, one imagines, would also have been far from salutary.) Then there was the Second World War to be dealt with: for Stalin this meant four years of twenty-hour days. So how were things going, under this particular Kremlin complexion? He was now sixty-five.

The war released great energies and talents in the Soviet people. But it also released half-forgotten or unexperienced emotions, faculties, mental states (responsibility, endeavour, initiative, pride); and these had won the war. Pasternak describes the general agonized yearning that the state would now begin to back off from its citizens – after thirty years of (in order) world war, revolution, civil war, famine, forced collectivization, more famine, terror and, again, world war. Stalin was quick to assure his people that the 'total claim' he made on them was not going to be reduced. I'm sure he sensed their awakened spirit; and I'm sure he didn't like it. Round about now we further note the development in Stalin of a fierce strain of national inferiority, which expressed itself as aggressive xenophobia combined with Great Russian hauteur. He felt inferior not just to the West but to the satellite countries of Central Europe, and killed army veterans who had seen what it was like in Bulgaria or Yogoslavia. His bitter isolationism, political and personal, was linking up with rearoused suspicions about the people, the people themselves, who seemed to him to be newly stirring.

In the period 1945–53 Stalinism entered its rancid, crapulent phase. The old addict was starting to pay for his 'excesses'. Since 1929 the Soviet Union had been a reflection of Stalin's mind. And now that mind was breaking up: infarctions, minor strokes, dizzy spells, faints. In common with another exhausted autarch, Macbeth, Stalin's way of life was fallen into the sere, the yellow leaf. Withered, parched, and above all *lurid*, in the botanical sense ('dingy yellowish brown'), and in every other: ghastly, wan, glaring, gaudy, sensational, and horrifying. And gutter-level: the level of the street corner and the upended milk crate. There would be more executions, deportations, conspiracies to establish 'conspiracies'; additional millions would be absorbed by the clogged gulag. But the theme of the period is fading vigour –

twitching, flailing. Atavisms, primitive stupidities, were ready to recrudesce. If the postwar years lack the phantasmagoric coherence of the 1930s, they still achieve an unexpectedly sordid symmetry. Even in his last excitations Stalin managed to fight his way to consummate historical disgrace.

Volkogonov reports that in January 1948 the Minister of the Interior, Kruglov, was called in by Stalin:

> [He] ordered him to devise 'concrete measures' for constructing new, additional concentration camps and prisons for special purposes ... 'Submit draft decrees in February,' he told Kruglov. 'We need special conditions for holding Trotskyites, Mensheviks, SRs, anarchists and Whites.' 'It will be done, Comrade Stalin, it will be done,' Kruglov assured him.

New camps, new prisons – for old, old crimes (the anarchists had been wiped out by Lenin in 1918). Stalin erratically revealed certain human qualities in his last years (a photograph of Nadezhda Alliluyeva would reappear on his desk), among them an elderly and irascible fear of change.* This fear now allied itself to a rancorous bid for autarky. There were old crimes, but there were also new crimes. PZ, for instance (Abasement Before the West), or VAD (Praising American Democracy), or the presumably more minor VAT (Praising American Technique). Then,

---

*With 25 million dead, and another 25 million homeless, with the loss of 70,000 villages, 1,700 towns, 32,000 factories, and a third of the national wealth, with 'banditism' (armed insurrection) down the length of the western border (guerrilla warfare would continue into the 1950s), and a serious though unacknowledged famine, the USSR, in 1945, was thrown back through time. The next lumbering Five Year Plan, drafted in that year, had in effect the same object as the first, industrialization, and made the usual demands for sacrifice, discipline and vigilance. This would have been congenial to Stalin – to his nostalgia for struggle.

from what at first seems to be an unexpected direction, there was suddenly another new crime: the crime of being Jewish.

Nothing quite explains this collapse into the gutter by Stalin, though his history of anti-Semitism turns out to be long and colourful. Khrushchev said he was dyed in the wool; and there are examples of Stalin's anti-Semitic crudities dating back to the teens of the century. 'Anti-Semitism is counterrevolution,' Lenin had tersely decided. And yet the Party was tainted with it as early as the 1920s. There seems to have been a policy of low-pressure ghettoization, in which the poorer Jews of the old Pale of Settlement in the East European Plain were encouraged to migrate to the Crimea. With Stalin's ascendancy came a change of desti-nation: the new Jewish Autonomous Region would be established in Birobidzhan, a 'desolate' area near the Chinese border.

This is Richard Overy:

> . . . Soviet propaganda made great play with the idea that the regime was protecting the culture and identity of the Jewish people. But [Birobidzhan's] remoteness from the traditional centres of Jewish culture . . . made it an unattractive prospect. Birobidzhan was a failed experiment in Soviet apartheid.

During the 1930s anti-Semitism became a part of Cheka policy, and in the years of the Terror such phrases as 'contact with Zionist circles' began to appear in its fabrications. The tenor of Stalin's prejudice is revealed in an anecdote describing a party attended by officials of the punitive organs in 1936, shortly after the executions of Zinoviev and Kamenev (both of them Jews). Conquest's version goes as follows:

> After a good deal of drinking all round, K. V. Pauker, who had been present at Zinoviev's execution in his capacity as head of

the NKVD [Cheka] Operative Department, gave a comical rendering of that event. Himself acting the part of Zinoviev, he was dragged in by two other officers. He hung from their arms moaning, 'Please, for God's sake, call Iosif Vissarionovich.' Stalin laughed heartily, and when Pauker repeated the perform-ance, adding as his own invention, 'Hear, Israel, our God is the only God!' Stalin was overcome with merriment and had to sign to Pauker to stop.

Of the eighteen defendants at the Bukharin/Yagoda trial of 1938, thirteen were Jews, including Trotsky and his son Sedov, tried in absentia. Among other things, this was a signal to Berlin. 'Molotov is not Bronstein,' as Ribbentrop duly observed.

One wonders whether Stalin's hatred of Trotsky, one of the most passionate in history (with three floors of the Lubyanka devoted to his destruction), was to some extent 'racial'. It is, anyway, all of a piece. Anti-Semitism is an announcement of inferiority and a protest against a level playing field – a protest against talent.* And this is true, too, of the most hysterical, demo-nizing, millenarian versions of the cult, according to which a tiny minority, the Jews, planned to achieve world domination. Now how would they manage that, without inordinate gifts? It is said that anti-Semitism differs from other prejudices because it is also a 'philosophy'. It is also a religion – the religion of the inadequate. When tracing the fateful synergy between Russia and Germany (soon to climax), we may recall that *The Protocols of the Elders of Zion*, the 'warrant for genocide' as it is called in

---

*On the other hand, one should not forget that support for Hitler was broad-based, and that Nazism had many distinguished admirers (among them Martin Heidegger and two Nobel Laureates in physics).

Norman Cohn's book of that name, was a fiction composed by the Tsarist secret police.*

The pact years of 1939–41 saw collaborative anti-Semitism between the two regimes. German Jews who had hoped to find safety in the USSR were first corralled, then delivered to the Gestapo. Meanwhile, Jewish refugees from the German-occupied countries were imprisoned or exiled to Central Asia or Siberia. In his half of partitioned Poland, Stalin combined general decapitation with a sustained attack on Jewish culture, banning religious holidays (including the Sabbath), bar mitzvahs and circumcisions, and dismantling the shtetls. After June 1941, Soviet policy went briefly into reverse, a switch apparently confirmed by Stalin's endorsement, ten months later, of the Jewish Anti-Fascist Committee. But the momentum of atavism was building. Conquest notes that Jewish activists interrogated by the Cheka in 1939 'were treated very badly', but 'the curses and imprecations never had any racial tone. When they were reinterrogated in 1942–43, anti-Semitic abuse had become the norm.' The shift in emphasis, like everything else, was top-down.

There were about 3 million Jews in the Soviet Union after the war, 1.25 million having died in the Holocaust. That Jewry faced the possibility of a second Holocaust, in successive decades, is strongly suggested by Stalin's sclerotic manoeuvrings in this

---

*'It was in the twelfth century,' Cohn writes, 'that [the Jews] were first accused of murdering Christian children, of torturing the consecrated wafer, and of poisoning the wells. It is true that popes and bishops frequently and emphatically condemned these fabrications; but the lower clergy continued to propagate them, and in the end they came to be generally believed.' As in his other classic work, *The Pursuit of the Millennium*, Cohn identifies the semieducated clerisy as the natural constituency for militant utopians as well as anti-Semites – a constituency that Stalin (or Stalin's mother) once hoped he would join. It was also Chernyshevsky's.

period, and particularly his decision of 1951: anti-Semitism went from covert to overt, from *Pravda*'s mutterings about 'rootless cosmopolitans' to a fully orchestrated propaganda campaign. Stalin was now ready to mobilize the atavism. Until 1951 his racially motivated arrests, executions, murders, purges and bannings had been largely clandestine. In the spring of that year he started developing the Slansky case in satellite Czechoslovakia (fourteen high-level Stalinists, eleven of them Jewish, were tried and executed, the charge being emended from 'bourgeois nationalism' to 'Zionism'). Further publicity was generated by a gang of Jewish 'wreckers' in Ukrainian industry in 1952. Then came 'the Doctors' Plot', and the propaganda juggernaut started preparing the public for a nationwide pogrom. Solzhenitsyn believes that the pogrom was to be launched at the beginning of March by the hanging of the 'doctor-murderers' in Red Square. But then, too, at the beginning of March something else happened: Stalin died.

Historians usually say that there would have been 'another terror' of uncertain scale; but what *kind* of terror? It wouldn't have been like the Great Terror, where public participation was confined to the delivery of denunciations. The Jewish terror would have modelled itself on the older Bolshevik idea or tactic of inciting one class to destroy another. It would have resembled the Red Terror of 1918 with the Jews very approximately in the role of the bourgeoisie. The Red Terror of 1918, Orlando Figes insists, was participatory, top-down but also bottom-up. It is tempting to see more mangled regression here, in Stalin, as he sets about provoking the baser energies of the masses, and more nostalgia for the days of struggle, the days, as Lenin called them, of 'chaos and enthusiasm'.

There are rational explanations for Stalin's surrender to the gutter voodoo. Conquest summarizes them (and they form a rebarbative brew):

> [His] attitude from 1942–43 seems to have been based in part on what he took to be Hitler's successful use of anti-Semitic demagogy. It was certainly also due to his increasing Russian nationalism, to which he felt most, or many, Jews were not truly assimilable. And the idea of a special Jewish predilection for capitalism is of course to be found in Marx.

The proximate cause of the final delirium was evidently the emergence of the state of Israel in 1948 and the arrival, later that year, of the new ambassador, Golda Meir, who attracted a crowd of 50,000 Jews outside the Moscow synagogue. This was a shocking display of 'spontaneity'; it also confronted Stalin with an active minority who owed an allegiance other than to 'the Soviet power'. He is supposed to have said: 'I can't swallow them, I can't spit them out.' In the end, it seems, he decided to do both. The Jews who survived the gauntlet were meant to end up in Birobidzhan on the Chinese border and in other parts of Siberia where, according to Solzhenitsyn, 'barracks had already been prepared for them'.

It is perhaps controversial to suggest that Iosif Stalin in his last years was capable of further spiritual decline. But one is struck by the loss, the utter evaporation, of his historical self-consciousness, suggesting some sort of erasure in a reasonably important part of Stalin's brain. 'Anti-Semitism is counterrevolution.' Anti-Semitism was the creed of the Whites, of the Tsarists – and of the Black Hundreds, the reactionary gangs with their knives and knuckledusters (sometimes equipped with guns – and vodka – by the gendarmerie), against whom the young Stalin might have stood in line on the streets of Russia's cities. Anti-Semitism was for the rabble and the Right. In turning to it, the world's premier statesman, as he then was, also squandered the vast moral capital that the USSR had accumulated during the war: Hitler's conqueror, incredibly, became Hitler's protégé. The various restrictions imposed on Soviet Jewry lacked the lewd pettines of some of the Nuremberg Laws of the 1930s;* but Stalin's signature is everywhere apparent. As his social fascism broadened to include ethnic fascism, Stalin added to his other innovations by becoming the first Holocaust-denier. It was dangerous to talk about 'Jewish martyrdom' (this was 'national egotism'), and the regime concertedly heckled the notion that the fate of the Jews was a significant aspect of the Second World War.† Chaotically Stalinesque, too, was the arrest of several Jews on the (probably trumped-up) charge of accusing the state of anti-Semitism.

One last deformed irony emerges from the strange dance, the *pas de deux* performed by the little moustache and the big moustache. In his final convulsion, 'the Doctors' Plot', the defendants (nearly all of them Jewish) were accused (falsely) of the quintessential, the defining, the exceptionalizing Nazi crime: medical murder.

---

*As part of an effort to improve the birth rate, German women, on each parturition, were awarded a crucifix tastelessly called the *Mutterkreuz*. Aryan households, at this time, were forbidden to employ any Jewess under the age of forty-five. No *Mutterkreuz* for *her*.

†Right up until 1989 the Auschwitz Museum itself was a monument to Holocaust denial. The part played by the Jews was deemphasized in favour of the Struggle Against Fascism. Similarly: 'The report produced in Kiev on Babi Yar talked of the death of "peaceful Soviet citizens", not of Jews' (Overy).

The Bedbug

When he adopted the 'reconciliation line' at the Congress of Victors in 1934, Maxim Gorky was profoundly mistaken in thinking that 'biographical therapy' was the way to Stalin's soul. Planetary preeminence didn't soften him in 1945. A few more mendacious hosannahs wouldn't have softened him in 1934. Stalin wasn't that kind of animal.

Writers were pushed, sometimes physically, sometimes spiritually, into all kinds of unfamiliar shapes by the Bolsheviks. Isaac Babel, shot in 1940, Osip Mandelstam, losing his mind en route to Kolyma in 1938 ('Am I real and will death really come?'): these men could tell themselves that they were martyrs to their art; and they were, and so were hundreds of others. Some more or less genuine writers tried to work 'towards' the Bolsheviks. Their success depended inversely on the size of their talent. Talentless writers could flatter the regime. Talented writers could not flatter the regime, or not for long. One thinks of Mayakovsky. His tough-guy verses about bayonets and pig-iron statistics have a smile somewhere behind them; and his play *The Bedbug* (a satire on bureaucratism) was considered subversive enough to be quietly quashed. But he compromised his talent, minor though it was. And it seems that you just can't do that. He killed himself in 1930.* The strangest and perhaps the sourest destiny of all, however, was that of Maxim Gorky.

'*I despise and hate them more and more,*' he wrote of the

---

*It was only after his suicide that Mayakovsky's work 'began to be introduced forcibly, like potatoes under Catherine the Great,' noted Pasternak: 'This was his second death.' Pasternak survived, without compromise. His lover, Olga Ivinskaya, was interrogated and sent to the gulag. The child she was carrying was stillborn in jail.

Bolsheviks, in June 1917. Gorky was not a 'hereditary proletarian', but he was certainly a hereditary plebeian: early poverty was followed by orphanhood; he took his first job at the age of nine. By the mid-1890s he was world-famous, and still in his twenties. His revolutionary credentials were also excellent. He was an enemy of the old regime, and had done time in prison. A friend of Lenin's since 1902, Gorky donned the black leather tunic and the knee-high boots for the failed revolution of 1905.* During the war his large apartment in Petersburg became a Bolshevik HQ. Gorky's disillusionment was gradual but steady. Two weeks after October he wrote the following:

> Lenin and Trotsky do not have the slightest idea of the meaning of freedom or the Rights of Man. They have already become poisoned with the filthy venom of power, and this is shown by their shameful attitude towards freedom of speech, the individual, and all those other civil liberties for which the democracy struggled.

In *A People's Tragedy* Orlando Figes uses Gorky as a moral anchor. In the typhoon of unreason, his is the voice of suffering sanity.

He was also a superenergetic philanthropist, saving many lives and easing many hardships during the Red Terror and the Civil War. Lenin, for a little while longer, was still listening to him, even though Gorky's newspaper, *Novaia zhin'* (new world), had been suppressed in 1918. It is extraordinary how many of Lenin's most-quoted utterances are to be found in his correspondence

---

*The Bolsheviks persisted with this outfit long after taking power. The squeak-and-glisten look, it seems, was admired by all the putschists of the first half of the twentieth century.

with Gorky: the one about the 'unutterable vileness' of all religion; the one about intellectuals being society's 'shit'; the one about the 'marvellous Georgian'. In power, Lenin grew sterner with his friend. Gorky's letters are now forceful pleas for particular leniencies and general moderation. Lenin fights his corner in his usual style, with the kind of debating tricks that would embarrass even the Oxford Union, and crowingly delivered:

> Reading your frank opinions on this matter, I recall a remark of yours: 'We artists are irresponsible people.' Exactly! You utter incredibly angry words – about what? About a few dozen (or perhaps even a few hundred) Kadet and near-Kadet gentry spending a few days in jail to prevent plots* ... which threaten the lives of thousands of workers and peasants. A calamity indeed! What injustice. A few days, or even weeks, in jail for intellectuals in order to prevent the massacre of thousands of workers and peasants! 'Artists are irresponsible people.'

Quite easily done.† Lenin's letters started to include threats. 'I cannot help saying: change your circumstances radically, your environment, your abode, *your occupation*, – otherwise life may disgust you for good' (July 1919). Italics added. To bring about the inevitable rift it would take the death of two poets and a famine.

---

*This is Lenin's thumbnail sketch of the Red Terror. Again, for perspective (and this applies to the years 1917–24): 'it is possible that more people were murdered by the Cheka than died in the battles of the civil war' (Figes).

†This letter of Lenin's has an equivalent in the Stalin archive: the one to Mikhail Sholokhov (who, according to Solzhenitsyn, *didn't* write *And Quiet Flows the Don*) about the peasantry. In rather more languid tones, Stalin assures his 'esteemed' comrade that the 'worthy reapers', whom he had only minimally inconvenienced, were not as worthy as they seemed: they were using terrorism to starve the towns.

When Moscow eventually started to admit that a quarter of the peasantry was dying of starvation, Gorky was chosen to lead the call for aid. When the famine was over, Lenin arrested all but two of the relief committee and told Gorky to go abroad 'for his health'. Then there were the deaths of the poets, Alexander Blok and Nikolai Gumilev. After a brief enthusiasm for October, and two famous poems in celebration of it, Blok wrote nothing after 1918, and died of hunger and despair in August 1921. Days later, Gumilev (the former husband of Anna Akhmatova) was arrested by the Petrograd Cheka – for monarchist sympathies, which he indeed professed. Gorky went at once to Moscow and obtained from Lenin an order for Gumilev's release. When he got back to Petrograd he found that Gumilev had already been shot, without trial. On being told of this, Gorky coughed up blood. His health was in any case poor. He emigrated in October.

In 1932 Gorky was induced to return to the USSR, from Italy, by Comrade Stalin. This was a propaganda coup for the regime, which made much of the deliverance of the great writer from 'fascist Italy'. He was awarded the Order of Lenin; a little palace in Moscow was made available for him, and a dacha (into which, on hearing of Gorky's difficulties with the stairs, Stalin sensitively installed an elevator); Tverskaia Street became Gorky Street, and his native Nizhnyi Novgorod became Gorky: this was large-scale lionization.* It must have been clear to Stalin that Gorky would eventually give him trouble. There would be a man, there would be a problem. Stalin, I am sure, was excited by the idea of breaking

---

*Other things were named after Gorky – a weaving factory, for instance, and an airplane (the world's largest), which crashed. Solzhenitsyn, who is maximally hard on Maxim, eagerly reports that *camps* were named after him too – posthumously, no doubt. One of Stalin's rare jokes.

this big cat: breaking the talent, breaking the integrity, breaking the man.

As early as June 1929, during the second of his five reintroductory summer trips to Russia, Gorky comprehensively defiled himself. To counter the recent publication, in England, of a book about Solovki (*An Island Hell: A Soviet Prison in the Far North*), Gorky was sent on a visit to the cradle of the gulag. The camp was hurriedly Potemkinized. As Solzhenitsyn tells it, however, Gorky secured an uninvigilated ninety-minute conversation with a fourteen-year-old boy in the Children's Colony. He left the barracks 'streaming tears'.* In the Visitors' Book he praised 'the tireless sentinels of the Revolution, [who] are able, at the same time, to be remarkably bold creators of culture'; these views were published worldwide. 'Hardly had [Gorky's] steamer pulled away from the pier than they shot the boy' (Solzhenitsyn).

The second spectacular self-abasement occurred in 1933–34, when Gorky edited *The White Sea-Baltic Canal* (his co-editors included the Deputy Chief of the gulag). In the summer of 1933 a delegation of 120 writers visited the canal, which had just been completed, and thirty-six of them contributed to the volume, which lauded the project as 'a uniquely successful effort at the mass transformation of former enemies of the proletariat'. Built by slave labour (mostly kulaks), the canal was meant to connect the two fleets by a mighty waterway. In the end it cost perhaps 150,000 lives, and it was useless.† Gorky had long been a close

---

*The boy told him, inter alia, about the 'mosquito treatment': these insects, like airborne piranha, could turn a man into a skeleton within hours. Prisoners were also strapped to logs and then bounced down the stone steps of the fortress.

†Not deep enough. Solzhenitsyn visited the site many years later. He was there all day, and saw two barges.

friend of the hard-line but candid and realistic Kirov, the Leningrad boss, in whose fief the canal was built. The book itself was evidence enough: manifestly and monotonously fraudulent, sickly and craven. Gorky's incidental pronouncements, around now, are unrecognizable. He speaks the dialect of the regime in a tone of icy triumphalism.

It was the murder of Kirov (December 1934) that penetrated Gorky's spiritual coma. Stalin expected this. A matter of hours after the killing, Cheka troops ringed Gorky's Crimean villa – to protect him, or to contain him lest he speak out? The parallel tracks now entered the chicane. Urged by Stalin to join the condemnation of individual terror (after the Kirov killing), Gorky replied that he condemned state terror too: this amounted to an accusation of murder. When Gorky returned to Moscow the organs moved in closer. He told friends that he was under 'house arrest'. His quarantine was bizarrely symbolized by the fact that the copies of *Pravda* he saw were specially rigged up for him ('reports of arrests,' as Tucker notes, 'were replaced by news about the crab catch and the like'). Isolation increased in May 1935 when his adopted son, Maxim Peshkov, who acted as his go-between, died mysteriously after a minor illness. Gorky's own pulmonary trouble grew worse. Stalin, accompanied by Molotov and Voroshilov, paid a visit to his bedside. He died on 18 June 1936, and was buried with full honours. Two months later his old friend Kamenev came to the dock (and to eventual execution) in a trial that Gorky had been expected to denounce.

No personage in history, we may think, has a weaker claim to the benefit of the doubt, but Stalin is less thoroughly implicated in the death of Gorky (and Gorky's son) than in the death of Kirov. Moving from the 'quiet terror' of Party expulsions to the percussion of the Great Terror itself, Stalin was now at his most anarchically improvisational, a mad gymnast of multiple deceit, filling a hole here, plugging a gap there, in the vibrating edifice of his reality. In the later trial of Bukharin and others (1938) it was claimed that Gorky was killed by his doctors, who were themselves the creatures of head Chekist Yagoda. Yagoda was of course executed; and so were Drs Levin and Kazakov.* The Gorky 'murder', a bumbling, piecemeal business (the doctors induced him to stand near bonfires and to visit people who had colds), sounds embarrassingly feeble, and drenches the event in an undeserved improbability. The entire case feels extemporized: Yagoda's plot was presented as a terroristic move against the leadership, and so Gorky (his shade would not have been happy to learn) was liquidated as one of the stauncher Stalinists. Anyway, there seems to be a rule, and it may be metaphysical: when Stalin wished for a death, then that wish came true.

Gorky, then, was trying to regain his integrity. But why did he lose it in the first place? Solzhenitsyn is unsparing:

> I used to ascribe Gorky's pitiful conduct after his return from Italy and right up to his death to his delusions and folly. But his recently published correspondence of the 1920s provides a reason for explaining it on lesser grounds: material self-interest. In Sorrento Gorky was astonished to discover that no world fame had accrued to him, nor money either . . . It became clear that both for money and to revive his fame he had to return to the Soviet Union and accept all the attached conditions . . . And Stalin killed him to no purpose, out of excessive caution: Gorky would have sung hymns of praise to 1937 too.

---

*Other doctors were implicated, and in such numbers (Conquest tells us) that they were collectively known as 'Gorkyists' in the prisons and camps.

We understand Solzhenitsyn's anger (that last sentence contains two definitive insults), but we cannot quite accede to it. Vanity, venality – perhaps; but Gorky was stumbling, groping, suffering. He returned to Russia because on some level he felt, perhaps conceitedly, that he could moderate the system – moderate Stalin – from within. He pawned his soul, and then tried to redeem it.

Anomalously, Gorky was allowed a last trip to the Crimea – for his health. One night, escaping the supervision of his doctors, he climbed out of a window and crept into the garden. Tucker writes (he is paraphrasing his source): 'Gorky looked up at the sky. Then he walked to a tree, clasped its branches in his arms, and stood there weeping.' He had much to weep about. In general, writers never find out how strong their talent is: that investigation begins with their obituaries. In the USSR, writers found out how good they were when they were still alive. If the talent was strong, only luck or silence could save them. If the talent was weak, they could compromise and survive. Thus, for the writers, the Bolsheviks wielded promethean power: they summoned posterity and inserted it into the here and now.

A certain document was found among Gorky's papers. On reading it Yagoda swore and said, 'No matter how much you feed a wolf, he keeps looking back towards the woods.' (This is a unique occurrence: Yagoda, here, is more generous than Solzhenitsyn.) In the document Gorky had imagined Stalin as a flea – a flea that had grown to vast and uncontrollable proportions, 'insatiable for humanity's blood' (in Conquest's gloss) 'yet essentially parasitical'. And perhaps we should make that giant flea a giant bedbug, for Stalin craved, and brought about, the politicization of sleep. He murdered sleep.

With a solemnity that can be easily imagined, Stalin himself led Gorky's funeral march. The passionate friendship the two men shared now established itself in Soviet myth. A fortnight later the three journals Gorky edited were closed down and their staffs arrested, along with others of his entourage.

Demian Bedny: Demian the Poor. Maxim Gorky: Maxim the Bitter. Iosif Grozny: Iosif the Terrible.

End

This is how Ivan went, in 1584: '[he] began grievously to swell in his cods, with which he had most horribly offended above fifty years together, boasting of a thousand virgins he had deflowered'.* The soothsayers were called in, and Ivan sought relief in the fondling of jewelry. He died while attempting to begin a game of chess:

> He sets his men† . . . the Emperor in his loose gown, shirt and linen hose, faints and falls backwards. Great outcry and stir, one sent for aqua vita another to the apothecary for 'marigold and rose water' and to call his ghostly father and the physicians. In the mean he was strangled and stark dead.

'Was strangled' here means 'asphyxiated', because Ivan died of natural causes. As, scandalously, did Stalin. He took rather longer to go. And, such was his incredible talent for death, he showed that he could kill people violently even from his coffin.

---

*This and subsequent quotes are from an account by Sir Jerome Horsey of the Muscovy Company in London.

†'All saving his king, which by no means he could make stand in his place with all the rest upon the plain board' (Horsey's note, which sounds too good to be true).

One of the hundred and more Jewish artists executed between 1948 and 1953 was the legendary actor Solomon Mikhoels. He was not arrested; he was lured, murdered, and left in the street, where a Cheka truck drove over him. The regime was content at first to decide that the death was accidental, but later it was put about that he had indeed been murdered – by the CIA, to stop him from exposing an American spy ring. Mikhoels had performed, privately, in the Kremlin. He had done Shakespeare for Stalin. He had done Lear for Stalin. I contend that this was a great historical moment. Lear was of course a totalitarian from birth – there are differences – but *Lear* remains the central visionary meditation on the totalitarian mind. Did Stalin's nose twitch when he heard Mikhoels, his future victim, flaying him from the stage?

> They flattered me like a dog . . . To say 'ay' and 'no' to every-thing that I said! . . . When the rain came to wet me once and the wind to make me chatter, when the thunder would not peace at my bidding; there I found 'em, there I smelt 'em out. Go to, they are not men of their words: they told me I was everything: 'tis a lie – I am not ague-proof.

And nor of course was Koba. Khrushchev reports him as being unwontedly cheerful on the evening of 28 February (and unwontedly drunk);* other accounts describe a night of sombre denunciations from the head of the table, and Stalin's silent and disgusted departure (at the usual hour: 4 A.M.). The standing dinner invitation to Kuntsevo had always been a mixed blessing. In more youthful days the Kremlin cronies had amused

---

*Stalin, it seems, drank moderately by Russian standards. But he postponed giving up smoking (cigarettes and pipe) until the fruitlessly late date of 1952.

themselves with bun fights, songs, jokes, japes. A typical prank was the placement of a ripe tomato on the chair of the drunken Poskrebyshev (was this, one wonders, before or after his wife was shot – or both?). Stalin enjoyed the spectacle of humiliation – getting Khrushchev to dance Cossack-style, for example. But these men were already humiliated, long before 1953. By then Poskrebyshev was gone (fired, merely) and the others, particularly Beria and Malenkov, were regarded with intense suspicion. 'I'm finished,' Stalin had recently been heard to say to himself: 'I trust no one, not even myself.' Svetlana says of this period that a visit to her father would physically wipe her out for several days; and Svetlana was in no fear of her life.

On 1 March Stalin stirred at midday, as usual. In the pantry the light came on: MAKE TEA. The servants waited in vain for the plodding instruction, BRING TEA IN. Not until 11 P.M. did the duty officers summon the nerve to investigate. Koba was lying in soiled pyjamas on the dining-room floor near a bottle of mineral water and a copy of *Pravda*. His beseeching eyes were full of terror. When he tried to speak he could only produce 'a buzzing sound' – the giant flea, the bedbug, reduced to an insect hum. No doubt he had had time to ponder an uncomfortable fact: all the Kremlin doctors were being tortured in jail, and his personal physician of many years, Vinogradov, was, moreover (at the insistence of Stalin himself), 'in irons'.

Beria, apparently fresh from some debauch, made a flying visit on the night of 1 March. But it wasn't until the next morning that a team of (non-Jewish) doctors was assembled and set to work, spurred on by Beria's obscenities and threats, while members of the Politburo paced about in the adjoining room. One finds oneself tending to linger over the medical documents (is it the novelty of a natural death?), with their portrait of total powerlessness. Extracts:

> . . . the patient was lying on a divan on his back, his head turned to the left, his eyes closed, with moderate hyperemia [excess of blood] of the face; there had been involuntary urination (his clothes were soaked in urine) . . . The heart tones were dull . . . The patient is in an unconscious state . . . There is no movement in the right extremities and occasional disturbance in the left.
>
> Diagnosis: hypertonic disease, generalized atherosclerosis with predominant damage of the cerebral blood vessels, right-handed hemiplegia as a result of middle left cerebral arterial haemorrhaging; atherosclerotic cardiosclerosis, nephrosclerosis. The patient's condition is extremely serious.

Because the patient, in other words, had had a massive stroke. The doctors applied leeches – four behind either ear, contentedly and innocently sucking the bedbug's blood. Magnesium sulphate was administered by enema and hypodermic. Stalin's right side was paralysed; his left side twitched at random. Over the next five days, as the doctors trembled over their work, Vasily Dzhugashvili would sometimes stagger in and shout, 'They've killed my father, the bastards!' At 9:50 P.M. on 5 March Stalin began sweating heavily. His blue face turned bluer. Svetlana watched and waited. This is her valediction:

> For the last twelve hours the lack of oxygen became acute. His face and lips blackened . . . The death agony was terrible. He literally choked to death as we watched. At what seemed like the very last moment, he opened his eyes and cast a glance over everyone in the room. It was a terrible glance, insane or perhaps angry, and full of fear of death . . . [Then] he suddenly lifted his left hand as though he were pointing to something

up above and bringing down a curse on all. The gesture was incomprehensible and full of menace.

What was he doing? He was groping for his power.

Stalin was dead – but he wasn't yet done. He had always loved grinding people together, pestling them together, leaving them without air and space, without recourse; he had always loved hemming and cooping them, penning them, pinning them: the Lubyanka reception 'kennel', with three prisoners for every yard of floor space; Ivanovo, with 323 men in a cell intended for twenty, or Strakhovich, with twenty-eight men in a cell intended for solitary confinement; or thirty-six in a single train compartment, or a black maria packed so tight that the *urkas* can't even pickpocket, or the zeks trussed in pairs and stacked like logs in the back of the truck – en route to execution . . . On the day of Stalin's funeral vast multitudes, ecstatic with false grief and false love, flowed through Moscow in dangerous densities. When, in a tightening crowd, your movements are no longer your own and you have to fight to breathe, a simple and sorrowful realization asserts itself through your panic: that if death comes, it will be brought here by life, too much life, a superabundance of life. And what were they all doing there anyway – mourning *him*? On that day well over a hundred people died of asphyxiation in the streets of Moscow. So Stalin, embalmed in his coffin, went on doing what he was really good at: crushing Russians.

Negative Perfection

While preparing for the demonstration trial of the SRs, Lenin wrote to the People's Commissar of Justice (May 1922):

Comrade Kursky!
As a sequel to our conversation, I am sending you an outline of a supplementary paragraph for the Criminal Code . . . The basic concept, I hope, is clear . . .: openly to set forth a statute which is both principled and politically truthful (and not just juridically narrow) to supply motivation for the *essence* and the *justification* of terror, its necessity, its limits.

The court must not exclude terror. It would be self-deception or deceit to promise this, and in order to provide it with a foundation and to legalize it in a principled way, clearly and without hypocrisy and without embellishment, it is necessary to formulate it as broadly as possible, for only revolutionary righteousness and a revolutionary conscience will provide the conditions for applying it more or less broadly in practice.

With Communist greetings,

LENIN

'Terror is a powerful means of policy,' said Trotsky, 'and one would have to be a hypocrite not to understand this.'

Both men, we see, are anxious to avoid being hypocritical.* No, let us not have any hypocrisy. Terror, if you must. But let us not have any hypocrisy. Lenin's letter to Kursky elaborates on an earlier suggestion: 'Comrade Kursky! In my opinion we ought to extend the use of execution by shooting (allowing the substitution of exile abroad) to all activities of the Mensheviks, SR's, etc.'

---

*N. V. Krylenko (who was prosecutor at the SR trial, and sometime Commissar of Justice) held that *laws* were hypocritical. 'It is one of the most widespread sophistries of bourgeois science to maintain that the court . . . is an institution whose task it is to realize some sort of special "justice" that stands above classes . . . "Let justice prevail in courts" – one can hardly conceive more bitter mockery of reality than this.' In July 1938 Stalin was given a list of 138 names; the words 'Shoot all 138' accompany his signature. Krylenko's name was on that list. His trial lasted twenty minutes (the paperwork minimum), and the protocol ran to nineteen lines. Was that unhypocritical enough for him?

Looking at the thing from the PR point of view, Lenin goes on: 'We ought to find a formulation that would connect these activities *with the international bourgeoisie*.' His italics; and his hypocrisy. State terror is state hysteria; any attempt, however coldly undertaken, 'to legalize it in a principled way, and without hypocrisy' will turn out to be hypocritical. And how do we construe Trotsky's pronouncement? One would 'have to be a hypocrite,' he argues, 'not to understand' that 'terror is a powerful means of policy.' 'Not to understand', here, is a euphemism for 'not to act on': his political opponents, after all, don't mind his *understanding* it. Trotsky ought to have used the word 'sentimentalist' in place of 'hypocrite'. Everyone knows that terror is unsentimental. We still need persuading that terror is unhypocritical. More generally, we take it on board that Lenin and Trotsky were alert to the danger of hypocrisy.

In fact, of course, hypocrisy boomed under the Bolsheviks, like hyperinflation. I do not intend it as a witticism when I say that hypocrisy became the life and soul of the Party – indeed, this understates the case. Hypocrisy didn't know what had hit it in October 1917. Until then, hypocrisy had had its moments, in politics, in religion, in commerce; it had played its part in innumerable social interactions; and it had starred in many Victorian novels, and so on; but it had never been asked to saturate one sixth of the planet. Looking back, hypocrisy might have smiled at its earlier reticence, for it soon grew accustomed to the commanding heights.

This vice flourishes when words and deeds abandon all contiguity. Before examining the word 'revolution' (square one), let us consider square two: 'the dictatorship of the proletariat'. Barely more than a footnote in Marx, the phrase was fetishized by the Bolsheviks as 'vanguardism': the elite revolutionaries establish a dictatorship in the *name* of the proletariat; the proletariat, over time, outgrows mere 'trade-union consciousness', and catches up with the vanguard; the vanguard, the state, then famously 'withers away', and full Communism is 'realized'. The Bolsheviks, as we are aware, got stuck in the first phase of the process and never moved beyond it (though in a sense they did manage to wither away, a 'short' century later, leaving nothing behind them). Lenin was being hypocritical, therefore, when he outlawed the trade unions on the grounds that the proletariat already enjoyed dictatorial power.

Russia never experienced the dictatorship of the proletariat.

What Russia experienced was the dictatorship of the proletarian.

Russia experienced Stalin, and negative perfection.

(1) During the famine of 1933 Moscow continued its Russification policy in the Ukraine, purging all institutions (including the Chamber of Weights and Measures and the Geodesic Board). One official who had come under attack, Skrypnyk, responded spiritedly: he counterattacked, and then shot himself. The official obituary described his suicide as 'an act of faintheartedness particularly unworthy of a member of the Central Committee of the All-Union Communist Party'.

(2) From *The Great Terror*: 'The absolutely certain way for a defendant to get himself shot was to refuse to plead guilty. He would then not go before an open court at all, but either perish under the rigours of the preliminary investigation, or be shot, like Rudzutak, after a twenty-minute closed trial. The logic of Stalin's courts was different from what is customary elsewhere. The only chance of avoiding death was to admit to everything,

and to put the worst possible construction on all one's activities. It is true that even this seldom saved a man's life.'

(3) During Collectivization, when the peasants were slaughtering their cattle, the chief of grain procurement in the Ukraine, who could expect to feast his way through the coming struggle (i.e., terror-famine), is quoted as saying: 'for the first time in their sordid history the Russian peasants have eaten their fill of meat.'

(4) This is Robert Tucker on the execution of Kamenev and Zinoviev, whose lives Stalin had originally promised to spare: 'He not only humiliated, exploited, and destroyed them, but he caused them to die knowing they had publicly abased and besmirched themselves and very many others, taken on the guilt for *his* murder of Kirov, *his* supreme duplicity, and *his* terrorist conspiracy against the party-state. They had confessed to representing a variety of fascism when he was introducing just that in Russia by, among other things, this very pseudo-trial; and they wound up grovelling at their murderer's feet and glorifying him – *all for nothing but to serve his purposes*.'* In his forty-third unanswered letter to Stalin, Bukharin wrote: 'I feel towards you, towards the Party, towards the cause nothing but great and boundless love. I embrace you in my thoughts . . .' Few murderers have asked this of their victims – to go to their deaths with endearments on their lips. But this was the size of the defeat, the size of the deficit, that Stalin insisted on.

---

*This crescendo of indignation could have continued. Kamenev's wife was arrested in 1935 and shot in 1941; his older son was arrested in 1937 and shot in 1939 (his younger son survived a Cheka orphanage and the gulag). Zinoviev's three brothers were shot, as was one of his sisters; three other sisters, together with three nephews (one of whom was shot), a niece, a brother-in-law and a cousin were sent to camp; his son Stefan was shot.

(5) Occasionally requests for clemency were passed around the table by the leadership. One such, from an innocent military commander on the eve of his execution, was footnoted: 'A pack of lies. Shoot him – I. Stalin'; 'Agreed. Blackguard! A dog's death for a dog – Beria'; 'Maniac – Voroshilov'; 'Swine! – Kaganovich.'

(6) In 1948 Stalin made the following addition to his official biography, the *Short Course*: 'At the various stages of the War Stalin's genius found the correct solution that took account of all the circumstances . . . His military mastership was displayed both in defence and offence. His genius enabled him to divine the enemy's plans and defeat them.' Stalin then made this addition to that addition: 'Although he performed his task of leader of the Party with consummate skill and enjoyed the unreserved support of the entire Soviet people, Stalin never allowed his work to be marred by the slightest hint of vanity, conceit or self-adulation.'

(7) Increasingly, as the Terror-Famine gripped, peasants stole grain to stay alive. A new law politicized this crime, declaring that all such pilferers were to be treated as enemies of the people, and would receive the *tenner* or the *super*. 'By the beginning of 1933,' writes Volkogonov, 'more than 50,000 people, many of them starving, had been sentenced.' Using the *word* 'famine' carried the same penalty. The 'worthy reapers', in Stalin's facetious formulation, didn't know that they were starving as a matter of government policy. But they did know that they were starving. And it was a capital crime to remark on it. In essence, people were being killed, quickly, for the capital crime of saying that they were being killed slowly.

You see why Solzhenitsyn needs his expletives, his italics, his exclamation marks, his thrashing sarcasm. On the chain gang they had you sing:

> We Canal Army Men are a tough people.
> But not in that lies our chief trait;
> We were caught up by a great epoch
> To be put on the path that leads straight.

Or, at the amateur theatricals, bursting from the breast:

> And even the most beautiful song
> Cannot tell, no, cannot do justice
> To this country than which there is nothing more wondrous,
> The country in which you and I live.

. . . Oh, they will drive you to the point where you will weep just to be back with company commander Kurilko ['I'll make you suck the snot from corpses!'], walking along the short and simple execution road, through open-and-above-board Solovki slavery.

My Lord! What canal is there deep enough for us to drown *that* past in?*

The Gulag Archipelago, Volume Two, pp. 119–20.

PART III

WHEN WE DEAD AWAKEN

Letter to a Friend

Chalet La Galana,
Calle Los Picaflores,
Esquina Los Biguá,
José Ignacio,
Maldonado,
Uruguay.

10 February 2001.

Comrade Hitchens!

I *like* the way the Bolsheviki hailed each other in their letters, and will be disappointed if inquiry reveals that the exclamation mark was a national habit – just as the Americans favour the businesslike colon, while the British stick with the diffident yet intimate comma. I *like* the comrades' 'shock' greeting, with its suggestion that the recipient may have fallen into some deviationist reverie, and its further suggestion that he had better snap out of it and reattend, on pain of death, to his quotas. I like the air of menace, of vigilance, of *sleeplessness*. Considering my current location, I might have followed what was presumably the practice at POUM* and opened my

---

* *Partido Obrero de Unificatión Marxista*, the heretical sect of Catalonia, savaged by the Cheka during the Spanish Civil War for its Trotskyist bent.

communication with an inverted exclamation mark, as well, obliging the comrade to tense up even quicker.

The northern hemisphere, at least in the months that *we* call winter, is, I fear, a fool's game. Here we all wander about the place with the grateful and trusting smile of a recently rescued Bambi. It is a land of thousand-mile beaches, spectacular *tormentas*, and flipped and wriggling beetles the size of Gregor Samsa. Fernanda has learned how to swim, Clio has learned how to talk, and I have learned how to say one very versatile sentence in Spanish – *Yo siento mucho, pero no puedo ayudar* (oh and the equally all-purpose *Yo no sé nada*).* All I lack is the presence of my other children. I miss them. And I miss my sister Sally, whom you knew. I have of late, but wherefore I know not, lost all my mirth. Now I *do* know wherefore – but it took some time. 'I have of late, but wherefore I know not, lost all my mirth, foregone all custom of exercises; and indeed, it goes so heavily with my disposition that this goodly frame, the earth, seems to me a sterile promontory; this most excellent canopy, the air, look you, this brave o'erhanging firmament, this majestical roof fretted with golden fire: why, it appeareth nothing to me but a foul and pestilent congregation of vapours.' It took me a while to find this speech, because I was sure Hamlet was in colloquy with Horatio – rather than with Rosencrantz and Guildenstern, which makes Hamlet's dejection even more soiled and thrown-away . . . The key phrase is 'but wherefore I know not'. Hamlet doesn't fully see that his metaphysical miseries constitute a subliminal symptom of grief; and this was exactly my case. I thought I was sick, I

*'I'm very sorry, but I can be of no help.' 'I don't know anything.'

thought I was *dying* (maybe that is what bereavement actually asks of you). Literature gives us these warnings about the main events, but we don't *recognize* the warnings until the events have come and gone. Isabel, my senior in the loss of a sibling, told me that you just have to take it, like weather – yes, like sleet in your face. Other skies ask other questions. Even the candid blue of Uruguay. But more of this another time, and there will be more of this, much more of this, and then more, and then more.

Just before we left we had a couple of very good evenings with the Conquests. Bob said to me, 'Do you remember my suggesting, long ago, that you should call your next novel *The Cupid Stunts*?' I said that I did, and adduced the analogous *Cunning Stunts* from Nabokov (is it from *Transparent Things?*). Then (dry, professorial) he said, 'Of course there's also *The Cotton Runts*.'* I asked him, 'What is *The Cotton Runts*?' And he said, 'A social-realist novel about Lancashire slum children affected by the collapse of the textile industry' . . . If Nietzsche is right, and a joke is an epigram on the death of a feeling, then *this* joke is a massacre. I laughed for so long that he got going too; as it subsided he took off his glasses and removed a tear with his little finger. I think I reminded him of Kingsley – for the Amis men double over when they laugh, and scrunch up their eyes to remove all possible distractions. More curiously, he reminds *me* of Kingsley. Because he is really *terrifyingly* unchanged, isn't he? Remember in the *Letters*, when Kingsley and Larkin have been exchanging sincere and eloquent

*The Nabokov quote is naturally another matter, but American readers should be told that the word being quibbled with here means, in English, something like 'moronic bastard', and has no sexual connotation.

complaints about old age, and Kingsley says incredulously that 'Bob just goes on as if nothing has happened'? (Liddie* says he simply 'wakes up happy'. Christ, is *that* what you've got to do?) In his Seven Ages limerick[†] he is still hovering between lines three and four – in his mid-eighties. How is he getting on with his memoirs? Will we learn about his Pierce Brosnan period at the Foreign Office? When you see them next, give them my love and say that I'll be over in June. Now back to business.

Comrade Hitchens! There is probably not that much in these pages that you don't already know. You already know, in that case, that Bolshevism presents a record of baseness and inanity that exhausts all dictionaries; indeed, heaven stops the nose at it. So it is still obscure to me why you wouldn't want to put more distance between yourself and these events than you do, with your reverence for Lenin and your unregretted disciple-ship of Trotsky. These two men did not just precede Stalin. They created a fully functioning police state for his later use. And they showed him a remarkable thing: that it was possible to run a country with a formula of dead freedom, lies and violence – and unpunctuated self-righteousness. During one of our four or five evenings on the subject, you quietly stressed that Lenin's performance was 'not hypocritical'. I wonder at that. Isn't

---

*Liddie Neece, the fourth Mrs Robert Conquest. 'Liddie and I are getting married,' he told my father. 'Bob, you can't do that. Not *again*.' 'Well, I thought – one for the road.' That was twenty-two years ago.

[†]Seven ages: first puking and mewling:
Then very pissed off with one's schooling;
   Then fucks; and then fights;
   Then judging chaps' rights;
Then sitting in slippers; then drooling.

unpunctuated self-righteousness, in a man presiding over the less than perfect world of the Soviet Union, 1917–24, automatically *not* not hypocritical? Off the record, Lenin was capable of telling the truth, blandly conceding that certain policies had had certain (unpleasant) results. But nothing here qualifies Bunin's judgment, with which I increasingly concur: Lenin, 'that congenital moral imbecile'. I will return later, if I may, to Trotsky.

The arc of the late Dmitri Volkogonov is an interesting one, is it not? His *Stalin: Triumph and Tragedy* appeared in 1989; and although the cover of my paperback is wreathed in quotes like 'a massive indictment' and so on, it is in fact comparatively lenient. In 1988 Volkogonov didn't know that Stalin was responsible for the fates of his parents (and two uncles). He found out later, and directly, in the archives: his father was shot in the Terror for possessing some work of Bukharin's, and his mother died in 'exile' – that is, as a police-harassed woman of the road. Dmitri was nine years old in 1937; he sensed what life was like, but he had already eaten the ideology . . . His *Stalin* has blind spots, tacit assumptions (he is almost jocose on the repressions of the clergy). Because he was still a believer: a political believer. The disappearance of that belief was complex, and partly independent of filial outrage, coming 'like the melancholy of a spiritual hangover'.* A queasy counterrevolution of the mind, the heart, the soul, the gut. Volkogonov's subsequent books in his trilogy, *Trotsky: The Eternal Revolutionary* (1992)

---

*These feelings are described in *Autopsy for an Empire*. Volkogonov died shortly after completing it, in 1995.

and *Lenin: A New Biography (1994),*[*] continue a curve of *mounting* disgust and despair. 'Perhaps the only thing I achieved in this life,' he wrote (when his life was ending), 'was to break with the faith I had held for so long.' The workings of Volkogonov's internal *perestroika* are altogether alien to me; but this quietly extraordinary remark is a goad to the imagination.

You must understand the process better than I do, because you have undergone it, or partly undergone it. *Your* restructuring remains incomplete. Why? An admiration for Lenin and Trotsky is meaningless without an admiration for terror. They would not want your admiration if it failed to include an admiration for terror. Do you admire terror? I know you admire freedom. A while ago I told you that 1989 was a turning point in your evolution as a writer. Until then your prose had always given me the impression of less than complete disclosure – the sense that certain truths might have to be postponable. Then you lost that inhibition, and your writing voice gained a new quality: freedom.

Seen in terms of freedom and freedom alone, October was not a political revolution riding on the back of a popular revolution (February). It was a counterrevolution. The 'unrest' of 1921 – in the armed forces (mutiny at Kronstadt and elsewhere), in the post-Civil War remains of the proletariat (strikes, demonstrations, riots), and in the countryside (peasant rebellion involving millions) – constituted a popular revolution far more thoroughgoing than those of 1917 and 1905.[†] The Bolsheviki, of course, called this a counterrevolution, and bloodily suppressed

---

*Dates of publication in Russia. They appeared in reverse order in the West.

†The Kronstadt sailors, and other groups, actually called themselves *revolutionaries* and fought under the red flag.

it. Whereas, in fact, *their* revolution was the counterrevolution. That was the elephant – the trumpeting, snorting, farting mammoth – in the Kremlin living room. Established on an abyss of untruth, Bolshevism was committed to its career of slapstick mendacity, attaining universal and ideal truthlessness under Stalin. The fragile freedom of the interrevolutionary period was replaced by unfreedom, dead freedom, as Vasily Grossman puts it. And that's what matters:

> The history of humanity is the history of human freedom ... Freedom is not, as Engels thought, 'the recognition of necessity'. Freedom is the opposite of necessity. Freedom is necessity overcome. Progress is, in essence, the progress of human freedom. Yes, and after all, life itself is freedom. The evolution of life is the evolution of freedom.

So may I make a suggestion? You should reread the twenty-four volumes of Lenin's works in the following way: every time you see the words 'counterrevolution' or 'counterrevolutionary' you should take out the 'counter'; and every time you see the words 'revolution' or 'revolutionary' you should put the 'counter' back in again.

Your boy Trotsky. No, I haven't read Isaac Deutscher's *The Prophet Armed* and *The Prophet Unarmed* and *The Prophet Outcast*, but I have read Volkogonov's *Trotsky: The Eternal Revolutionary* (make that *Counterrevolutionary*. And what's all this 'eternal' stuff and 'prophet' stuff? What was he a prophet of? A Communist England? A Communist USA?). As is certainly not the case with Lenin (I groaned with deep recognition when I recently learned that he couldn't pronounce his r's: not a good start, I think, for a Russian revolutionary), the attraction to Trotsky is intelligible, and has some human basis.

For one thing, he had literary talent – there is always a lulling quality in his rhythms; and he was a great encapsulator. When the Kronstadt sailors (his 'flower and beauty of the revolution' – and make that 'counterrevolution') inaugurated their articulate and principled rebellion, he said, 'Now the middle peasant speaks to us with naval guns' – because the armed forces had started responding to state terrorism in the countryside. (As against that, he suppressed the sailors with exemplary Bolshevik mercilessness, and never mentioned this postponable truth in his various memoirs.) Trotsky's slogan at Brest-Litovsk ('Neither war nor peace') was insubordinate and gravely counterproductive – but it was original: I can hear that German general saying, '*Unerhört!*' And so on. But Trotsky was never a contender for the leadership. In that struggle he was a mere poseur (reading French novels during meetings of the Central Committee): a Congress election result of 1921 put Trotsky tenth (and he didn't come tenth because he was more humane than the other nine). More basically, Trotsky was a murdering bastard and a fucking liar. And he did it with gusto. He was a nun-killer – they all were. The only thing that can be entered on the other side of the ledger is that he paid a price that was very nearly commensurate. Death was visited on him and all his clan. It is shaking to read the list of Bronsteins, and near-Bronsteins, destroyed by Stalin. When Trotsky publicly offered Stalin the job of 'gravedigger of the Revolution' (and make that 'Counterrevolution'), it was said that he would not be forgiven 'unto the fourth generation'. And so it might have proved. Murder came to almost everyone who had ever known him or talked to him or seen him up close; hundreds of thousands, millions of innocent people lost their lives for some imagined connection to him and his name. So far as I am aware there is in Trotsky's writing no reference to what this felt like. He seems simply to have accepted it – that he became a lightning rod for death. But then they were all charged up with the electricity of violence.

We come back to where we started. As you rightly intuit, the gravamen ('essence, worst part, of accusation') runs as follows: under Bolshevism the value of human life collapsed. You claim that the value of human life had *already* collapsed – because of the world war. Well, this argument would have more weight behind it if a) there had been a similar collapse (i.e., total, and lasting thirty-five years) in any other combatant country, and if b) a single Old Bolshevik had spent a single day at the front, or indeed in the army (though it is true that Stalin got as far as failing his medical: that withered left arm plus 'a defective foot'). The 'full-time revolutionaries' spent the war years abroad, or in state-subsidized and unsupervised internal exile, or in the embarrassingly congenial Tsarist prisons, rereading that idiot Chernyshevsky. (Trotsky said that he enjoyed his stays in the Peter and Paul Fortress: he had all his comforts, and didn't have to worry about getting arrested.) The full-timers nursed their impotence until that night in October, when they saw that power was lying on the streets of Petrograd and picked it up 'like a feather'. That summer the Party slogan was 'Down with capital punishment, reinstated by Kerensky!' In fact, the Bolsheviki had more in mind than capital punishment. 'We must rid ourselves once and for all,' said Trotsky, 'of the Quaker-Papist babble about the sanctity of human life.' What they had in mind was vanguard violence: a violence 'not seen for centuries' (Conquest); a violence 'whose scope and inhumanity far exceeded anything in the national past' (Malia).

I know a little about Russian Jacobinism, the writings of Sergey Nechaev et al. (kill everyone over the age of twenty-five, and so on), but it isn't clear to me how the paradise-via-inferno idea survived a moment's thought in the first place. Let us laboriously imagine that the 'paradise' Trotsky promised to 'build' suddenly appeared on the bulldozed site of 1921. Knowing that 15 million lives had been sacrificed to its creation, would you want to live in it? A paradise so bought is no paradise. I take it you would not want to second Eric Hobsbawm's disgraceful 'Yes' to a paradise so bought. Means define ends, as Kolakowski said – and means, in the USSR, were all you were ever going to get. And the contradiction within the contradiction is this: the militant utopian, the perfectibilizer, from the outset, is in a malevolent rage at the obvious fact of human imperfectibility. Nadezhda Mandelstam talks of the 'satanic arrogance' of the Bolsheviki. There is also infernal insecurity and disaffection, and infernal despair.

Bukharin is apt in his demolition of the permanent-revolution theory propounded by Stalin (and, with variations, by Trotsky):

> This strange theory elevates the actual fact that the class struggle is now intensifying into some sort of inevitable law of our development. According to this strange theory, it would seem that the farther we go in our advance towards socialism, the more difficulties will accumulate, the more intense the class struggle would become, so that at the very gates of socialism, apparently, we will have to either start a civil war or perish from hunger and lay down our bones to die.

Now, Hitch, I want to leave you with two images. I cannot find the source in either case, and maybe there has been some unwarranted elaboration in my mind. Anyway.

In the early months of the Great Patriotic War there were reports of pitched battles between troops and their Cheka 'blocking units'.* Imagine such a battle, with machine guns (certainly), tanks (possibly), and a third army just across the field . . .

The second image is more notional. Trotsky's *other* theory of permanent revolution (we should call it Permrev) consisted of the vain hope for a series of revolutions in foreign lands, the process concluding with global socialism. Some prominent comrade further remarked that only then, when Communism ruled the earth, would the *really* warm work of class struggle be ready to begin . . . And I instantly pictured a scorpion stinging itself to death. Scorpions have of course been known to do this – when surrounded by fire, for example. But where *is* the fire, on a Communist planet? It is a fire in the self. It is self-hatred and life-hatred. After all, the scorpion has an excellent 'objective' reason for killing the scorpion: it's *alive*, isn't it?

Not with anti-Communist greetings, then, because these thoughts are part of no package, but with fraternal love, as always,

Martin

The Beginnings of the Search for Decorum

One evening in the autumn of 1999 my wife and I, together with the Conquests, attended a political meeting at Conway Hall in

---

*'Above all, it was Trotsky,' writes Niall Ferguson in *The Pity of War*, 'who in December 1918 ordered the formation of "blocking units" equipped with machine guns, whose role was simply to shoot front-line soldiers who attempted to retreat.'

Red Lion Square, Holborn, London, just over the road from the old *New Statesman* offices in Lincoln's Inn Fields. We had come to hear the Hitchens brothers, Christopher (pro) and Peter (anti), discussing the European Union. So: a very boring subject indeed. But the debate was lively, and the audience passionately inter-active: fierce questions posed in fierce regional accents, drunken braying by 'name' journalists, and, from various rotund politicos, the occasionally resonant 'hear hear' – which, if I remember my James Fenton aright (he was evoking a lethargic afternoon in the House of Commons), sounded like 'erdle erdle' and made you think of an enormous stomach digesting an enormous meal. At one point, reminiscing, Christopher said that he knew this building well, having spent many an evening in it with many 'an old comrade'. The audience responded as Christopher knew it would (his remark was delivered with a practised air): the audi-ence responded with affectionate laughter.

Afterwards I asked Conquest, 'Did *you* laugh?'

'*Yes*,' he said.

And I said, 'And so did I.'

Why is it? Why is it? If Christopher had referred to his many evenings with many 'an old blackshirt', the audience would have . . . Well, with such an affiliation in his past, Christopher would not be Christopher – or anyone else of the slightest distinction whatsoever. Is *that* the difference between the little moustache and the big moustache, between Satan and Beelzebub? One elicits spontaneous fury, and the other elicits spontaneous laughter? And what kind of laughter is it? It is, of course, the laughter of universal fondness for that old, old idea about the perfect society. It is also the laughter of forgetting. It forgets the demonic energy unconsciously embedded in that hope. It forgets the Twenty Million.

And this isn't right:

Everybody knows of Auschwitz and Belsen. Nobody knows of Vorkuta and Solovetsky.

Everybody knows of Himmler and Eichmann. Nobody knows of Yezhov and Dzerzhinsky.

Everybody knows of the 6 million of the Holocaust. Nobody knows of the 6 million of the Terror-Famine.*

Yet *I* know, and *I* laughed. And *Conquest* laughed. Why won't laughter do the decent thing? Why won't laughter excuse itself and leave the room?

Let us go back, for a moment, to Tibor Szamuely. Given eight years in the gulag for privately referring to Georgi Malenkov as a 'fat pig', Tibor was imprisoned en route to Vorkuta. This is my father's account from his *Memoirs*:

> The big daily event in a Soviet gaol is the delivery of the copy of *Pravda*, and it was Tibor's right and duty, as the Professor, to read the contents out to the cell [which contained several dozen inmates] . . . It appeared that Stalin had protested *in person* to the UN or one of its offshoots about the inhuman conditions under which some Greek Communist prisoners

---

*When Austria's Haider praises one of Hitler's employment policies, Europe spits him out, convulsively, as if he were a bad oyster. Russia's Putin praises Stalin, echoes Stalin ('to liquidate the oligarchs as a class'), and proposes to mint coins bearing Stalin's profile. He is welcomed at Downing Street, and has tea with the Queen . . . More substantively, between 1945 and 1966, writes Solzhenitsyn, '*eighty-six thousand* Nazi criminals had been convicted in West Germany . . . And during the same period, in our country (according to the reports of the Military Collegium of the Supreme Court), about *ten men* have been convicted.' In the 1980s, Molotov and Kaganovich, two elderly Eichmanns, were living on state pensions in Moscow.

were being held at the end of the civil war there – inadequate exercise, meagre rations, food parcels only once a week, gross overcrowding on a scale comparable with (say) Czarism, insufficient visiting, and suchlike enormities. After a moment's stunned silence, every prisoner broke into hysterical laughter, the tears running down their faces, embracing, rolling over and over on the floor, old feuds forgotten, for minutes. Indeed, the mood of euphoria lasted not for minutes but, in short bursts, for days. A careless spray of urine over one of the sleepers nearest the bucket would bring not the usual howl of rage, or worse, but a cry from the offender of, 'Now, now, Comrade! Remember the sufferings of our Greek fellow-fighters for peace against the Western oppressor!' and an answering guffaw.*

Russia, 1917–53: what is its genre? It is not a tragedy, like *Lear*, not an anti-comedy, like *Troilus and Cressida*, nor yet a problem comedy, like *Measure for Measure*. It is a black farce, like *Titus Andronicus*. And the black farce is very Russian, from *Dead Souls* to *Laughter in the Dark* . . . It seems that humour cannot be evicted from the gap between words and deeds. In the USSR, that gap covered eleven time zones. The enemy of the people was the regime. The dictatorship of the proletariat was a lie; Union was a lie, and Soviet was a lie, and Socialist was a lie, and Republics was a lie. *Comrade* was a lie. The Revolution was a lie.

Butyrki Nights

I too, now, am obliged to confess – not to a lie but to a sin, and a chronic one.

*Solzhenitsyn recalls a quaveringly passionate speech by a Greek writer, in Moscow, on behalf of the imprisoned Communists. Maybe he 'did not understand the shamelessness of his appeal, and maybe, too, in Greece they do not have the proverb: "Why grieve for others when there is sobbing at home?"'

The Butyrki was the best prison in Moscow. (A curious statement, some may well feel; but this is a confession I find I am having to back my way into.) Or, to put it another way, there were worse prisons in Moscow than the Butyrki (sometimes transliterated as Butyrka). The Butyrki was the largest of the three main prisons for 'politicals' only, and less feared than the other two, the Lubyanka and (especially) the Lefortovo. More feared than the Lefortovo was Sukhanovka, called 'the dacha' (it was coincidentally close to Lenin's Gorky estate). Solzhenitsyn knows of only one coherent survivor of Sukhanovka, a place, it seems, of strenuously enforced silence and continual torture.* The Butyrki, built by the Tsars to contain the Pugachev rebels, was cleaner and better-run than the Taganka and other prisons where politicals cohabited with ordinary crooks and *urkas*. Solzhenitsyn, again, had some stimulating times in the Butyrki. The standard of prisoner was astonishingly high, with academicians and scientists (and novelists) milling about the cells. It was like the *sharashka* (a laboratory behind barbed wire in the gulag) described in *The First Circle*: any physicist would have been proud to work there.

Fate had it that one evening I was alone in the house with my six-month-old daughter. (Another curious statement, perhaps, at this juncture, but I am slowly getting to the point.) Without preamble she embarked on a weeping fit that began at the outer limit of primordial despair, and then steadily escalated. Far from

---

* *The Gulag Archipelago*: 'Sukhanovka was the most terrible prison [the Cheka] had. Its very name was used to intimidate prisoners; interrogators would hiss it threateningly. And you'd not be able to question those who had been there: either they were insane and talking only disconnected nonsense, or they were dead.'

soothing her, my kisses and murmurings might as well have been molten pincers, skilfully applied. After an hour I was relieved by the nanny I had summoned from her home. The weeping ceased at once. I staggered into the garden and started weeping myself. Her cries had reminded me of the clinically explicable anguish of my younger boy, who, at the age of one, was an undiagnosed asthmatic. She had reminded me of the perfect equipoise of nausea and grief, as the parent contemplates inexpressible distress.

'The sounds she was making,' I said unsmilingly to my wife on her return, 'would not have been out of place in the deepest cellars of the Butyrki Prison in Moscow during the Great Terror. That's why I cracked and called Caterina.'

If I had been better informed, at that point, I would have said Sukhanovka instead of Butyrki, and that would have been the end of it. For Butyrki, I am afraid, is now established as one of my daughter's chief nicknames, along with its diminutives, Butyrklet, the Butyrkster, the Butyrkstress, and so on. The cognomen is widely current in the family; Butyrki's four-year-old sister uses it – with an excellent and out-of-nowhere Russian accent (these days, even *Butyrki* can say 'Butyrki'); and what a sigh went up in our household, one morning, when I drew attention to Eugenia Ginzburg's chapter heading, 'Butyrki Nights' . . .

It isn't right, is it? My youngest daughter has passed her second birthday, and her cries are not particularly horrifying any more, and I still call her Butyrki. Because the name is now all braided through with feeling for her. Nearly always, when I use it, I imagine a wall-eyed skinhead in a German high-rise (and I'm sure such a person exists) with a daughter called Treblinka. Treblinka was one of the five ad hoc death camps, with no other function (unlike Auschwitz). I am not as bad as the wall-eyed skinhead. But the Butyrki was a place of inexpressible distress. In 1937 it held 30,000 prisoners crushed together. And it isn't right. Because my daughter's name is Clio: muse of history.

The Forty Days of Kengir

There was that time in December 1975, when V. S. Pritchett (perhaps passing Oleg Kerensky on the stairs) came to the offices of the *New Statesman* in Lincoln's Inn Fields with his review of *The Gulag Archipelago* (Parts III–IV, which comprise Volume Two of the trilogy)* tucked under his arm. Pritchett's piece went first to the literary editor, Claire Tomalin, and then to me, her deputy. Having read its conclusion—

> Exactness and an exacting, unceasing irony is Solzhenitsyn's aim: the camps made him a self-searching man and when people say to him, 'Why drag all that up from the bad times?,' his answer is that a country's or a dogma's evasion of its own past, on this excuse or that, is as fatal to the quality of life as it is to the private heart. He is not a political; he is without rhetoric or doublethink; he is an awakener.

—I turned back to see if Claire had provided a title. She had: 'When We Dead Awaken' (the reference is to the Ibsen play). I remember I gave a sudden nod and thought: the argument is over now. We can move on from the argument. To what? Well, to

---

*In his introduction to the abridged single-volume *Gulag* (first published in 1999, and recommended only as a kind of crib), Edward E. Ericson gives the following American sales figures: 2,244,000 for Volume One, 500,000 for Volume Two, and 100,000 for Volume Three. These figures are representative worldwide, and point to the limits of our stamina and appetite. In fact, *The Gulag Archipelago* simply goes on getting better, and, of course, achieves an impregnable unity.

remembrance, naturally. And also, perhaps, to a search for decorum.

On page 13 of Volume One, in self-lacerating mood, Solzhenitsyn writes: 'We didn't love freedom enough.' Then: 'We purely and simply *deserved* everything that came after.' In the Preface to Volume Three he is less severe, and more persuasive: the Communist regime survived 'not because there has not been any struggle against it from inside, not because people docilely surrendered to it, but because it is inhumanly strong, in a way as yet unimaginable to the West'. Among the elements of the state's strength was its capacity to astonish, to dumbfound – and thus to delude. As Conquest says, 'the reality of Stalin's activities was often disbelieved because they seemed to be unbelievable. His whole style consisted of doing what had previously been thought morally or physically inconceivable.'

In 1949 Stalin decided partly to isolate the politicals, the 'fascists', in special camps (known as the Special Camps), presumably to protect the common criminals from ideological contamination. The decision backfired because the 'whole system of oppression in his reign', as Solzhenitsyn writes, 'was based on keeping malcontents apart, preventing them from reading each other's eyes'. In the Special Camps the politicals became political; and the result was rebellion. Their first move expressed a terrible logic: they started to kill all the stoolies. They called it *chopping*, but the process was surgical and cold-blooded – a masked man with a knife in the middle of the night. The stoolies no longer strolled to the camp mailbox with their denunciations, no longer named names for the commandants (even under savage interrogation). And the terror from below continued: 'You whose conscience is unclean – this night you die!' Soon the trusties 'started *escaping* into the Disciplinary Barracks', where they sought safety in the Isolators, gratefully agreeing 'never again to breathe clean air or see sunlight'. The authorities responded with typical enterprise: suspected ringleaders were singled out and delivered to the stoolies for beatings and torture in the prison within the prison.

Solzhenitsyn himself, at Ekibastuz in 1952, took part in an extraordinary protest: a work strike and a hunger strike. Even the *goners* – the *wicks*, the garbage-eaters – joined this fast of the starving. With only one year left to serve, and the near-certain prospect, now, of a fresh sentence, Solzhenitsyn nonetheless entered into the unreadable afflatus: defiance, despair, elation, and, most dizzyingly, a moral *nausea*, a perverse fear of freedom. At the end of the third day came a shout from the window – 'Hut nine! ... Nine has surrendered! ... Nine's going to the mess hall!' Solzhenitsyn magnificently proceeds:

> Two hundred and fifty pathetic little figures, darker than ever against the sunset, cowed and crestfallen, were trailing slant-wise across the camp ... Some, feebler than the rest, were led by the arm or the hand, and so uncertain were their steps that they looked like blind men with their guides. Many, too, held mess tins or mugs in their hands, and this mean prisonware, carried in expectation of a supper too copious to gulp down onto constricted stomachs, these tins and cups held out like begging bowls, were more degrading and slavish and pitiable than anything else about them.
>
> I felt myself weeping. I glanced at my companions as I wiped away my tears, and saw theirs.
>
> Hut No. 9 had spoken, and decided for us all ...
>
> We went away from the windows without a word.
>
> It was then that I learned the meaning of Polish pride, and

understood their recklessly brave rebellions. The Polish engineer Jerzy Wegierski . . . was now in our team. He was serving his ninth and last year. Even when he was a work assigner no one had ever heard him raise his voice. He was always quiet, polite, and gentle.

But now – his face was distorted with rage, scorn, and suffering, as he tore his eyes away from that procession of beggars, and cried in an angry, steely voice:

'Foreman! Don't wake me for supper! I shan't be going!'

He clambered up onto the top bunk, turned his face to the wall – and didn't get up again. That night we went to eat – but he didn't get up! He never received parcels, he was quite alone, he was always short of food – but he wouldn't get up. In his mind's eye the steam from a bowl of mush could not veil the ideal of freedom.

After Stalin's death in March 1953 came the 'Voroshilov amnesty'; 'utterly faithful to the spirit of the deceased', it liberated not the politicals but the *urkas*. There was a riot in Camp Division No. 12 in Karlag, and 'a major rebellion' at Norilsk. But the seismic disturbances really began with the fall (and execution) of Beria, in July.* That month there was a full-scale strike at Vorkuta. Machine guns were mounted; the men went back to work; but Pit 29, shielded by a hill from the rest of the camp, refused to believe that the strike had collapsed. These men were called out on to the parade ground, where they faced eleven truckloads of soldiers. Threatened with 'harsh measures' unless they picked up their tools, the prisoners in the front line linked arms and stood their ground. There were three volleys, and sixty-six dead.

Beria's fall, and his execution on criminal charges, was an

---

*The Politburo moved against Beria with extreme wariness. The man chosen to arrest him was no lesser figure than the war-winner, Marshal Zhukov.

affront to the prestige of every Chekist, and so was the dramatic wage cut that followed it. The response, again, had a brutal symmetry: to prove their usefulness they started to foment disorder by openly and randomly killing innocent prisoners. This terror from halfway up – the terror of the janitoriat – seems to have been especially unignorable at the prison complex in Kengir, near Karaganda in Kazakhstan. They killed a young girl who hung her stockings out to dry 'near' the perimeter fence. They would lure others to the boundary, with the promise of tobacco, say, and shoot them down. They riddled a returning work team with dumdum bullets. And it worked. In *The Gulag Archipelago* the chapter called 'The Forty Days of Kengir' runs to fifty pages. The disturbances would blossom into the greatest and most heroic rebellion in the history of the camps.

Yet again, and as always, the authorities reacted with maximum cunning, perfidy, and miscalculation* – though not yet with maximum violence. The year, remember, is 1954. They injected 650 *urkas* into troublous Section Three. *They* would turn it around, would steal, would rape (a women's camp was by now part of the rebellion), would wound, would murder, would set

---

*To risk bathos, we should incidentally consider, as an illustration of the Chekist personality, the matter of Khrushchev's car. When the cabal figureheaded by a trembling Brezhnev (who once fainted before Kaganovich's wrath) finally ousted him, Khrushchev lived on in disgraced and much-monitored retirement (the bathroom, too, was bugged, and Khrushchev stoutly denounced the Politburo for spending good rubles just 'to eavesdrop on my farts'). They gave Khrushchev a car. Much thought had gone into Khrushchev's car. It was a low-to-middling kind of car, and went wrong all the time (which was meant to be humiliating). But the point was that the car had private plates, and not government plates. This was intended to suggest that Khrushchev was *corrupt*. You want to say, 'Make your point.' Either a reeking rattletrap with government plates, or, with private plates, a burnished limousine.

man against man, which was always the whole idea. But it was different now, in the camps, in Kengir (and elsewhere); there was bursting *esprit*; the old camp ethos, perfunctorily yet profoundly expressed in the motto 'You die today, me I'll wait a bit,' was undergoing revolution. And what appeared was, of all things, a little universalist utopia (so *this* is what it looks like), with equality and respect between all persons, and nothing to be gained by preferment. Naturally the dawning utopia, which was incarcerated and doomed to extreme punishment, had its iron fist. When the *urkas* were trucked in, their leaders were visited by a delegation from the politicals' military wing. You are outnumbered, they said, and we have changed. Join us, or we will kill you all. The *urkas* joined, and were purified. In May/June 1954, Section Three became a civil society.

Everyone at Kengir knew what awaited them. And to take on the enemy, the state, at *that* level, second-generation and downward-selected and now enraged, an enemy of lead and steel. On 22 June it was announced that the rebels' demands would be met. On 25 June, in the early dawn, the Cheka came in with snipers, artillery, aircraft, machine guns and tanks. There were over 700 dead and wounded. Then the normal course of resentencings and executions . . .

Let us remember, as Solzhenitsyn does, the Socialist Revolutionaries of Vyatka Prison in 1923, who 'barricaded themselves in a cell, poured kerosene over all the mattresses and *incinerated themselves*'. And the hunger-striker Arnold Rappaport, who 'starved until he could see the light through his hands'. And, at Kengir, the young couple who threw themselves beneath the tracks of the tank, the women who formed a human shield around the men and received the bayonets, the old zeks on the barricade who ripped off their shirts, 'pointed to their bony chests and ribs, and shouted to the machine gunners: "Come on, then, shoot! Strike down your fathers!"'

And let us try to remember the utterly invisible victims, whose numbers no one will ever tabulate. In the 'ancient, slow-moving' village of Kady, in the remote province of Ivanovo, in the year of 1937, some minor officials were accused of attempting to overthrow the Soviet government by disrupting the local supply of bread. Among those shot (after a risible public trial) was the head of the District Consumer Cooperatives, Vasily Vlasov: honest, fearless, and innocent. Solzhenitsyn adds, in fine print at the foot of the page:

> One little note on eight-year-old Zoya Vlasova. She loved her father intensely. She could no longer go to school. (They teased her: 'Your papa is a wrecker!' She would get in a fight: 'My papa is good!') She lived only one year after the trial. Up to then she had never been ill. During that year *she did not once smile*; she went about with head hung low, and the old women prophesied: 'She keeps looking at the earth; she is going to die soon.' She died of inflammation of the brain, and as she was dying she kept calling out: 'Where is my papa? Give me my papa!' When we count up the millions who perished in the camps, we forget to multiply them by two, by three.

As the stars are known to the Night

In the search for decorum our feelings must have access to the high style. Laughter, as we have seen, will never absent itself from the black farce of Bolshevism; laughter will never raise its hands to its lips, bidding adieu. By now we recognize the kind of laughter we hear; we hear it when we witness epiphanic moral sordor.

But there is also a plane of emotion that excludes laughter. The high style excludes laughter.

In November 2000 it fell to me to help arrange my younger sister's funeral. My father, in the last year of his life, told me that in his most defenceless insomnias he tended to worry about Sally and what it would be like for her when he was dead: the loss of general support, the loss of purpose, of *raison*. And so it proved. A long depression was followed by a sudden illness. When I arrived at the hospital she was in intensive care and had already lost consciousness. She never regained it, and died four days later. I was apprised of this death, not by any change in my sister's demeanour, but by the twining coils of the monitor screen. She, or the respirator she was attached to, continued to breathe, to pant ardently: a corpse with a heaving chest. Then they disconnected her, and she could be approached and kissed without horror. And I asked her a question I had asked many times before, but would now have no cause to ask again: 'Oh, Sally, what have you *done*?' Many times, as a child, I silently promised to protect her. And I didn't do that, did I? No one could have protected her, perhaps. But those promises, never uttered, are still inside me and are still a part of me.

At St Dominic's Priory Church in Kentish Town my wife and I discussed the service with Father John Farrell (Sally had converted some years earlier). The music (Bach), the readings (Romans 8, Matthew 11), the hymns ('To Be a Pilgrim', 'Jerusalem' – Blake, with his burning utopianism: 'I will not cease from mental fight, / Nor shall my sword sleep in my hand, / Till we have built Jerusalem / In England's green and pleasant land.'). It was also agreed that I should recite the poem written for Sally by Philip Larkin ('Tightly-folded bud, / I have wished you something / None

of the others would . . .'), 'Born Yesterday', which bears the shockingly recent date of 20 January 1954.

We moved into the church proper, where my wife (who did
it all, really) talked on with Father Farrell while I stood, suscep-
tibly, by the door. My thoughts were already returning to the con-
solations of habit (the study, the desk) when I noticed the plaque
to the war dead of the parish, and the poetry, the war poetry, of
their names (Bellord, Cody, Gubbins, Lawless, Notherway, Scrim-
shaw). Beneath was a stanza of verse etched in stone:

> They shall grow not old, as we that are left grow old:
> Age shall not weary them, nor the years condemn.
> At the going down of the sun and in the morning
> We will remember them.

As these lines heaved their way through me, I naturally thought
first of their connection to my sister. But again the sudden nod,
and the thought that, yes, this would about answer to the Twenty
Million.

I had recently come across this poem in one of my father's
anthologies, and I looked it up that evening: 'For the Fallen' by
Laurence Binyon. The fallen are the British dead of World War
I.* And it is not inappropriate, it is not indecorous, that war
poetry should resonate with our thoughts about the Twenty
Million. A war was prosecuted against them and against human
nature – by their own people. *War poetry*, which is summarized
in a single line of Wilfred Owen's – from 'Strange Meeting', where

---

*The poem's 'tone may give it the appearance of a commentary after the event
[reads my father's note]; in fact Binyon wrote it within the first few weeks of war'.
Like Kipling at the same stage, he seemed to grasp the dimensions of what was
about to unfold.

the dead poet meets his dead opposite or double from the other side, who says: 'I am the enemy you killed, my friend . . .'

Binyon was a distinguished scholar and translator (he did *The Divine Comedy* in the 1930s), and a good, affable, yet unarguably minor poet. But here something happened: an uncovenanted expansion. Despite its opening sonorities, 'The Fallen' is not a glorification of war; it is an attempt at maximum *consolation*, in the high style; and it answers to our theme:

> They shall grow not old, as we that are left grow old:
> Age shall not weary them, nor the years condemn.
> At the going down of the sun and in the morning
> We will remember them.
>
> They mingle not with their laughing comrades again;
> They sit no more at familiar tables of home;
> They have no lot in our labour of the day-time;
> They sleep beyond England's foam.
>
> But where our desires and our hopes profound,
> Felt as a well-spring that is hidden from sight,
> To the innermost heart of their own land they are known
> As the stars are known to the Night.
>
> As the stars that shall be bright when we are dust,
> Moving in marches on the heavenly plain;
> As the stars that are starry in the time of our darkness,
> To the end, to the end, they remain.

Afterword: Letter to My Father's Ghost

Dearest Dad,

I experimented with 'Dearest Kingsley', in recognition of your changed status; but I spend a lot of time in your mental company – and why break the habit of half a lifetime?

If you could so much as glance at the dedication page of my last book you would know at once that the thing you greatly feared is come upon you, and that which you were afraid of is come unto you. The dedication page reads:

To Kingsley
and Sally

For these are my Amis dead. She survived you by half a decade. Her last years were quiet, and quietly comfortable (she managed your legacy with care). There was no sudden precipitant. Her last days were peaceful, and there was no pain. Don't despair: the story has a happier ending. I suppose, too, that there is one chance in a googolplex that she is now at your side. Supposing she isn't, and yet also supposing that you actually get my news, I suggest that you spend a few years of your eternity recuperating from it – and then come back to this letter. Rest, rest, perturbed spirit.

I will return to the happier ending. But before we get there . . . 'I do not want to be personal,' wrote Nabokov to Edmund Wilson, before going on, very gently, to analyse his friend's forgivable, even likeable, but in the end fatally woolly utopianism. I do not want to be personal either (you didn't like people who were personal), but I do want to talk briefly about a couple of differences between you and me. As father and son we have an unusual thing in common: 'we are both English

novelists', as you once put it, 'who are *some* good'. But you
were a poet, too. And that accounts for the main dissimilarity
between my prose and yours. The other dissimilarities may be
almost entirely generational. If our birthdates had been trans-
posed, then I might have written your novels and you might
have written mine. Remember the rule (truer in our case than
in most): you are your dad and your dad is you. Just to round
this off: you wrote, very largely, about the bourgeoisie in your
fiction, i.e., the middle classes – a category seldom seen in
mine, where I make do with the aristocracy, the intelligentsia,
the lumpenproletariat, and the *urkas*.

You are your dad and your . . . But not quite. The other
difference is political, and basic. You were ideological and I am
not. Of course, you believed, and believed in, Soviet
Communism for fifteen years. There were, as Bob says, no
rational justifications for doing so. But I can give you some
good excuses: middle-class guilt; 'an unfocused dissatisfaction
with the way things are' (as you described it), or unusual
hatred of the status quo; a desire to scandalize parental, or
paternal, conservatism; and the not quite entirely delusional
sense that you were involving yourself directly in world affairs.
It was also a symmetrical convenience – for Stalin – that a
true description of the Soviet Union *exactly* resembled a
demented slander of the Soviet Union. As the admirable and
pitiable Viktor Kravchenko wrote, in his *I Chose Freedom*
(1946: N.B.): 'This scene outside the [Cheka building, where
the families of the arrested wept and screamed] I shall never
be able to expunge from my memory. A great theatrical
genius, hoping to convey mass despair, macabre and boundless
sorrow, could not have invented anything more terrifying' . . .

But I don't want to reproach you for credulity – you were not alone in believing. It's the 'believing *in*' bit that interests me.

In your essay 'Why Lucky Jim Turned Right', written when you were forty-five, you said, explaining your earlier affiliation:

> We are dealing with a conflict of feeling and intelligence, a form of wilful self-deception whereby a part of the mind knows full well that its overall belief is false or wicked, but the emotional need to believe is so strong that that knowledge remains, as it were, encysted, isolated, powerless to influence word or deed.

This is well said. But what is the basis of the 'emotional need'? I will now juxtapose two sentences from the last two paragraphs of the piece:

> You cannot *decide* to have brotherhood; if you start trying to enforce it, you will before long find yourself enforcing something very different, and much worse than the mere absence of brotherhood.

And:

> The ideal of the brotherhood of man, the building of the Just City, is one that cannot be discarded without lifelong feelings of disappointment and loss.

Sentence one seems to me so obvious, and so elementary, that sentence two has no meaning – indeed, no content. Just what *is* this Just City? What would it look like? What would its citizens be saying to each other and doing all day? What would laughter be like, in the Just City? (And what would you find to write about in it?) *This* is the time to start asking *why. Zachto?* Why? What for? To what end? Your 'emotional need' was not a

positive but a negative force. Not romantic. Not idealistic. The
'very nobility' of that ideal, you say, 'makes the results of its
breakdown doubly horrifying'. But the breakdown, the igno-
bility, is inherent in the ideal. This is the joke, isn't it? And it's
a joke about human nature: the absurd assiduity, the droll
dispatch, with which utopia becomes dystopia, with which
heaven becomes hell . . . The 'conflict' you describe is, in the
end, not a conflict between 'feeling and intelligence'. It is,
funnily enough, a conflict between hope and despair.

I quote the following with only token complacency (it is not
merely 'derivative', as claimed; it is kleptomaniacal):

> '. . . although Eden, then, is the "goal" of human life, it remains
> strictly an imaginative goal, not a social construct, even as a
> possibility. The argument applies also to the literary utopias,
> which are not the dreary fascist states popularisers try to extrap-
> olate from them, but, rather, analogies of the well-tempered
> mind: rigidly disciplined, highly selective as regards art, and so
> on. Thus Blake, like Milton, saw the hidden world, the animal
> world in which we are condemned to live, as the inevitable
> complement to man's imagination. Man was never meant to
> escape death, jealousy, pain, libido – what Wordsworth calls
> "the human heart by which we live". Perhaps this is why Blake
> paints the created Adam with a serpent already coiled round
> his thigh.'
>
> So ended my short, derivative, *Roget*-roughaged essay . . .

When I wrote that I was about twenty-two; and my student
narrator was nineteen – the same age as you were when you
'joined'. And so, Dad, probably to my detriment, I never felt the
call of political faith (and probably one should feel it, one
should be zealous, for a while). Nobody can be 'against' the Just
City. This is among the reasons people feel entitled to kill

people who get in the way of it. But when you threw in your lot with the agnostics, the gradualists (and also found another ideology: anti-Communism), you aligned yourself with those who have *more* faith in human nature than the believers. More faith in – and more affection for. Enough. And now the happier ending.

Anonymously present at Sally's funeral was Sally's daughter. Remember, you and I saw her when she was a baby (in the summer of 1979), just before her adoption. The baby, who was perfect, was called Heidi, named after Sally's very unencouraging new mentor. She is not called Heidi any longer. Sally, then, was twenty-four. Catherine, now, is twenty-two.

She had never met her mother. The funeral was supposed to be a goodbye to her birth identity. As we reconstructed it later, though, she saw our clan at the church and thought – that's my clan too. She wrote to 'The Amis Family' via the undertaker (and what a sinister word that turns out to be). I wrote back: we would meet. A little later, when it was all becoming very much worse for me (the cud in my throat tasted like a decisive diminution of love of life), I wrote again. I said that soon I would be going for three months to the other side of the world; and before I could do that I needed to see the semblance of my sister. She came (with her foster-parents), and she was perfect. You will have to imagine the strange precision of the way she physically occupied the space that Sally had vacated – the same weight of presence, and then a certain smile, a certain glance.

Last spring we took her to Spain to meet her grandmother, and her step-grandfather, and her uncles Philip and Jaime. Catherine was also accompanied by four cousins: my Louis and

Jacob, whom you will admiringly remember, and my Fernanda and Clio, two of the three granddaughters you never met. So all your grandchildren were there bar two: my Delilah Seale, and Philip's Jessica. The clan suffers its losses but continues to expand. There have been four additions in the last six years. Mum said that if we spring too many more grandchildren on her she's going to have to start strangling them like kittens. Catherine said afterwards, 'It was like a dream.' I know you would have taken to her very much, and especially and instantly for this proof of both her nature and her nurture: she's one of the last thirty or forty people in the English-speaking world who doesn't say 'between you and I'.

Last winter, over in Uruguay, as we were about to begin our evening game of catch, Fernanda, who had just turned four, seized the ball with a look of demure triumph on her face. The ball was an inflated globe; and on its surface a dead bee had alighted. The bees were dying in their hundreds as the southern summer ended. They would fizz greedily around the lamps on the veranda, then drop. This was the thing they wanted to do before they died . . . Of course, a dead bee can still sting. Fernanda's smile abruptly disappeared and she said in a strong, proud, declarative voice (before shedding the necessary tears), 'Something just hurt me *very much*.' Well, that was exactly how I was feeling about Sally's death. Remembering her, and you, and you and her, has filled me with an exhaustion that no amount of sleep can seem to reach. But the exhaustion is not onerous. It is appropriate. It feels like decorum. Naturally, it feels like self-pity, too. But pity and self-pity can sometimes be the selfsame thing. Death does that. Don't you find?

Stalin (whom, incredibly, you served for twelve years, inconspicuously, infinitesimally – but still incredibly) once said that, while every death is a tragedy, the death of a million is a mere statistic. The second half of the aphorism is of course wholly false: a million deaths are, at the very least, a million tragedies. The first half of the aphorism is perfectly sound – but only as far as it goes. In fact, every life is a tragedy, too. Every life cleaves to the tragic curve.

This letter comes at the end of a book subtitled 'Laughter and the Twenty Million'. You might consider it an odd conclusion. Sally, of course, has nothing whatever in common with the Twenty Million. Nothing but death, and perhaps a semblance of reawakening.

Your middle child hails you and embraces you.

Permissions

The author and publishers wish to thank the following for permission to reprint copyright material:

The Estate of Vladimir Nabokov for permission to reprint material from *Dear Bunny, Dear Volodya: The Nabokov-Wilson Letters, 1940–1971* edited by Simon Karlinsky, all rights reserved; Viking Penguin, a Division of Penguin Putnam, Inc. for permission to reprint material from *Kolyma: The Arctic Death Camps* by Robert Conquest © 1978 by Robert Conquest; HarperCollins Publishers Ltd for permission to reprint material from *Forever Flowing: A Novel* by Vasily Grossman, translated by Thomas P. Whitney © 1970 by Possev-Verlag, English translation © 1972 by Thomas P. Whitney and material from *The Rise and Fall of the Soviet Union* by Dmitri Volkogonov, translated and edited by Harold Shukman © 1998 Novosti Publishers, English translation © 1998 by Harold Shukman; The Random House Group Ltd and HarperCollins Publishers, Inc. for permission to reprint 1370 words from *The Gulag Archipelago 1918–1956: An Experiment in Literary Investigation I–II* by Aleksandr I. Solzhenitsyn © 1973 by Aleksandr I. Solzhenitsyn, English translation © 1973, 1974 by Harper & Row Publishers, Inc., published by The Harvill Press, and 730 words from *The Gulag Archipelago 1918–1956: An Experiment in Literary Investigation III–IV* by Aleksandr I. Solzhenitsyn © 1974 by Aleksandr I. Solzhenitsyn, English translation © 1975 by Harper & Row Publishers, Inc., published by The Harvill Press; Curtis Brown, Ltd and Oxford University Press, Inc. for permission to reprint material from *The Harvest of Sorrow* by Robert Conquest © 1986

Index

Martin Amis

TIME'S ARROW

Shortlisted for the Booker Prize

'Amis's most daring and ambitious novel'
Daily Telegraph

'Amis's backwards world is rigorously imagined. It is a world of pathos and cruel hilarity...but the crux, the test of his vision, is what he does with Auschwitz'
James Wood, *Guardian*

Time's Arrow tells the story, backwards, of the life of Nazi war criminal, Doctor Tod T Friendly. He dies and then feels markedly better, breaks up with his lovers as a prelude to seducing them and mangles his patients before he sends them home...

Escaping from the body of the dying doctor who had worked in Nazi concentration camps, the doctor's consciousness begins living the doctor's life backwards.

'The devastatingly sustained black irony stands comparison with Swift's *A Modest Proposal*. It is, I think, Amis's finest achievement to date'
Financial Times

Also available in Vintage

Martin Amis

LONDON FIELDS

'A true story, a murder story, a love story and a thriller
bursting with humour, sex and often dazzling language'
Independent

'An electrifying writer who likes to shock his fans and share
his sharply contemporary concerns...Amis is a maddening
master you need to read – the best of his generation'
Mail on Sunday

London Fields is a brilliant, funny and multi-layered novel.
It is a book in which the narrator, Samson Young, enters the
Black Cross, a thoroughly undesirable public house, and
finds the main players of his drama assembled, just waiting
to begin. It's a gift of a story from real life...all Samson has
to do is write it as it happens.

'Martin Amis's most ambitious, intelligent and nourishing
novel to date...Keith Talent is a brilliant comic creation...as
a fictional minor crook, he is in the major league, lying and
cheating on the scale of Greene's Pinkie Brown and Saul
Bellow's Rinaldo Cantabile'
Jay McInerney, *Observer*

'*London Fields*, its pastoral title savagely inappropriate to
its inner-city setting, vibrates, like all Amis's work, with the
force fields of sinister, destructive energies. At the core of its
surreal fable are four figures locked in lethal alignment'
Peter Kemp, *Sunday Times*

V

VINTAGE

Martin Amis

HEAVY WATER

'Cracking prose…highly inventive, inimitably
stylish and funny'
The Times

'Brilliant…A remarkable feat of rhetorical beauty and overwhelming truth…A terrific collection…brilliantly varied,
constantly surprising chips of a superb imagination'
Mail on Sunday

In Martin Amis's short stories whole worlds are created – or
inverted. In 'Straight Fiction', everyone is gay, apart from
the beleaguered 'straight' community; in 'Career Move',
screenplay writers submit their works to little magazines,
while poets are flown first-class to Los Angeles; in 'The
Janitor of Mars', a sardonic robot gives us some strange
news about life in the solar system. In 'Let Me Count the
Times' a man has a mad affair with himself. 'Heavy Water',
portrays the exhaustion of working-class culture, and 'State
of England' its weird resuscitation. And in 'The Coincidence
of the Arts' an English baronet becomes entangled with an
African-American chess hustler.

'Amis is immaculate as a comic stylist…irresistible'
Daily Telegraph

'This volume is essential reading for anyone remotely interested in where we are and how we got here'
Sunday Times

V

VINTAGE

BY MARTIN AMIS
ALSO AVAILABLE IN VINTAGE

☐	Einstein's Monsters	0099768917	£6.99
☐	Experience	0099285827	£7.99
☐	Heavy Water	0099272660	£6.99
☐	London Fields	0099748614	£7.99
☐	Night Train	0099748711	£6.99
☐	Other People	0099769018	£6.99
☐	The Rachel Papers	0099455420	£6.99
☐	Time's Arrow	0099455358	£6.99
☐	The War Against Cliché	0099422220	£8.99

FREE POST AND PACKING
Overseas customers allow £2.00 per paperback

BY PHONE: 01624 677237

BY POST: Random House Books
C/o Bookpost, PO Box 29, Douglas
Isle of Man, IM99 1BQ

BY FAX: 01624 670923

BY EMAIL: bookshop@enterprise.net

Cheques (payable to Bookpost) and credit cards accepted

Prices and availability subject to change without notice.
Allow 28 days for delivery.
When placing your order, please mention if you do not wish to receive
any additional information.

www.randomhouse.co.uk/vintage